GOVERNMENT BEYOND THE CENTRE

SERIES EDITORS: GERRY STOKER AND DAVID WILSON

The world of sub-central governance and administration – including local authorities, quasi-governmental bodies and the agencies of public–private partnerships – has seen massive changes in the United Kingdom and other western democracies. The original aim of the **Government Beyond the Centre** series was to bring the study of this often-neglected world into the mainstream of social science research, applying the spotlight of critical analysis to what had traditionally been the preserve of institutional public administration approaches.

The replacement of traditional models of government by new models of governance has affected central government, too, with the contracting out of many traditional functions, the increasing importance of relationships with devolved and supranational authorities, and the emergence of new holistic models based on partnership and collaboration.

This series focuses on the agenda of change in governance both at sub-central level and in the new patterns of relationships surrounding the core executive. Its objective is to provide up-to-date and informative accounts of the new forms of management and administration and the structures of power and influence that are emerging, and of the economic, political and ideological forces that underline them.

The series will be of interest to students and practitioners in central and local government, public management and social policy, and all those interested in the reshaping of the governmental institutions which have a daily and major impact on our lives.

Government Beyond the Centre
Series Standing Order
ISBN 0-333-71696–5 hardcover
ISBN 0-333-69337–X paperback
(outside North America only)

You can receive future titles in this series as they are published by placing a standing order. Please contact your bookseller or, in the case of difficulty, write to us at the address below with your name and address, the title of the series and an ISBN quoted above.

Customer Services Department, Macmillan Distribution Ltd
Houndmills, Basingstoke, Hampshire RG21 6XS, England

GOVERNMENT BEYOND THE CENTRE

SERIES EDITORS: GERRY STOKER AND DAVID WILSON

Towards Holistic Governance

The New Reform Agenda

**Perri 6, Diana Leat, Kimberly Seltzer
and Gerry Stoker**

palgrave

First published 2002 by
PALGRAVE
Houndmills, Basingstoke, Hampshire RG21 6XS and
175 Fifth Avenue, New York, N. Y. 10010
Companies and representatives throughout the world

PALGRAVE is the new global academic imprint of
St. Martin's Press LLC Scholarly and Reference Division and
Palgrave Publishers Ltd (formerly Macmillan Press Ltd).

ISBN 0-333-92891-1 hardcover
ISBN 0-333-92892-X paperback

This book is printed on paper suitable for recycling and made from fully managed and sustained forest sources.

A catalogue record for this book is available from the British Library.

Library of Congress Cataloging-in-Publication Data
Towards holistic governance : the new reform agenda / Perri 6 ... [et al.].
   p. cm. – (Government beyond the centre)
Includes bibliographical references and index.
ISBN 0-333-92891-1
 1. Public administration–Great Britain. 2. Great Britain–Politics and government–1997- I. 6, Perri, 1960- II. Series.

JN318 .T69 2002
351–dc21

2001058771

10 9 8 7 6 5 4 3 2 1
11 10 09 08 07 06 05 04 03 02

Printed in China

Contents

List of Figures

Acknowledgements

We are grateful to our publisher, Steven Kennedy, for unfailing patience and tact as an editor, and for invaluable guidance at critical points in the preparation of this book, and to Keith Povey for his labours to turn our text into something readable.

In a project of this nature, four authors accumulate a great many debts. The project was directed by Perri 6, who did much of the synthesis and data interpretation, and wrote the first complete draft of the text; all the field work was done by Diana Leat (local case studies in England, interviews in Australia) and by Kim Seltzer (telephone interviews on central government initiatives in Britain, case studies in the USA), who also prepared many of the initial analyses and some of the literature review; Siân Gibson conducted much of the early research interviews on local case studies in England, document collection, and some of the conceptual development. Gerry Stoker brought conceptual and theoretical rigour to the work and edited the draft text.

The research was funded by the Esmée Fairbairn Charitable Trust, and we are grateful to the Director, Margaret Hyde; by Sequent Computers, and we are grateful to Nick Penston, now at CISCO and to his successors Rob Green and NB Quin, Sequent Computers; and by ICL UK, where we are grateful to Gill Ringland and John Wolfe and Ian Perkins.

We are grateful to all the people who gave generously of their time and ideas, and in particular to Wendy Wallace, Zoë Reid and Arun Patel.

Particular thanks for their comments, suggestions and support go to the members of the Advisory Group: Robin Young, then of Cabinet Office; Jeremy Cowper, Better Government Unit, Cabinet Office; Genie Turton, then Government Office Director, Government Office for London; Francis Aldhouse, Deputy Data Protection Registrar; Paul Vevers, then Director of Audit Support, Audit Commission; Brian Briscoe, Chief Executive, Local Government Association; Annie Faulder, then Deputy Chief Executive, Kirklees Metropolitan Council; Sarah Tanburn, then Director of Strategy and Information, Hertfordshire County Council; Elizabeth Ransom, Director, Public Sector Consulting, KPMG Consulting; and Professor Vernon Bogdanor, Department of Politics, Oxford University.

Ian Christie, Tom Bentley, Geoff Mulgan, Ravi Gurumurthy, and Gavin Mensah-Coker provided invaluable comments on some of our early material. Professor Sir Adrian Webb, Vice Chancellor of Glamorgan University provided us with valuable comments on some chapters.

We are also grateful to Professor Patrick Dunleavy, Department of Government, and Professor Julian Le Grand, Department of Social Policy at the London School of Economics, for their criticisms of some of our arguments.

We are grateful to successive directors (Geoff Mulgan, and Tom Bentley), staff and trustees of Demos for supporting our research, and for publishing the first output from our work, *Governing in the round: strategies for holistic government*, from which we have drawn some material in most chapters of the present book, and who have generously given us permission to re-use it here, although often with extensive changes and amendments.

None of these people bears any responsibility for our errors, nor should they be assumed to agree with our arguments.

PERRI 6
DIANA LEAT
KIMBERLY SELTZER
GERRY STOKER

Introduction

The search for a more holistic approach to policy and management looks set to be as much a hallmark of public service reform in the early twenty-first century as the changes introduced under the rubric of 'new public management' or 'reinventing government' were in the closing decades of the twentieth.

This book is intended to provide a state-of-the art review both of the character and prospects of existing initiatives to foster 'joined-up government' and a grounded assessment of the possibilities and limits of moving substantially further to establish a new form of holistic governance centrally focused on delivering integrated policies and practices delivering genuinely desirable outcomes to meet real needs.

Our intention is not to write a utopian tract, although in contrast to the gloomy prognoses of many – especially academic – commentators, we do argue that it is possible to reconstruct our institutions of public administration in ways that can deliver more effective services and better economic and social outcomes for our communities. We do not underestimate the scale of the challenge, but believe that the challenge can be met and have attempted to provide at least a provisional route map for those who are interested in travelling down the path of reform. For this reason we have tried throughout the book to test our arguments against real developments and experiences both in the UK – where the New Labour government has been an early enthusiast and pathfinder for 'joined-up government' just as its predecessors were for privatisation and contracting out – and elsewhere.

Outline of chapters

The book begins with two chapters that provide an introduction to the practice of holistic governance. Chapter 1 presents a brief history of the aspiration for holistic government in the United Kingdom and notes the association of that aspiration with centrist politics. The emergence of a centre–left New Labour political force in the UK has once again brought the ambition to construct an effective and integrated government machine into prominence.

As Chapter 1 makes clear, it is difficult to overestimate the scale of the challenge that New Labour has set itself in reconstructing the delivery of the UK's public services and the customer – citizen interface with government. Yet the challenge has also been taken up in parts of Australia, New Zealand, Canada and the United States. It would be a mistake to claim that the UK is somehow in the lead in developing holistic governance forms and it is certainly not a view that this book promotes: rather we draw on the good, bad and indifferent experience of the UK in the New Labour years in government from 1997 to establish an argument about how the aspiration for holistic governance could be developed and brought to fruition.

Chapter 2 begins the serious business of defining what is involved in holistic governance. The chapter lays the conceptual groundwork for the remainder of the book. It presents an understanding of holistic governance in contrast to baronial, turf war or muddling through forms of governance. True holistic government emerges where government agencies and their partners share reinforcing objectives and can identify a shared commitment to a range of mutually supportive tools to achieve that objective. Perhaps full holism will be achieved only rarely but the aim is to move more governance processes in that direction. It is important to stress that holism is not opposed to specialisation. Rather, its enemy is fragmentation. The key challenge is how to give recognition to the need for a division of labour in any bureaucracy and its beneficial contribution of expertise while weeding out those roots of fragmented governance that undermine the system's capacity to get things done. The enemies of holism include both benign features of government such as current accountability systems and the more malign influence of, for example, professional capture of agencies. Holism rests on a view that something can be done to challenge the forces of fragmentation and sets for itself a task of reconstruction that extends all the way through from the formulation of inputs to the identification of appropriate outcomes.

Chapter 3 presents the case for and against holistic government. Holism has attracted many criticisms and we group them under three headings. There are critiques that suggest the goals of holism are futile, that reforms will end up making no real difference. Then there are arguments that the advent of holism will jeopardise current positive features of our system of governance. Finally there are those that argue that holism will have perverse and unintended impacts on our systems of governance. So the case against it is that it won't work, it would be undesirable if it did, and even if it wasn't undesirable – like many reform strategies – it will produce perverse and unwanted unintended consequences. These are serious challenges and before the meat of the development of holistic government is considered, Chapter 3 provides a systematic response to the critics. We recognise that the advocates of holism make strong and bold claims but our case is not for ushering in some new utopia. Rather, it is that the critics overdo their fatalism. We are not suggesting that holism will sweep all before it but equally we do not see it as inevitably blocked by either value-driven objections or overwhelming implementation problems.

Our case for cautious optimism starts from the theoretical perspective outlined in Chapter 4. We offer a rather different way of looking at institutions to that which tends to dominate the academic literature. Drawing on the work of Mary Douglas and other neo-Durkheimians we present an understanding of how social relations are constructed along certain lines that can co-exist in tension with one another. Hierarchist, communitarian, individualistic and fatalist tropes or ways of organising are identified and seen as providing different answers to basic organisational problems of coordination that lies at the heart of holistic governance. Holism, however, is not delivered by imposing any one of these tropes, for example by promoting extensively the scope of hierarchy, but rather by finding a new mix between the tropes that enables the system to work better. It is the subtlety of the neo-Durkheimian perspective that enables us to see the possibility of achieving a new organisational settlement. We do not and must not expect humans suddenly to behave in a new way or all come to think and act in the same way. Rather, by working with the grain of the complex forces within organisations, we argue, it is possible to imagine and achieve a new settlement that will bring beneficial consequences.

Chapter 5 describes the dilemmas of how to develop a successful reform strategy for holistic governance. It notes the inevitability of both top–down and bottom–up elements to any successful reform strategy. We begin with an understanding of how risks can be managed in any strategy, and argue for a balance between anticipation and resilience. The chapter illustrates how too heavy-handed and centralist an approach has caused problems, by examining risks and failures in the experience of reform in the first term of the new UK Labour government (1997–2001). Finally, we present the key lessons from the vast organisational change literature on strategies for the development of innovations of this kind. We note how crises are often crucial in stimulating change, how champions and ownership for reform have to be won and finally how successful change needs to be embedded in institutional reforms and the reconstruction of incentives.

Chapter 6 deals with the issue of how holistic working is established on the ground in co-operative relations between agencies and organisations. It examines how trust is created and how it is a key ingredient in successful holistic governance. The chapter draws on our research to show some of the most common forms of organisational resistance to holistic working and how key resources can be found to overcome resistance. We look at some of the skills and tactics of holistic working, and although the practical skills for undertaking joined-up working are similar to those generally involved in complex management contexts, we identify the special skills in what one of the respondents described as 'managing out of control'.

Chapter 7 looks at the way that information technology systems might contribute to more successful holistic working. It examines its contribution to service delivery, to the organisation of citizen input into the decision-making process and to the process of decision-making or governance. The difficulties posed by the potential threat to privacy by the greater and more effective use of information technology are also addressed. The chapter notes that ethical concerns over privacy have so far only been dealt with in a piecemeal manner and argues that a more systematic approach will have to be developed in the future.

Accountability, which is at the heart of holistic working, provides the focus of attention for Chapter 8. We argue that far from undermining accountability, holistic working offers the prospect of a more demanding and effective commitment to accountability. There is a tension sometimes between holistic working and existing forms of accountability that stretches back through the traditional silo structures of government. Yet it is possible to reconstruct accountability in tune with accountability principles. The chapter emphasises the key role in scrutiny and oversight functions in ensuring holistic working. In many respects creating accountability through mechanisms such as those witnessed in embryonic form in some of our case studies provide a stronger drive to holistic working than reorganising with executive structures.

Chapter 9 deals with the issue of finance and in many ways presents a sceptical analysis of what makes holistic governance work. Despite the much-vaunted experiments in holistic budgeting, we are not convinced that budget formation and allocation are the most important tools for holistic working. Rather, we think cultural changes in ways of working are the real keys to successful holism. The chapter reviews some of the more grandiose attempts at holistic budgeting before outlining how budgets can play a useful but limited role in holistic working.

Chapter 10 provides an overarching assessment of the prospects for holistic working. We show how holistic working could be institutionalised and, although it is not yet fully established in any country – and certainly not the UK – we see no inherent reason why it could not become the established form of governance for the early part of the twenty-first century.

We are not suggesting by this, however, that holistic working will dominate public management and government forever, we although do argue that its time has come in the present period. The embryonic forms we have observed suggest that there are no insurmountable obstacles to its establishment as the new dominant paradigm and practice.

About the research

This book is based on several years of study and research into initiatives in coordination and integration in public services, public management and policy making in the UK and elsewhere. It is not, however, a research report. Rather, it presents an argument about what is feasible, and it offers an interpretation of the evidence, which draws upon both the wider literature and our empirical case study for illustration.

In this section, we briefly summarise the nature of the research upon which this book is based. We have attempted to survey the academic literature as internationally as possible: this was principally carried out by 6 and Seltzer. The practitioner literature is so vast that no one could possibly read it all in a lifetime, and getting across a reasonable sample of it would require a much larger team than we could have brought together. Most of our empirical work was conducted in the UK: this consisted of nine local case studies using face-to-face interviews, mainly conducted by Leat and an extensive programme of telephone interviews with civil servants on UK national level initiatives conducted by Seltzer. The latter are discussed in Chapter 1. We have also drawn upon some of Seltzer's work on initiatives in the US.

Although the argument of the entire book is informed by our case studies, we make most extensive use of the interview material with public managers in the nine local initiatives in England in Chapters 5 (strategy), 6 (interorganisational relationships), 8 (accountability) and 9 (finance). We conducted the interviews and obtained documents locally during 1999 and early 2000. However, we continued to examine developments and to reflect on them in the text until mid-2001.

The nine initiatives are summarised in Figure 0.1. (All the names have been changed to protect the anonymity of our interviewees, who often spoke to us with a candour that would not have been possible if they were to be identifiable.)

Of these initiatives, one is involved in policy making and one wholly oriented to service provision. Within the group, some are centrally funded, some wholly locally funded; some involve only local bodies, and some

Figure 0.1 *Nine local initiatives*

Local initiative	Key activity	Functions coordinated or integrated	Lead agency, if any	Structure
Mixborough Early Years Initiative	Integrated early years provision	Social services, education, early years play, childcare	Local authority	Local authority managed agency
Eastwoodshire Young Citizens Programme	Cross-agency pro-active work to identify and intervene early to help young people at risk of involvement in crime or delinquency	Social services, police, youth justice, education welfare	Local authority	Local authority managed agency
Southbrookborough Partnership	Integrated services for people with learning disabilities	Social services, health services	Local authority and health authority equally	Jointly owned subsidiary
Midcaster City Centre Company	Integrated city centre management for economic development	Economic development, development control, vocational training, business community support	Local authority, chamber of commerce	Arms length company
Beltham Single Regeneration Budget programme	Coordinated area economic development	County council, district council later unitary authority (re transport, land use planning and development control, vocational training, etc.), police authority, careers service, business partnership, health authority, race equality council, Training and Enterprise Council, council for voluntary service, etc.	Unitary authority	Arms length partnership body

Norlingshire Environmental Audit	Integrated environmental audit and planning process	Environmental protection, land use planning, economic development, business community, health authorities, voluntary organisations, utility companies	County council	Forum convened by county council
Redbrickham Social Strategy Focus Group	Integrated city-wide policy process for community and economic development	Economic development, land use planning, community development, business community, voluntary sector, police, probation, Training and Enterprise Council, Benefits Agency, regional office of government	City council	Forum convened by city council
Riverborough Local Service Centre, Alberton	One-stop shop for individual services and case support	All local authority departments	Borough council	Borough council agency
Uplandton Partnership	Integrated policy planning and economic development	Borough and county council's economic development, education, land use planning functions, health authority, police, employment services, schools, colleges, voluntary organisations, churches.. Housing associations, youth and community and careers services	Borough council	Arms length partnership body

involve local offices of centrally accountable agencies. However, all sprang up in response to concerns felt locally. Interviews were conducted with chief officers and, where possible, with leading elected or appointed members. Questioning focused on the origins of initiatives, the perception of obstacles and problems, opportunities and conditions for 'success', defined very simply by ability to survive as an integrated or coordinating entity, beyond the initial phase.

In addition, we conducted telephone interviews and world wide web searches on several initiatives from around the world that have achieved particular prominence in recent practitioner and policy making debates. These included:

- Centrelink Australia – integrated service provider
- New Zealand Strategic Result Areas Initiative
- E-government in Canada
- Oregon Shines – integrated policy benchmarking
- US federal Department of Housing and Urban Development – multi-skilled employee teams programme
- Florida full service schools programme
- Michigan, Vermont, Missouri and California integrated children and families programmes

It should be clear from this brief list of major initiatives across the Anglophone world, and from comparative reviews of particular types of integration such as one-stop shop programmes in Europe (see Hagen and Kubicek, 2000), just how widespread are the recent programmes of holistic working across governments.

The purpose of this book is to see what can be learned from this international trend about effective and sustainable holistic government.

1 Holism Past and Present

In this chapter we explore the history of the aspiration for holistic government. This aspiration, we show, wells up cyclically and is related to cycles over which centrist politics erupt in political history.

The imperative for coordination and integration in government is far from new, although the precise forms, preferred instruments and particular problems have changed over time. Collaboration, coordination and integration between agencies of government, whether described as 'joined-up', 'holistic' 'coordinated' or 'integrated', have long been principally conceived as a goal for public administration within states. Holistic governance is not new. Indeed, in some ways, achieving coordination across the organisational instruments by which goals are pursued is an eternal problem – perhaps, *the* eternal problem – in governance. Concern and priority for this waxes and wanes over decades, but it surely cannot wholly die away.

Nevertheless, the conscious design of the civilian executive and administrative machinery of government – as distinct from, say, the design of constitutional arrangements for the allocation of legitimate authority – is a concern of politics that has arisen essentially since the eighteenth century. It is not that civilian public servants did not exist before then, although certainly they were not employed in such numbers. Rather, it is that the range of tasks entrusted to civilian public services remained relatively narrow until that century.

Previous initiatives in holistic governance

In the eighteenth century a rising concern for the management of civilian populations came to the centre of what it is to govern in what Foucault (1991) called 'bio-politics'. Thus, in Prussia and elsewhere, government statistical bureaus emerged to gather, collate and analyse new kinds of measures on civilian populations (Hacking, 1990). These activities required more modest administrative machinery than was previously thought necessary.

The range of government tasks began to grow in the nineteenth century with the development of the urban and industrial economies and new

9

forms of transport and communications. All of these led to increased political demands for new forms of regulation and public investment in, for
example, public health (Porter, 1999), policing (in the modern sense), early
forms of land use planning control, health and safety and other regulation
of the labour process, and so forth. The advent of global colonialism
required new forms of civilian administration overseas. The development
of new financial instruments soon created a pressing demand, for innovation in regulation (Polanyi, 1944). In turn, this called for new forms of
organisation of civilian government. As a result almost all the forms of
organisation that dominate our lives today were invented in the nineteenth
century. Key new forms of organisation invented in that period include the
professional civil service, local government, the joint stock company, the
charitable trust, the co-operative and the friendly society or industrial and
provident societies in Britain, and in continental Europe, by the beginning
of the twentieth century, the association and foundation forms (6, 1998a).

The major drivers of both functional growth and reorganisation of the
civilian public service in the twentieth century have been, of course, first,
the advent of total warfare in which civilians were targets and combatants
on a scale not previously experienced within Europe, and second, the polit
ically irresistible demands for welfare programmes. Welfare measures
emerged ranging from basic schooling, pensions and unemployment insur-
ance, rented housing and medicine free at the point of use, all the way to
major middle class welfare programmes such as subsidies for home ownership and tertiary education.

In the British case, the basic principles of both organisation and interorganisational relationship can be traced back to the mid-nineteenth century.
The Northcote-Trevelyan report of 1854, as implemented with sometimes
more and sometimes less reluctance and conflict over the following
decades, instituted the process of the professionalisation of the civil service, and in particular the substitution of recruitment on merit instead of
patronage and, in some cases, nepotism and corruption. During the second
half of the nineteenth century, however, more attention was given to probity in the recruitment system than to structure of the civil service. The
main structural changes were to give greater authority to the Treasury over
the service as a whole, both individually and organisationally, to secure
greater Parliamentary scrutiny over taxation, budgeting and expenditure
(Silberman, 1993). The assumption about the relationship between organisational coordination and individual recruitment, promotion and career
development seems to have been that the creation of a professional class of
educated generalists would provide the personnel basis on which coordination across functions could be achieved.

The same century saw the steady development of another kind of rationalisation. This took the form of the Benthamite utilitarian tradition that organisational form should follow task, and that the design of administrative organisation should follow the rationality of policy design, rather than reflect the balance of political forces and their special interests. It was this outlook that inspired Edwin Chadwick's reforms of local government and public health (Challis *et al.*, 1988, pp. 5–7). He was neither the first nor the last to find that interests, politics and institutions and what Weber (1947) called *Wertrationalität* can limit the scope for reorganisation along the lines desired by the narrower concerns of utilitarian professionals, or what Weber called *Zweckrationalität*.

At the end of the Great War, the Haldane Committee's report of 1918 represents an important point of reconsolidation in the principles of functional organisation (Jordan, 1994). Having considered the alternatives to organising departments by function or similar activity or service provided by related professions, Haldane dismissed them as unworkable for various reasons. Organising by clientele (papers, insured persons, children, unemployed, were the categories imagined) would lead, it was argued, to 'Lilliputian administration'. Terri-torially organised governance might be appropriate for colonies and for those subaltern functions allocated to local authorities, but not for great departments of state. In the United States, of course, clientele based government is politically much more legitimate, and indeed often conceded at both state and federal level as a way to respond to the demands of particular interests. For coordination between departments, Haldane considered that we should look to the Cabinet: coordination should be a matter of political initiative in every case rather than a matter for civil servants to initiate. Nor should it be institutionalised in the organisational structure below the level of the Cabinet, lest political authority over civil service – which had been fought for with such determination over the previous century – be undermined.

One way to interpret the 1945 settlement by Clement Attlee's Labour Government that reorganised and massively extended the British welfare state is that it was designed, in part, to bring coordination to what was perceived as a fragmented system of voluntary and public provision. The system was seen to be competing ineffectively, covering target clienteles patchily, and failing to bring together appropriate packages of services. The growth in the range of activities for which local government was made responsible during the twentieth century was often justified on the grounds that bringing together several functions under the aegis of a single elected authority would better enable the coordination of those services than a system of wholly separate boards. This case was made with some vigour in respect of the municipally owned utilities (Chandler, 2000).

Towards the end of the 1960s a new wave of concern arose about the failings of coordination within the British welfare state and within local government, and urgent efforts were seen as necessary to remedy these defects. The Seebohm Committee, which reported in 1968, provides a particularly clear example. Its concern was the lack of coordination and integration within the personal social services. Its analysis identified problems of inefficient duplication in some fields and inadequate coverage in others, difficulty of access by the public, lack of clarity in both the division of labour between professionals and appropriate relationships between different professions. It also recognised issues concerning lack of foresight and anticipation in the process of investing in the development of new services to respond to changing demand. Debates that arose in the Seebohm enquiry continue to resonate through debates about coordination today: for instance, whether to coordinate around defined clienteles which may be scattered geographically, or whether to coordinate around small geographically defined neighbourhoods or 'patches'; how to manage relationships between health care provided by the National Health Service and social care provided by local government; how to balance and deploy generic and specialist staff (Challis, 1990).

Seebohm's solution was typical of its time and of the wave of initiatives in holistic working that followed during the 1970s. It proposed integration under the umbrella of a single giant executive agency, which, in the case of the public personal social services, was to be the local authority social services department under the director of social services who would personally hold legal powers and duties. The preference for structural reorganisation was characteristic of the 1960s and early 1970s, as the mergers of central departments under the Heath administration of 1970 to 1974 showed. By the 1970s, however, interest was already shifting to coordinating tools of budgetary and informational kinds. While the present wave of initiatives tends to privilege these kinds of tools, the creation in 1997 of the vast Department for the Environment, Transport and the Regions shows that the instrument of structural reorganisation is far from wholly eschewed.

While the Seebohm committee was one of many in the late 1960s under the first Wilson administration concerned with coordination at the local level, its exact contemporary devoted to the question of reorganisation at the centre was the Fulton Committee. Its report, also published in 1968, has become a byword in public administration for the vaulting ambition of rationalism. Like Seebohm, Fulton was preoccupied with the balancing of generalists and specialists in the overall mix, and with the division of labour between them. For Fulton, as for Haldane, cross-departmental coordination was a matter for the political executive, but, unlike Haldane, the role of the Cabinet Office was stressed. The Fulton report was never fully implemented and by the 1970s the Heath administration was more concerned with other strategies for coordination from the centre than with coordination through the division of labour between types of staff.

At the centre, the creation of the Central Policy Review Staff was envisaged by some radical centralists as the germ of a Prime Minister's department, and by others as providing the centre with a long range capacity necessary for future policy level coordination. Certainly, it was expected to take the lead in what would come to be called 'cross-cutting issues' under the Blair administration thirty years later. The Joint Framework for Social Policies presented in 1975, although published under the second Wilson government and written by new politically approved staff, reflected the Heathite vision of a centrally set coordinating framework for policy (Challis *et al.*, 1988).

Just as the 1970s were the era of coordination from the centre and gigantism in central government, so they were too in local government, with the emphasis across the main parties on corporate management techniques and big structures accountable to a political centre, as advocated by the Redcliffe-Maud Royal Commission on Local Government and the Bains report.

One leading commentator and sometimes policy advisor has described the ambitions for holism in the 1970s as based upon too rationalistic a conception of how decisions can be made in government, and upon assumptions about interorganisational relationships that were too altruistic. By contrast, he argues, the 1980s were characterised by the opposite extreme, or attempts to induce whatever coordination and integration might seem practicable based upon equally overly simple accounts of decision-making and interorganisational relationships as based upon bargaining under general incentives to work together (Webb, 1991).

Indeed, the 1980s represented a period in British politics, no doubt in reaction against the priorities and perceived failures of the previous decade, where government was much less concerned with coordination. The Central Policy Review Staff was abolished fairly early, and no effort was made to resurrect anything like the Joint Framework. The impact of such reforms as the Financial Management Initiative, the creation of the Next Steps agencies, and other programmes of creating dedicated agencies began to increase fragmentation along the functional lines. Indeed such bodies – in particular the Urban Development Corporations – were justified famously by Michael Heseltine because they would 'focus like a laser beam' and be 'single-minded'. The rise of New Management reforms with their emphasis on separating client and producer roles rather encouraged fragmentation, as governments engaged in what came to be called 'steering rather than rowing', following Osborne and Gaebler (1992).

Nevertheless, by the end of the 1980s and even more so in the 1990s, the British Conservative governments began to feel the need to correct some of the fragmenting effects of their own reform directions. Even as early as 1983 there were modest initiatives in joint finance and joint planning between health and social services. On his return to the Department of the Environment in the 1990s, Heseltine began to talk of the need for partnership and launch a range of initiatives which encouraged joint working. It was not until the arrival of New Labour in 1997 that joined-up government became a key slogan and objective.

The cyclical pattern behind interest in holistic governance

The following aspirations seem to rise and fall together in the history of government reform:

- *Problem-solving government*: that certain felt problems should be addressed and solved by government action (even – or especially – if that government action is oriented to creating and sustaining certain kinds of markets), rather than the argument being accepted in advance that these problems are insoluble or that any solution would be worse than the problem;
- *Effectiveness in policy design and implementation*: for effectiveness of governments' social, domestic and economic policies in their publicly stated terms and for their publicly stated goals of social problem-solving, rather than for other implicit goals, symbolic reassurance or simply to provide selective benefits to important interest groups;
- *Rational design*: for systems of accountability, evaluation, data collection on performance and outcomes, and financing within governance systems that are designed to serve that end;
- *Integration*: for more specific coordination between agencies as a key feature of that design;
- *Prioritisation*: for more effort to devise systematic, even formula-based strategies by which to settle priorities between problems and available solutions for the attention of politicians, for the allocation of resources, for the allocation of effort in scrutiny and oversight, rather than simply relying on politics, pressure, media interest and the diligence of interest groups and lobbies and a responsive culture of democratic political

government that allocates according to popular concerns, decibels of interest group voice and media pressure; and

- *Anticipation and prevention*: for increased institutionalisation of fore-sight and anticipation, and the use of more preventive mechanisms in the design of policies and specific interventions in particular cases.

These aspirations were very clear in the politics of the New Liberals and the debate about the goal of 'National Efficiency' in Edwardian times. These ideas clearly informed the Webbs' minority report on the review of the poor laws in 1909. Despite the commitment to functional organisation at the heart of its recommendations, the 1918 Haldane report stressed the importance of cabinet coordination at the top of the system. The same basic principles inspired Harold Macmillan's 1938 *Middle Way* which stressed coordination. The same imperative lay behind the Heath government's programmes for zero-based budgeting, programme analysis and review (PAR), the creation of the Central Policy Review Staff, and the Joint Framework for Social Policies which the CPRS produced in 1975 (Challis *et al.*, 1988, chapter 1), just as they can be found underpinning the programme of Michael Heseltine for one-stop shops and the single regen-eration budget on his return to government in the 1990s, and Roger Freeman's vision for *government direct*. These themes are echoed in the New Labour programme for holistic government and its analogues in the Australian, New Zealand and US administrations of the late 1990s and early 2000s. Turning from reform of central government administration and policy-making to the local level, much the same trajectory can be dis-cerned with the interest in coordination in the 1960s around the time of the Redcliffe-Maud report finding later echoes in the 1970s debates about 'corporate' management (Cockburn, 1977).

In the UK it is possible to see a range of motivations in this cyclical concern with holism. The first is that one purpose of holistic governance is to engage in priority setting in a different way. Budgeting methods such as zero-based budgeting, and evaluation and scrutiny techniques such as pro-gramme analysis and review in the 1970s or the role of holistic spending review in the late 1990s, emphasise the importance of the aspiration to be systematic and not 'merely' responsively political in setting priorities.

The second is that another objective is to underpin organisational change with cognitive change, and specifically with a greater role for anticipation and foresight. It is no coincidence that the 1970s and the late 1990s were both periods in which there was great interest in futures work in government, and when the centre committed resources to large-scale scenario building exercises.

The third is the importance of strengthening the capability of the political centre to make decisions, whether that is the centre of central or of local government. Finally, the fourth is that holistic working requires rethinking the role of professions and professionals: issues of recruitment, status, retention, training and personnel management inevitably become central.

A roughly similar story but with slightly different chronology can be told for the United States (Agranoff, 1991). The 1960s and 1970s saw a wave of local, state and federal initiatives in holistic working, which were in retrospect judged too ambitious, and by the end of the Carter administration in the late 1970s, although major academic assessments could be made (Agranoff and Pattakos, 1979), governmental interest was waning. Under Reagan, the attention shifted to other priorities. Only in the 1990s with the encouragement of a Democratic President was the timid and quiet experimentation in holistic working at state and local level brought together, given a central policy commitment, and integrated into the second wave of public management reform. Again, it was the relatively centrist administrations of Ford and Carter in the 1970s, and Clinton in the 1990s, that gave greatest priority to holistic working. While the near social democratic (by US standards) administration of Johnson in the 1960s largely assumed that coordination would develop in any case – the error behind that assumption was the subject of one of the defining texts of political science, namely, Pressman and Wildavsky's (1973) study of implementation failure. Failure was due, in part, to failure of appropriate levels of coordination and integration.

Explaining the rise and fall of holism: centrist politics

What can be learned from this brief and schematic reminder of the chronology of twentieth century reforms and the recurrent themes of previous initiatives in coordination? Why do these ideas keep coming back in slightly different forms? The answer may lie in their resonance with a particular centrist style of politics and its internal contradictions but also in its capacity to leave behind an influential institutional legacy.

It is not unreasonable to argue that, despite the rhetoric of radicalism associated with the Webbs, as well as Heseltine and Blair, these are essentially centrist governments. Contrary to the arguments of critics such as Rhodes (2000, pp. 69–74), the commitments of holistic working, coordination and problem-solving government are not the peculiar domain of the socialist left at all. Genuine radicals of the socialist left have always objected to the idea that utilitarian policy effectiveness should be put above the goal of securing the interests of particular social classes or groups, and have been highly suspicious of utilitarian instrumentality in policy design. Equally, the genuine radicals of the liberal and libertarian right have always rejected the very idea of anticipation and prevention (Wildavsky, 1988), while many on the more authority-oriented right, whether from disdain or fatalism, reject the idea of problem-solving as being at the heart of governance (Oakeshott, 1947). What radicals of all stripes have in common is a commitment to raw politics above policy. Whatever the actual content of radical politics, the effect of such radicalism in government is often to allow the division of labour in government and public services to develop in ways that are later seen to call for institutional coordination and ordering. In theory, some radicals want to roll back government altogether, but in practice, the difficulties of doing this typically limit them to curtailing its growth, cutting certain activities and using outsourcing and other mechanisms to reform the delivery, in ways that further the processes of fragmentation.

Centrism is based on attempting to institutionalise social peace between rival forms of social organisation. It is not necessarily an unprincipled fudge, or simply technocratic. Moreover, the focus on effectiveness and coordination on defined tasks and instrumental rationality of the centrist programmes for public administration has a deep connection with centrist efforts to limit the polarisation of political culture.

The second common factor between these centrist movements and governments for coordinated effective government is that they often see themselves as correcting the excesses of a previous direction in policy and public administration towards fragmentation or incoherence. Just as the advocates of joined-up government today see their programme as responding to the problems inherited from the New Management era, so the Fabian and New Liberal rationalisers immediately before and after the First World War were reacting to the consequences of the Victorian reforms of the civil service and local government. Similarly the Heathite Tories of the 1970s saw themselves as correcting the chaotic system of governance inherited from the post-war welfare settlement.

The third factor is a consequence of the second. The successive waves of centrist rationalism are based on programmes of social peace between capital and labour and on attempting to focus on more modest goals than the governments they replaced or the movements they displaced. Today, this means combating social exclusion rather than achieving equality; in the Edwardian era it meant efficiency rather than ever expanding global domination or vast social transformation.

Crucially, reforms in public administration launched by centrist governments contain elements that are irreversible and which lay down new
sedimentary layers of institutional structure into systems of governance,
which survive succeeding waves of radicalism and centrism. The history of
government reform is not simply the story of an unending cycle between
centrism and one of a small group of radicalisms, each disorganising the
institutional reforms of its predecessor. Institutionalisation in structures of
government, in the formation of professions, in the design of systems of
accountability and budgeting may be difficult to achieve, but it is achieved
more often and more deeply than is imagined by those critics who see only
failure at the end of each wave. Indeed, the hand of Trevelyan is still visible in the recruitment, promotion and grading of the British civil service,
just as that of Chadwick can be discerned in the basic model of local government. The Heath government of the 1970s, notwithstanding its failures
in other fields, left the legacies of its gigantism in departmental structure,
of its commitment to long range central policy-making. That administration's belief that reform of the budget process is the key to better government is deep and lasting in British government, and is among the centrist
reforms currently being attempted across the English-speaking world. This
tends to discredit the critics who suggest that because the advocates of
holistic government cannot expect to achieve all their goals, they can
expect to achieve nothing at all.

Centrism has, at its heart, the aspiration that the imperatives of practical
politics and instrumental policy management can at least in some measure
be aligned. Cynics argue that this is utopian and, of course, if taken liter-
ally and applied across all fields of governance, it would be. Cynics rightly
point to the ways in which centrist governments fail, and their programmes
for rational government reform are undermined by the power of political
interests, the power of institutions, the intractability of social problems
to programmatic treatment. Of course, no one believes in the myth that
politics and policy can always or indefinitely reinforce one another – that
is the fallacy that 'all good things go together', as the late Isaiah Berlin
put it (Berlin 1990). The complete dominance of utilitarian technical
design of organisational structures – even if there could be agreement on
what that would be – is indeed politically unrealistic and, in a liberal
democracy, the absolute dominance of a single design principle may be
undesirable.

Centrist projects achieve more than some critics allow and their basic
imperatives continue to well up in democracies and their programmes
achieve a degree of institutionalisation. The empirical focus of this book is
on the latest centrist project to emerge in British politics: New Labour.

The roots of the New Labour agenda for 'joining up'

The government that came to power in June 1997 in Britain, after eighteen years in opposition, arrived with a programme that certainly required very large-scale change in the public sector if it was to be delivered. However, there was nothing in the New Labour manifesto that indicated how central the aspiration for holistic governance would become. The commitment did, however, take shape surprisingly quickly. There were several reasons for this.

First, there were important proximate causes. Many of the huge number of task forces and policy reviews commissioned in the first few weeks in office produced recommendations for more integration and coordination across fields of policy formulation and implementation. Second, policy inheritance was an important factor. The incoming government inherited from the previous administration a number of major initiatives towards integration that it had neither ideological reason nor political desire to abandon. These included the reformed elements of the Urban Programme and the electronic government programme for single points of access for citizens and businesses to all public services which had been taken forward by Roger Freeman, as he then was, as Chancellor of the Duchy of Lancaster, or minister in the Cabinet Office, and Mr Heseltine's attempt when he was at Trade and Industry to produce a one-stop-shop for business dealings with government.

Second, we must consider some forces that combine long-standing institutionalised pressures within the centre–left with more conjunctural considerations. The impetus for integration first came to seem urgent and take shape in social policy. For New Labour's commitment to combat what they termed social exclusion soon required a wide range of integrative activities. The growing demographic and therefore political importance of older voters brought higher up the agenda the imperative for greater integration between health and social care, which had been a gnawing problem for many decades.

Moreover, the decision to accept the very tough public spending restrictions set in the final budget of the outgoing Conservative Chancellor of the Exchequer (finance minister) Kenneth Clarke – so tough that, had the Conservatives been re-elected, it is quite possible they themselves would have relaxed them – left New Labour with a problem. The fear – entirely reasonable, given the history of past Labour governments – was that a significant initial increase in public expenditure, even if (or perhaps especially if!) accompanied by an increase in the ordinary or higher rates of personal income tax, would trigger pressures on the price of government debt which was running at high levels, or on the exchange rate for an already overvalued currency, or on general inflation and hence on interest rates. Such measures also carried political risks, given that polling data suggested strongly that much of the electorate was prepared to trust new Labour only on the basis that people could believe in their fiscal orthodoxy. This may be taken as a kind of informal institutional constraint. However, in the particular political setting, it created a conjunctural pressure. Some kind of initiative was required for the public services that could take forward the government's agenda without requiring large increases in spending in the short term or major structural re-organisation which might prove a distraction. The aspiration for what Prime Minister Tony Blair was calling 'joined-up' government even as early as a month after the election in his first social policy speeches (for example, the major speech on the Aylesbury estate in South London in July 1997) fitted the requirement well.

Further, movements in the marketplace of ideas may have had an impact, at least on short-run timing and the availability of the particular form that the aspiration for holistic governance. During the mid-1990s, there had been a growing chorus of criticism by academic political scientists and influential practitioners of 'fragmented government' especially at the local level (e.g., Clarke and Stewart, 1997; Alexander with Orr, 1995; Hodgkin and Newell, 1996). In contrast, much of the earlier academic and practitioner literature criticising the reinvention reforms of the 1980s and early 1990s was focused on issues concerning the role of private finance, the private sector, the role of contracts, transaction costs, and so on. In the second half of 1997 the aspiration for integration was beginning to take shape among senior civil servants. There is a disagreement over who first used the phrase 'joined-up government'. One candidate for the prize is Sir Robin Mountfield, a permanent secretary who retired in 1999 (Mountfield, 2000). Another is Geoff Mulgan, now the Director of the central think tank, the Performance and Innovation Unit. It has been said of each that they used the phrase before the general election. In 1997 too, the first full-scale manifesto for holistic governance in Britain was published, under the title *Holistic Government* (written by Perri 6), which quickly gained the attention and interest of many national and local policy-makers. However, without the other factors, this would hardly have been decisive: after all, most such documents sink without trace.

Finally, as so often is the case (John, 1998; Hood, 1994), causal factors in the market place of ideas cannot readily be distinguished from the effects of political and policy networks (Knoke, 1990). The development of the integration agenda in New Zealand, in some states of the USA and in Australia at both commonwealth and state level in the 1990s certainly had an impact on the British debate and on New Labour in particular.

The New Labour government put much greater effort than had the Major administration on the active search for policy ideas from other countries. Links with the Clinton administration at federal level in the USA have been well documented, but many senior policy staff from London were sent to examine other countries ranging from Singapore to Victoria in Australia. The trailblazing role of the second wave of New Zealand reforms (see below) to put in place key over-arching strategic objectives around which coordination and integration were to occur was of particular significance. Whilst in no sense could the British reforms be described as a straightforward case of policy transfer (probably, there are no such cases in the history of governance), some lessons were clearly taken, whether or not 'correctly'.

Of these various causal factors, one that many political scientists would typically expect to look for behind any policy change is signally absent. This is the self-interest of junior to middle ranking civil servants or local government officers and the self-interest of the great public sector professions. This is entirely deliberate, for these are the groups that have no immediate institutionally produced interest in holistic governance. By contrast, some and perhaps many senior civil servants and local government chief officers may see in the agenda an opportunity for, and a means to pursue, 'bureau-shaping', or focusing their offices on interesting policy work and policy management (Dunleavy, 1991). That is not to say that the institutional interests of middle and junior ranking civil servants and local government officers or the great professions are actually threatened by holistic governance, although that may also be true in some cases. However, they are not active forces for holism, and, depending on one's view about the trend in the relative power of these groups over public policy formulation and implementation, this may or may not be a significant limitation in the aspiration for the institutionalisation of holistic governance. Certainly active obstruction by these groups can make successfully implemented policy change very difficult, and this has been documented many times for many countries in literature on street level bureaucracy, 'bottom-up' policy implementation, professional capture, and so forth. However, these forces alone are not necessarily entirely decisive. It should be remembered that much of the literature that made the strongest claims for the power of such groups to capture or block reform in government was actually written in the 1970s (e.g., Niskanen, 1971; Lipsky, 1980). It was shortly after that period that politicians, perhaps in reaction to similar perceptions about the flow of power, began to try to seize back the initiative. In the Thatcher and Reagan administrations, the relative power of these groups over policy formulation seemed to decline. That is not say that perfect implementation is even remotely likely, or that political author-ity is now absolute, or that middle and junior ranking officials and profes-sionals have been neutered: far from it. Rather, we wish only to suggest that the gloomy literature of the 1970s that the self-interest of public servants would typically be decisive needs to be read with some qualification today.

Certainly, there have been many New Labour commitments, which, as we shall see in Chapters 5 and 6, have quickly come into conflict with their holistic government agenda. The five specific pledges about public services offered on a credit card sized piece of paper to millions of voters in the 1997 election campaign were all framed in terms of activities or inputs. In particular, the efforts required of health managers to achieve the waiting time reductions promised have often not only distracted energy from, but actively got in the way of, other kinds of initiatives that might have yielded more health gain through joint working.

Other major initiatives of the New Labour government will probably be shown to have had an ambivalent relationship with the holistic governance agenda. Consider the impact of the devolution of powers to Scotland, for example. On the one hand, this may make some cross-border linkages slightly more difficult to organise, and when, sooner or later, the priorities of the Scottish Parliament start to diverge significantly from those of Westminster, this could become an important problem. On the other hand, the creation of the Parliament and the reorganisation of the civil service structure and development of new political relationships between Edinburgh and the local authorities represents a major opportunity to develop forms of holistic working in Scotland (Leicester and Mackay, 1998), which could include significant refocusing on genuine outcome measures (Ralls and Thomson, 1999).

The New Labour holistic governance programme

In the period prior to public expenditure announcements in the summer of 2000, the New Labour government managed to introduce a plethora of – indeed, perhaps too many, as we shall see in Chapters 5 and 6 – initiatives in holistic working, some of which we now briefly review. Some initiatives are led and conducted by a single department, but because they are con-ducted in ways that cut across the work of many departments, do not them-selves involve service provision, and are designed to be based on outcomes rather than functions, play an important role in holistic governance. The Comprehensive Spending Review (CSR), for example, conducted by the Treasury alone, is one of the most important of this kind. In the first CSR, there were a small number of studies conducted to measure expenditure on clienteles and problems; in the second CSR published in 2000, there were fifteen. Whereas the first set of Public Service Agreements between the Treasury and the spending departments contained targets largely expressed in input and activity terms, the series published with the second CSR contained far more expressed in outcome terms, albeit often with qualifications. However, the calculations of what is currently being spent, broken down by outcome, are not published: only expenditure totals for specific cross-cutting budgets are provided (HM Treasury, 2000).

Some initiatives are 'joined-up' principally at the centre in policy formulation and oversight, but their delivery and implementation is mainly the responsibility of a single department or agency or at most two. This is the case, for example, with the welfare-to-work programme called New Deal. The Treasury, the Department of Social Security and the Department for Education and Employment are the three principal policy actors in the New Deal, and even commentators who are generally sceptical about holistic governance consider that the arrangements for joint policy development and oversight at the centre seem to be working well (Smith, Marsh and Richards, 2000). At the local level, the Employment Service is often the lead agency, and the local benefits offices play a role more akin to what we shall (see Chapter 2) call coordination rather than integration.

Other initiatives involve many agencies in both policy development and implementation. A particularly important theme in New Labour's social policy has been the way in which resources, expertise and organisational attention to problems have been focused on particular *neighbourhoods*, being areas significantly smaller than local authorities' jurisdictions, where problems are considered to be particularly severe. This spatial concentration is crucial both to the forms of social policy analysis favoured by ministers and to the organisational style. 'Zones' have been created around particular neighbourhoods, in which large consortia of central and local public agencies, voluntary bodies and private companies are to be assembled, often with a lead agency, and with specific budgets and authorisations to tackle problems.

There are now Education Action Zones, Health Action Zones and Employment Action Zones, and there are other areas that are eligible to bid for special funds such as the New Deal for Communities programme, and in addition, there are some special initiatives targeted in deprived neighbourhoods, such as the funding available for those Healthy Living Centres which are not located in Health Action Zones. The centres have both public health preventive roles and also a role in bridging barriers between health and social service provision for priority clienteles such as children and elderly people. In some cases, partnerships and consortia running zones can apply for waivers of particular regulations that are believed to obstruct joint working or achievement of key outcomes. These are conceived within the framework of the social exclusion strategy which stresses 'neighbourhood renewal'. There are risks in such defining of deprived areas. This kind of 'production of locality' (Appadurai, 1996, chapter 9) can result in areas being stigmatised, which can drive down house prices, encourage the healthiest, best educated and most employable to leave, further reduce quality of life, and make the initiatives self-defeating. However, they can provide the more imaginative and entrepreneurial public managers with opportunities to bring together agencies around a shared focus. The different types of zones have national networks through which ideas, good practice, problems and issues of professional development can be shared.

Some joint initiatives are defined around *outcomes* but not particularly focused geographically upon neighbourhoods, such as the crime reduction initiatives, which involve more partnerships between local authorities, the police and a variety of other agencies. Crime and Disorder Partnerships of several kinds are offered special funding.

A different approach to programmes requiring joint implementation at the local level involving a great many agencies, is to define funds and interventions around *clienteles* rather than around problems or outcomes. This is the strategy taken in the Surestart programme, which is designed to bring together childcare, primary health care, early education and play and family support in key neighbourhoods where child poverty is identified as being severe. In the 2000 spending review, the geographical scale of the programme is being expanded and another small scale programme for Early Excellence Centres is now being merged with SureStart. Another clientele defined programme of a different kind is Better Government for Older People, which offers not money but a status, national publicity and recognition to local initiatives in integrated service provision for older people.

Other such initiatives are defined around *problem areas*, but not around outcomes or clientèles. The initiatives in coordination across the criminal justice system are a good example of this approach, in which several budget heads are used to support local joint working initiatives to create seamless housing and employment support and rehabilitation for offenders and ex-offenders. One strand of this is the integrated information system for all the agencies involved in the criminal justice process, code named IBIS.

Then there is at least one programme defined around joint work to build *generic inter-organisational capacity* in fragile areas. The New Deal for Communities is a modestly funded discretionary budget open to bids from local authorities and community organisations, with the aims of promoting volunteering, supporting and developing small new community groups and networks between them, and of developing experiments in devolved joint forms of neighbourhood management.

There are also several budgets that can be used on ministerial initiative or on competitive bidding for joint working, but which are not defined specifically by outcome, clientele, problem area or generic organisational capacity, but which are entirely *generic*. The Invest to Save Budget can be used to support such things as integrated electronic service-delivery, co-location of agencies and 'one stop shops'. In the 2000 Comprehensive Spending Review, a new Policy Innovation Fund was created to support innovations of various kind, with a bias towards initiatives in holistic working.

There are also re-badged forms and new cases of quite traditional forms of holistic working, including joint planning programmes for rural areas conducted between the Ministry for Agriculture, Fisheries and Food, and the Department for the Environment, Transport and the Regions, joint finance and planning support for health and local authority social service collaboration.

A major and distinct category of New Labour initiative in holistic working in government is the use of the powers of the centre to exercise *regulation* of local government activity to encourage holism. The government came to office committed to replace the eighteen-year-old compulsory competitive tendering scheme with a new system. The replacement came to be known as Best Value, after the duty on local authorities to look for the 'best value' design and provider. However, unlike its predecessor, Best Value does enable imaginative authorities to package up services in quite new ways before seeking quotations from private providers, and it also permits cross-sectoral partnerships to bid. Potentially still more important, local authority plans must specify goals, which should be expressed in outcome terms, and derive their service plans from these goals. The plans must be consulted and there is a stringent inspection regime placed on local authorities, as well as traditional forms of audit, all of which are intended to exert pressure for more holistic working. Although this does allow important elements of discretion not permitted under the compulsory competitive tendering régime, the national framework, national standards and centrally set standard spending assessment system retain many elements of central influence over the objectives that local authorities can set. In addition, the Beacon Council programme will offer those authorities that satisfy national inspection of the quality of particular services over a period for which they apply for and are granted the status, eventually the possibility of greater fiscal autonomy.

The local government movement has sought to agree a series of compacts with the new Labour administration to govern a range of opportunities for more autonomy, in return for guarantees of achieving high standards of service provision. The Local Government Association (LGA) coordinates a programme of its members under the rubric, New Commitment to Regeneration, which seeks to bring integration not the swathe of special initiatives that have been the principal instruments of New Labour's approach but through coordination of the big mainstream budgets. The LGA has also proposed a 'local challenge' scheme that would extend the Beacon Council programme by offering the centre guaranteed improvement on agreed outcomes, to be achieved through integrated working, but instead of greater fiscal autonomy, the scheme would provide councils granted the status for a particular field, waivers from particular regulations that they could show were obstructing their performance: in this, it takes ideas from the Scandinavian 'free commune' schemes (6, 1999b). What eventually emerged in 2000 was a commitment to local public service agreements.

New Labour's style of holism, then, has been centralist, but has not been characterised by the adoption of a single grand method, in the way that the 1970s initiatives relying on particular models of budgeting and planning were. It has relied heavily on a plethora of special initiatives, and most of the emphasis has been on holism in social policy, by contrast with, for example, the aspirations for holistic macro-economic policy that dominated in the 1970s, or business support that were the hallmark of the Heseltine era, or the integration around environmental policy that has been more important in some other countries.

Conclusion

There are cycles in the priority attached by policy-makers to coordination and integration across the public services, and the recent and current upswing follows this pattern. The basic pattern is that interest rises with the waxing of centrism, and declines with its waning. In each political generation which has seen such a recrudescence of interest and effort in coordination across public services and policy-making, the same issues arise. The interest in coordination is linked with a shift, however nuanced, towards more anticipatory styles of policy-making, towards greater confidence that government has a positive – if limited and far from omnipotent – role to play in solving problems, that society's problems are not simply conditions to be lived with. Each return to emphasis upon coordination and integration directs the attention of policy-makers to the same issues – the disciplines that can effectively be placed upon policy-makers themselves to coordinate among themselves centrally the design of budgets, the crafting of appropriate boundaries between organisations, the dilemmas of centralisation and devolution of responsibility, the scope and limits of the aspiration for greater 'rationality' – understood in various ways – in policy formulation and implementation.

The exact techniques pursued and the particular aspirations raised differ between periods of effort towards holistic governance. These differences are unlikely to reflect any simple process of unclouded learning from the past, for institutional memory within political parties and central civil service systems is remarkably weak, and in any case, there are sharp limits upon how far those focused on the present and what seem to be its peculiar challenges, looking with the particular blinkers of their age, really can learn from the past. However, the recent British experiment is an important one to study, not only because of the very high priority attached to it from the very centre of government, but because it can be compared with other initiatives around the world, and because the central and local dimensions can be examined.

2 Understanding Holistic Governance: Towards a Conceptual Framework

In this chapter, we present the basic conceptual framework that informs the argument of the rest of the book. The chapter begins by considering the basic issues. What is being integrated? What is meant by coordination? How does it differ from integration? What is meant by 'holism' and how it is different from 'joined-up' government?

The chapter then asks, 'if holism is the solution, then what was the problem?' Our answer is that the problem is one of fragmented governance, and we offer an account of what is meant by fragmentation, showing that it is not the same thing as specialisation. We explore the roots of the exacerbation of fragmentation in the reforms of the 1980s and early 1990s. We show that the aspiration for holistic governance is an optimistic one, committed to the view that fragmentation is a problem that can be overcome, not a condition to be lived with.

Finally, the chapter examines in more detail the goals that holism requires, the range of particular activities or mechanisms involved, and concludes by offering a taxonomy of types of holism, along a spectrum, which will then be drawn upon in later chapters.

Dimensions of holistic governance: what is to be integrated?

We begin with an account of what it is that holists want to integrate. The challenge for holistic governance is to bring coherence at all the key levels of activity, namely,

- *Policy*: the process of making, formulating the content of policy, and then exercising oversight or scrutiny over its implementation;
- *Regulation*: the organisation, content and impact of regulation of individuals, private organisations and within government;
- *Service provision*: the organisation, content and impact of service provision; and

- *Scrutiny*: the evaluation, audit, interpretation and appraisal of performance in policy, regulation or service provision.

Figure 2.1 identifies three basic dimensions along which holistic working may be undertaken.

Firstly, there can be integration between different tiers of governance, or within the same tier – between local authority departments, between local and central agencies, between local agencies and programmes of particular Directorates-General of the Commission of the European Communities, or between local trading standards officers, national trade regulators and the global standards and trading authorities, or within a global network of national environmental or data protection regulators.

Next, there can be coordination within functions – getting the three armed forces to collaborate, persuading all the divisions of the Ministry of Defence to work together – or between few or many functions – just health and social care, or all the agencies involved in inner city renewal.

Finally, integration may work within the public sector, between public authorities and voluntary bodies (typically ones in receipt of government contracts or grants) or with private, proprietary companies.

Figure 2.1 *The dimensions of holistic working*

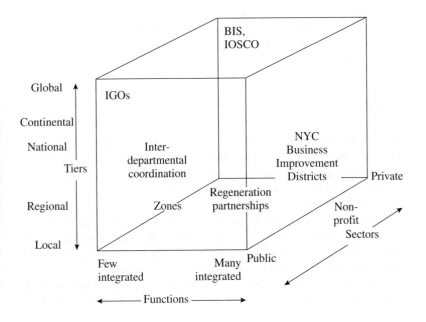

Figure 2.1 brings together these measures to give a three-dimensional space in which we situate a number of illustrative examples of holistic working. Consider first the case of many inter-governmental organisations (IGOs). By definition, they score highly on the vertical axis of the tiers of governance spanned; however, on the horizontal axis, most are so specialised that they integrate only a few functions; on the interior perspectival axis, they typically include only public sector bodies (Cupitt *et al.*, 1997 [1996]). Therefore, they are located at the upper left near the front of the box. The forms of global private governance such as the Bank for International Settlements in Basle (Reinicke, 1998, chapter 4; Wiener, 1999, chapter 3) and the International Organisation of Securities Commissions (http://www.iosco.org/) are also at the top, but at the back of the box reflecting their purely private ownership and private authority, but at the left because of their limited number of functions. At the bottom right at the back are the Business Improvement Districts of New York City, in which many functions in very small neighbourhoods dealing with only a few tiers of neighbourhood governance are handed over exclusively to the private sector. The New Labour experiments with zones and regeneration partnerships are also near the base of the box because they deal with national and local, but not with transnational tiers of governance, although they can encompass public, private and non-profit agencies; zones are to the left of regeneration partnerships because they are addressed (at least in theory) to fewer functions. Inter-departmental collaboration within national government in the UK must increasingly deal also with corresponding Directorates-General of the European Commission, and so occupies a higher place on the vertical axis.

Understanding key terms

Throughout this book, we use a series of terms with specific meanings, which we now explain. First, we situate the concept of holistic government by characterising it in contrast with the 'joined-up', and with 'fragmented' government, before moving on to define the ways in which we use the terms 'coordination' and 'integration'.

To understand these terms, we need first to distinguish between goals and means. Later in this chapter, we shall present a more detailed account of the substance and content of goals and means *within* holistic governance, but for the present, we are concerned with the relationships *between* the goals and the means employed by different agencies, departments, or authorities, whatever their content. In the first case, objectives may be in outright conflict; secondly, they might be consistent with one another; finally, they might actually be mutually reinforcing. Likewise, the means, the policy instruments and practical arrangements by which agencies pursue these goals may have the same kinds of relationship with one another. At one extreme, interorganisational relationships may exhibit high levels of collaboration, or a stable and effective division of labour or at least effective competition that strikes a sensible balance between stimulating innovation (dynamic efficiency) and driving down costs for a given output (static efficiency). At the other extreme, there may be organisational duplication, conflict or wasteful or destructive competition. Cross-tabulating these dimensions against another gives a space in which five of the nine logically available spaces are of interest to the present argument. Figure 2.2 summarises these cases.

Consider first the case of a straightforward conflict between agencies at both the levels of goals and means. For example, a Department of Trade and Industry policy on promoting electronic commerce through deregulation might come into direct conflict with a policy of the Data Protection Commission to promote consumer privacy, both because business wants access to personal data and the right to mine, warehouse and analyse it as strategists want, while the regulatory body want to secure a goal and the right to use means that quite simply contradict the departmental commitments.

Figure 2.2 *The relationship between goals and means*

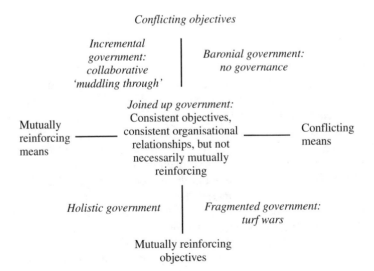

(We do not of course suggest that this is necessarily what is actually happening in Britain today!) The result is what we can call 'baronial government' in which department and agency engage in skirmishes and low level conflict to secure their own 'turf' and their independence and their control over the field, but in which people's expectations are reduced for the achievement of policy goals or the maintenance of the integrity of the means.

At the opposite end of the diagonal is true holistic government, which is defined as working back from a clear and mutually reinforcing set of objectives to identify a set of instruments which have the same happy relationship to one another. This is difficult to achieve, but the aspirations for many of the British government's zones and for some initiatives in budget reform described in later chapters of this book show that important experiments are being made in pursuit of the holistic grail. For example, to start with the goal of combating poverty in a defined neighbourhood and bringing together all the interventions – housing, employment, economic diversification, transport, social services, education, job training, leisure services and so on – that impact upon poverty, and re-engineering their professional practices and investment programmes, not only to collaborate as necessary but also to produce new rankings of their own functional goals to give appropriate and mutually consistent priorities to anti-poverty work is a demanding programme for any system of governance.

Where merely 'joined-up' initiatives ask the question 'what can we do together?', holistic initiatives ask 'who needs to be involved, and what basis, to achieve what we are all really here to achieve?' Therefore, 'joined-up' working is situated as the category where goals and means are consistent, but do not actually reinforce each other. For example, there is not necessarily a conflict between the goals of policy in the field of disability to put children with at least physical disabilities and the less severe learning difficulties into mainstream education, and the goals of the individual schools to secure high rates of GCSE passes. With the right kinds of support for mobility and classroom access, Braille-based software, and with commitment by teachers, children with a range of special needs can achieve grades at least as high as those of children with ordinary physical abilities from comparable backgrounds. However, these goals are not necessarily mutually supporting either. To make them consistent requires serious and consistent work over time, and in the absence of such work, at least the perception of a conflict can emerge. But joining up is at least possible, although fully holistic focusing on both general educational outcomes and disability achievement outcomes takes much more work still.

The situation where there are mutually reinforcing goals but destructive competition at the level of the instruments is well illustrated by the now standard case of the 'Berlin wall' between health and social care, long regarded as the test for successive projects for holism and integration in British public services (Webb, 1991). Both sides are concerned to promote the independence of older people; both want people out of hospitals and into more appropriate settings as soon as possible. However, the financial arrangements and perverse incentives, the professional rivalries, the local scarcities all militate against this. The problem is not specialism *per se*, but the poor design of the relationship between specialities. This is well described as fragmented government.

It might be imagined that where objectives conflict, the situation would be catastrophic. But this is not the case. Several generations of political scientists, and most famously the pathbreaking work of Lindblom (1955, 1959, 1979), have shown that it is in fact possible to set along tolerably well and to agree at a day-to-day level on what to do in practical terms, despite the fact each side in a relationship hopes for quite different outcomes from the agreed activities. Take the example of conflicting policy objectives within the criminal justice system. The overriding goal of the Crown Prosecution Service (CPS) is generally to bring to trial only those cases where they can secure convictions, and to achieve this, they are willing to engage in plea bargaining, by which guilty pleas on some charges are secured in return for dropping other charges. This can run counter not only to police goals of putting away some people for long periods but also to Home Office goals of deterrence. Yet in practice, an incremental, muddling along style has emerged in which the CPS tacitly agrees not to push plea bargaining too far, and the Home Office and the police accept that sometimes any conviction at all is better than none, when the evidence in the absence of a confession is weak. The system may be creaky, but it manages to stumble along without actually collapsing and without levels of crime being hugely adversely affected by these practical, often tacit, day-to-day settlements.

Much of this book is concerned with joined-up and holistic governance, since we generally consider baronial, fragmented and incremental government to be at best disappointing and at worst unacceptable. Cutting across both these categories, it is now important to distinguish between coordination and integration. For us, coordination refers to the development of ideas about joint and holistic working, joint information systems, dialogue between agencies, processes of planning, making decisions, while integration is concerned with their actual execution or implementation, through the development of common organisational structures and merged professional practices and interventions. Figure 2.3 shows the relationships between these key terms, and gives examples of each type.

Figure 2.3 *Defining the key terms*

Activity *Relationship between means and ends*	**Coordination** *Information, cognition, decision*	**Integration** *Execution, implementation, practical action*
Joined-up government Mutually consistent objectives, mutually consistent means, and means support objectives consistently	*Joined-up coordination* Most modest level – e.g. could be consistent with agreement by two agencies to work in separate fields, on an understanding of how to limit negative externalities	*Joined-up integration* e.g. Joint work but focused principally on prevention of negative externalities and of conflict between mission critical programmes
Holistic government Mutually reinforcing means, mutually reinforcing objectives, means support objectives in mutually reinforcing ways	*Holistic coordination* e.g. Understanding necessity for mutual involvement, but precise action not yet defined	*Holistic integration* Highest level of holistic governance, building fully seamless programmes

Wicked problems

The basic argument behind the holistic governance agenda is that government agencies are more likely to find solutions to the problems that citizens worry about most if their cultures, incentives, structures and other
capacities are oriented towards those problems, rather than towards the
efficient administration of processes. Most of the outcomes that matter are
the combined products of many departments, agencies and professions,
policies and practices (Smith, 1996). One definition of 'wicked problems'
is that they are precisely the ones that cross departmental boundaries and
resist the solutions that are readily available through the action of one
agency (Clarke and Stewart, 1997). It would appear that there is a lot of
wickedness in the world of public administration.

Medicine, for instance, does not produce health; indeed, health care
explains a very small proportion of health and illness. One well-known
estimate is that only about five years of the total twenty eight year increase
in British life expectancy over the course of the twentieth century can be
explained by the availability of medicine (Bunker *et al.*, 1994, summarised
in Tarlov, 1996; Wilkinson, 1996). Health is the product of factors relating

to diet, water quality, exercise, air quality, housing and working conditions, and behaviour, such as the use of nicotine, alcohol or other drugs, or
the take-up of dental checks. Likewise, crime is not much influenced –
sadly – by policing. Acquisitive crime is the product of aspirations and
expectations, of inhibitions and the acceptance of moral rules, cultures
(among young males in particular), the tolerance of others, the availability
of opportunities and the balance of rewards (Audit Commission, 1996,
1999). Employment and employability are the products of education, aspirations, class structure, labour markets, social networks, relationships
between housing, transport and the labour market, and so on. To promote
health, community safety and employability effectively therefore will take
the co-ordinated efforts of many public, private and voluntary agencies.

The second premise of the argument for holistic governance is that people have joined-up problems. That is to say, the problems that government
is expected to tackle are not neatly organised along the functional lines by
which government is itself organised.

Admittedly, some commentators have disputed this. Using an analysis
of data from the British Household Panel Survey (BHPS), a team from the
Centre for Social Exclusion at the London School of Economics argues
that socially excluded people do not have joined-up problems and therefore do not need joined-up solutions. (Burchardt, Le Grand and Piachaud,
1998.) They examine BHPS data for 1990 to 1995, focusing on five
dimensions of social exclusion:

- *consumption activity*: income half the mean equivalised household
  income;
- *savings activity*: not in owner-occupation, not contributing to or receiving an occupational or personal pension, savings less than £2000;
- *production activity*: not in employment or self-employment, full-time
  education or training, looking after children or retired and over pension-
  able age;
- *political activity*: did not vote in the 1992 general election, not a member of any political or campaigning organisation;
- *social activity*: lacking people to offer support of any of five kinds: someone you can count on to listen, help in a crisis, to relax with, to really
  appreciate you, to offer comfort.

They argue that in any single year fewer than 0.2 per cent of the subjects
were excluded in all five dimensions; 1–2 per cent were excluded in four
dimensions; about 5 per cent in three dimensions and 12 per cent in two
dimensions. The authors assert that this provides no evidence of the existence

of an 'underclass' cut off from 'normal' activity for long periods of time and that these five dimensions of social exclusion are not substantially related. Therefore, they conclude, integration is not necessary to address the problems of the socially excluded, as their problems are not multi-dimensional.

This argument has several weaknesses. First, the BHPS sample systematically under-represents socially excluded people, not least because it has a poor representation of prisoners, homeless people, people in care, illicit drug users, people with poor mental health. Second, the study treated health and housing indicators as mediating factors rather than dimensions that constitute social exclusion. The absence of any consideration of risk factors – such as poor health, education or housing, racial disadvantage or discrimination – means that the study fails to see the high levels of correlation that most studies find between these variables: (see, for instance, Amin and Oppenheim, 1992; Bradshaw, 1990; Dennehy, Smith and Harker, 1997; Audit Commission, 1996; Caprara and Rutter, 1995; HM Chief Inspector of Prisons for England and Wales, 1997; Bynner, 1998).

Third, the heart of the argument for holistic governance is that integrated working between professions, tiers and agencies across the public sector is typically necessary in order to address *any one* of the five dimensions selected by the LSE study. No matter how many people have multiple problems, even single problems must be tackled holistically.

Fragmented governance and its roots

The opposite of holism is fragmentation not specialism

In debates over many decades about coordination, integration, joint working and holism in governance, the same debates tend to recur. One is the debate about what the opposite of holism is, or is supposed to be. The question matters for two reasons. The first reason is diagnostic: if we can be clear what the opposite is, it should be easier to diagnose whether in a given field or country, that opposite condition is to be found and how widespread, institutionalised and problematic it is. The second is conceptual: if we can be clear about what the opposite of holism is, we should be clearer about kinds of interorganisational relationships, that might be valued on independent grounds and with which it might be consistent or inconsistent.

The issue becomes most urgent in connection with debates about the steady advance of differentiation or specialism and of the technical and professional division of labour, in service provision and in governance as in the rest of society (Durkheim, 1984 [1893]). Some critics of holistic interorganisational relationships contend that the aim is to undermine this kind of specialism. The claim is that the aim of holism is to replace professional expertise with less skilled generalist staff, which will either prove utterly infeasible, by flying in the face of all the historical trends, or, if it can be achieved, merely reduce service quality (Dunleavy, 1999).

Indeed, some advocates of holistic service design have talked from time to time of 'overcoming specialism' (for example, Bilton and Jones, 1994, p. 37). However, this is in fact a misunderstanding, which was corrected in the organisation studies literature over thirty years ago in the now canonical text of contingency theory by Lawrence and Lorsch (1967). They demonstrated that the most integrated firms – although their study concerned commercial organisations, sector is irrelevant to the point at issue – were also the most differentiated. They showed that the opposite of integration is not differentiation but *fragmentation*. Indeed a more careful reading of those who talk of 'overcoming' specialism shows that what is meant is the fragmentation that *poor coordination* between specialists can lead to. Indeed, the same concern underlay Durkheim's (1984 [1893]) original concern for securing what he called organic solidarity to sustain effectively, rather than undermine, the division of labour. Therefore, the first stage in understanding the nature of the holistic governance agenda is better to understand the nature of the fragmentation problem that it is seeking to address.

The problems of fragmentation

Functionally fragmented governance consists in the following kinds of problems or failures in interorganisational relations in relation to the 'wicked issues' (cf. the shorter list of problems offered by Peters, 1998, p. 296):

- *dumping of problems and costs by one agency on another*: when each agency focuses on its own priorities, it ends up leaving others to pick up the pieces – or not. Thus school exclusions have brought about serious problems of youth crime, which the criminal justice system has had to cope with;
- *conflicting programmes*: where two or more agencies serve conflicting policy goals, or where, despite serving the same or consistent policy goals, their interventions can undermine each other. (Here we are not principally concerned with conflicts for scarce resources such as

funding, although they can also have fragmenting impacts: for financial crises can also be opportunities, as we shall show in Chapters 5 and 6). For example, there can easily be conflicts between crime detection and prevention agencies' programmes for particular areas and the work of agencies dedicated to the rehabilitation of offenders or drug abusers, despite sharing a common goal of reducing crime;

- *duplication*: this causes waste and frustration to service users. The Social Exclusion Unit found that one London borough had to respond to six different regeneration initiatives (Social Exclusion Unit, 1998); One of our case study authorities was obliged to file more than 75 plans with central government departments;

- *conflicting goals*: the consequences of different services' goals can conflict sharply – anathema to holistic working. For example, the aspirations of the police to secure convictions that lead to punishment can readily conflict with those of youth services and probation for re-integration;

- *lack of or poor sequencing* of the appropriate kinds between interventions by different agencies or professions, arising from failure to communicate between agencies; for example, there are many cases where health promotion or education support interventions should precede classical social work interventions with families with young children, and if they had done so, the likelihood of children having to be taken into care would have been much reduced, but poor sequencing leads to avoidable but worse outcomes;

- *narrow exclusivity in responding to need*: where individual services assume they can provide a complete solution, without reference to other agencies, and end up failing to meet real needs. For example, before the establishment of Area Child Protection Committees, psychiatrists, education welfare officers, child-protection social workers and police officers all determined the manner and scope of their interventions separately. In our own case studies, for example, the Eastwoodshire county project on young people at risk found that many young people were the subject of attention by the police, social services and education welfare services, each operating in ignorance of what the others were doing;

- *inaccessibility of services, confusion about their availability*: people do not divide their problems into neat categories. As a result they often do not know where to find the most appropriate services. Someone who has been bereaved may need to sort out probate for the will, secure the termination of pension, benefit and tax arrangements, have access to medical services, organise the funeral, and even find some support for themselves. But, despite the many pilot projects, as yet there is no single point at which one can find the complete range of central and local public and private services necessary for dealing with this single life event. The same is true of the situation of someone coming up to retirement, giving birth, or giving up work to become a carer;

- *lacunae or gaps in service provision or interventions* that arise from a failure to think about the causation of wicked problems in the round, but from focusing on the available or inherited set of professional interventions. For example, programmes that have focused on long range crime prevention work have identified gaps in interventions in the early years of life that have only recently begun to be remedied, following such experiments as the High Scope/Perry School experiment in the USA (Crane, 1998; Weissberg *et al.*, 1997; Bright, 1997).

It is these problems that programmes of coordination, sequencing, integration, joined-up or holistic working in governance are intended to solve. For the sake of brevity, we shall refer to these problems collectively as ones of 'fragmented governance'. By contrast, where we speak of 'functionally fragmented governance', we are concerned with the organisation of interventions by function – rather than, say, by problem or outcome – that, on the theory behind holistic governance, is a key explanatory factor for fragmented governance.

Explaining the roots of fragmented governance

How have these problems of fragmented governance arisen? Even if it is accepted that functional fragmentation in public management is a key factor, how is it that this functional division has arisen, become institutionalised, become so readily accepted and so difficult effectively to overturn or else to discipline for more holistic ends? For it is essential for any well-designed and credible programme of holistic governance that it understands its 'enemy' well, and that its systems of governance are specifically designed to address the sources of the strength, durability, and legitimacy of the functionally fragmented system.

Broadly, we distinguish eight explanatory factors, grouped into two categories. The first group of five we call 'benign', because they seek to explain some part of the development and institutionalisation of functionally fragmented governance as the unanticipated consequences of governance strategies that are not in themselves necessarily undesirable. By contrast, and with an admitted slight exaggeration, we call the second group of three explanatory factors the 'malign' ones, explaining them suggests the role of self-interest by actors within systems of governance.

Within the benign group, the literature indicate the following five key factors, the unanticipated consequences of which have been to foster and institutionalise fragmentation:

1. *Greater ease of management and expenditure control on inputs* (Power, 1997; Carter, Klein and Day, 1993). The first challenge in the management and internal regulation of the public sector is to secure adequate systems of 'detectors' (Hood, 1983) in order to identify what monies it collects through taxes, fees and other sources, to track expenditures, to alert managers to losses and surpluses, and to plan future investments, requisitions and pro-grammes of revenue support or subsidy. How to do this? It is much easier to capture, record and analyse information about inputs – money spent, staff employed, numbers of goods procured, units of services procured, and so forth – than it is to acquire information about the difference actually made to reducing substantive social problems and increasing well-being. In some fields, such as personal social services, appropriate outcomes are notoriously difficult to define. Again, how is the universally desired outcome of 'employability' to be defined? A variety of definitions are offered, but none is simple to use or has the authoritative acceptance of conventional account-ing measures of cost (although, of course, even these are less straightforward to interpret and draw comparisons between, than is often claimed: Power, 1997). The control of expenditure is much easier, simpler and cheaper (in transaction costs terms) to conduct, if expenditures are correlated with straightforward and easily interpretable and comparable data. Therefore, public authorities tend to organise themselves in order to present their work in a fashion ready to be managed (to become auditable: Power, 1997).

2. *Accountability for probity* (Osborne and Gaebler, 1992). The second factor develops from the first. The later nineteenth century and the early twentieth century in Britain, Europe and North America was a period in which the central goal in government reform was to control, detect and prevent corruption in all its forms. Nepotism in recruitment, the sale of offices, lack of political neutrality of officers, abuse of funds, were the great evils which Victorian civil service reformers, American Progressive era reformers and Prussian meritocrats felt it most urgent to combat. Their commitment to probity in government required systems of accounting, of transparency, of measuring effort, rather than regulating behaviour. They naturally reached for the tools of measurement and regulation that were available, and they focused on the inputs of government – money, people, goods and units of services procured – because, as the first factor identi-fied showed, stocks and flows of such inputs are the easiest to measure and

control. Systems of audit, scrutiny by legislatures and evaluation were deliberately put in place around these measures of inputs, rather than around problems or outcomes, because the political priority for probity required that the available technologies, whatever their limitations, had to be used.

3. *Consumer-oriented government* (Peters, 1998). Users of public services do not have problems that come neatly divided into the categories defined by functionally organised public administration, and one of the goals of holistic working is to design interventions or else devolved capabilities that can respond to seamless combinations of problems. Nevertheless, consumers of services do not necessarily demand horizontal integration, and can often use 'voice' (Hirschman, 1970) to put pressure on managers for vertical and functional integration. In medicine, for example, increases in patient power have not typically resulted in patient pressure for better coordination of medical care with other services, bur rather for more and better functional organisation within medicine. The reasons for this are various but include the historic possibility of achieving transparency more readily in functional organisation (which is the converse of the first factor), the legitimacy with consumers of certain kinds of professional autonomy including that of physicians, and the visibility of such management units as hospitals and clinics.

4. *Strategic decisions for functional organisation.* As we saw in Chapter 1, at various points in the history of public administration, strategic decisions have been made to organise the civil service and local authorities on functional grounds. These decisions have been made for all sorts of reasons, including improved management focus, better performance management, greater political control, and so on, but the consequence has been functional fragmentation of governance.

5. *Democratic pressures for visible commitments to services in input or throughput terms.* Finally, democratic pressures themselves play an important role in explaining fragmentation. Citizens have long been keen to support demands for additional efforts that are framed in terms of putting more money, more staff, higher political priority or in some other way, increased levels of input, into functions. This is particularly obvious in the case of expenditure on socialised medical care. But it can also be seen in the politics of secondary education in recent years, where lower teacher–pupil ratios have been a popular demand rather than curriculum change for greater employability or greater integration of education with other programmes. How do these functionally defined and input-based demands come to be held so dear by significant sections of the public? Again, various factors are at work. One element is straightforward distrust

of politicians and the preference for changes that are measurable, observable, tangible. No doubt, too, the influence and even capture of professions over public opinion plays an important role. TV dramas, for example in the field of health care, tend to focus more on heroic professional intervention than skill management coordination of services. Indeed management is usually the repository for the 'bad guys' in such dramas.

The second group of explanatory factors, which point to self-interested behaviour, consists in three major forces:

1. *Politicians attempts to seize greater control over the executive and the administration.* The struggle of politicians to wrest greater control from bureaucrats, technocrats, career civil servants, and other interest groups is a perennial one. Control always calls for some form of 'divide and rule' strategy. Division by function not only has the merit of supporting easier and cheaper measurement, as the first factor above made clear, but also has the merit of enabling politicians to use existing systems of professional management, recruitment, status and career development as tools of control. Functional fragmentation therefore results from the greater priority that politicians attach to control by whatever means available, rather than by problem-solving.

The related but slightly larger point here might be put brutally: 'you can't take the politics out of government'. More exactly, constancy is neither a virtue nor a practical necessity in politics, and politicians have every incentive to ensure that they are not boxed in by their own policies. On more than one interpretation of what a politician essentially does as a political coalition builder, the essential skill and performance consists in exploiting inconsistencies between different strands of one's own policies, each of which is presented in order to appeal to a different constituency. Bluntly, technically sound public policy, as measured in utilitarian terms, is not the driving force of politics. Therefore, it is not reasonable to expect that politicians' commitments to holism will be expected to bind them when they feel the need to produce policies for simultaneous action that may undermine joint working. Politicians have to swing between different strands of their policy mix in order to sustain their coalition of fractious constituencies. From this it is sometimes concluded that in politics objectives can never be agreed for long periods, made consistent, nor can any set of trade-off(s) be accepted across tiers of governance or even across joint working arrangements within tiers. This makes holistic working very difficult, and gives politicians who want to use 'divide and rule' strategies to exploit policy inconsistencies, good reasons for preferring functional organisation and for accepting the consequent fragmentation.

2. *Professional capture, professional monopolies* (Klein, 1995). The role of the greater public sector professions in fostering functional fragmentation for their own ends cannot be overestimated. A key goal of professions is always to secure their autonomy in decision-making in their defined sphere. If the profession is heavily involved in delivering public services, the most rational strategy for securing that autonomy is to ensure that the organisation of the services follows the boundaries of the profession, and because professions are defined by the kinds of activities they undertake rather than by problem-solving in the round, this typically dictates a preference for functional organisation.

3. *Managerial maximisation of span of control.* Finally, functional organisation also suits senior civil servants. One widely respected account of the organisational goals of the most senior civil servants (Dunleavy, 1991, chapters 7–8) is that they seek to maximise, not their budgets as classical public choice theory would have had it, but the span of their control and influence, and they seek to shape the organisational model of the civil service to that end. Functional organisation creates a range of empires over which senior civil servants can preside.

A related argument is that functional organisation also suits street-level bureaucrats (as SLBs are defined in Lipsky, 1980). For, given the inherited starting point of functional fragmentation, they have learned to operate effectively within that structure, their implicit rationing and coping mechanisms for heavy, hard to control workloads and they have learned to maximise their discretion within such a system. Therefore, they have few incentives to do other than block attempts to institutionalise any alternative model.

Now, one conclusion that might be drawn from this list of factors is that the prospects for holistic governance are very dim indeed, if such an array of powerful institutional, technical, network and interest-based forces are on the side of functional fragmentation. However, it would be wrong to conclude that the holistic game is lost before it has begun. These detailed arguments are taken forward again in Chapter 10. For now it is sufficient to note that holism rests on a challenge to excessive fatalism when it comes to government intervention and institutional design.

Holism rests on a view that something can be done

As an approach to these wicked issues, the holistic governance agenda reflects a certain spectrum of ideological politics. For it is an essentially activist strategy. This sets the agenda against several clear political positions.

First, the holistic governance agenda is optimistic that wicked problems, however intractable to conventional functionally fragmented approaches, are not inherently insoluble. It therefore rejects one strand in conservative thought – not typically the dominant strand in post-Enlightenment conservative thought, but an important one – which is essentially fatalist. Holism denies that crime, unemployment, educational under-achievement, inability to exit from low paid and insecure and unskilled work, poverty, protracted ill-health for at least significant fractions of the population is inevitable. In Hirschman's (1991) terms, the challenge is to reject 'futility'.

The grounds on which fatalism has been argued are various. For some thinkers, deep biological flaws in the nature of at least some of the population are at the root of this, and it is argued that no intervention can remedy them or prevent their symptoms from developing. For others, the essential insolubility of misery lies more on the side of the weakness of any intervention than on the side of the constitution of the problem. Within this group, some hold that organisations and programmes of any kind are instruments that are too blunt to be effective, while others hold that for tackling these problems there is something peculiarly blunt about the tools of government.

Second, there are some variants of the latter position which hold that interventions designed, commissioned, inspired by government agencies, whether or not they are executed and implemented by public sector bodies, are unavoidably iatrogenic, that is, they cause more of the very same miseries they are supposed to reduce. Again, in Hirschman's words, these are 'perversity' arguments.

Third, the holistic governance agenda sets its face against the argument, which is made on both the hard left and the hard right, that it is better not to solve these basic social problems, because the price would be to undermine other values, other more deserving interests and damage solutions to other problems. So, for example, it is sometimes argued, sometimes *sotto voce* and sometimes explicitly, that poverty, low pay, unemployment and the consequent ill-health and other loss of life chances are unavoidable outcomes of measures that secure vital economic incentives, and that conversely, these incentives depend on the continuation of these problems for at least some people (although not necessarily the same individuals or households from period to period). Again, the common libertarian argument that the loss of freedom involved in higher levels of taxation and/or regulation required for serious efforts to tackle these wicked social problems is unacceptable (Nozick, 1974), is a case of this type. At the opposite political extreme, on the Marxian hard left, of course, effective melioration of social problems jeopardises the chances of mobilisation by the worst off, which is deemed more important. In Hirschman's (1991) terms, these are 'jeopardy' arguments.

Finally, there are combinations of jeopardy and futility arguments, as when it is argued that these problems can only be tackled effectively (whether by government or otherwise) at unacceptable costs, leaving most actually deployed interventions merely futile. Then there are combined perversity and jeopardy arguments, such as the claim that reducing unemployment below the optimal rate, if it can be done, not only creates more unemployment later on by expanding labour-intensive industries beyond levels that are economically sustainable, but also the only means by which it can be achieved are likely to stoke inflation.

This is not the place to offer a detailed empirical refutation of these claims. Indeed, as Hirschman (1991) stressed, in rather few cases are these arguments wholly empirical in nature. The ranking of costs implied in jeopardy arguments reflects particular values and sometimes priorities between the welfare of different groups in society; likewise, the arguments are highly sensitive to selection of periods over which effects (jeopardy, perversity) and non-effects (futility) of interventions are to be sought or ignored.

Nevertheless, it is worth pointing out that, if one is prepared to reformulate these as empirical arguments, there is evidence that suggests these three forms of null hypothesis cannot be sustained, at least in their pure forms. Evaluative work suggests that intervention can be successful. (See, for example, Bright, 1997, on crime, 1997; McGuire, 1995, on prevention of reoffending; Crane, 1998 on promotion of educational attainment; Naidoo and Wills, 1998, on health promotion; 6, 1997c, on a range of interventions around unemployment; Jackson, 1996, and Wood, 1989, on the prevention of environmental damage; Leat and 6, 1997, Scharf and Wenger, 1995, and Wenger, 1998 on delaying the onset of morbidity in old age.) Indeed, in general, careful empirical reviews in the fields of public health and environment suggest that, when reasonable ways of weighting costs and benefits or budgets and damage are used, the general claim of the perversity argument is not supported, and that when trading off risks against other risks, interventions cannot be designed that are risk-superior, in the sense that while trade-off(s) and costs are unavoidable, the losses need not wholly offset the gains (Graham and Wiener, 1996).

Like other centrist creeds holism suggests that government intervention can work. What is distinctive from other centrist agendas is the eponymous claim that in effective interventions, design for coordination and integration matters above all, that the problems of fragmented governance must be overcome before the aspirations for effective intervention can be defended.

The goals of holistic governance

The central formal goal, then, of holistic working is greater effectiveness in tackling the problems the public care most about. But there are also other, less ambitious goals. It is helpful to think about goals at each of four key levels: policy, client group, organisations and agencies (here we follow the helpful taxonomies developed by Agranoff and Pattakos, 1979, and revised and extended by Kagan and Neville, 1993). *Policy-level goals* describe the over-arching purpose of public intervention in a particular area. *Client-level goals* are concerned with meeting the needs of the clientele, or helping to reshape the clients' preferences. *Organisational goals* address the effective management of organisational relationships. *Agency-level goals* animate the work of the component agencies involved. Typically, client and agency level goals are generated and owned at the local level (Kagan *et al.*, 1995), while policy and organisational level goals may be formulated and responsibility taken for them at national or even supra-national level.

People will approach integrative working with a variety of motivations. In many partnerships, partners do not share common goals, but that fact does not necessarily undermine the capacity of each partner to achieve some of its goals. Most agencies pursue integrative work with multiple goals. But intelligent and effective holistic working typically requires that at least one of the agencies in the partnership has a clear and consistent set of goals. Figure 2.4 summarises some of the principal goals we have identified.

Once goals have been set, politicians and public managers have to take a series of framework decisions. The first is to fix the focus of integration for each level of operation.

At the highest level of ambition, the goal is to improve outcomes, for which it is usually necessary to integrate many processes (Hornbeck, 1991). If, for example, the policy aim is to enhance employability, some of the key factors are education, family, mobility and transport, social networks, attitude to risk, aspiration, housing and cost of childcare. The focus of involvement would be all the agencies, probably in both public and private sectors, which provide, regulate and promote policy initiatives in these areas.

At the client level, the focus of attention might be children, older people, carers or young adults at risk from crime or at risk of turning to crime. Here the aim would typically be to involve all those agencies that have a significant impact on the life chances of the chosen group. (The client group could equally be defined geographically, as is the case with the UK government's various programmes for Special Action Zones.)

Figure 2.4   *Goals and purposes for holistic working*

Focus level	Inputs	Throughputs*	Outputs	Outcomes
policy goals	policy coherence	better policy management	better quality of service-delivery	more effective cure, palliation or prevention/ greater control over clienteles
client goals	encourage citizens' or users' views and/or involvement	greater acceptance by clients of service process	comprehensive service delivery/more accessible services	greater public legitimacy, community building
organisational goals	avoid duplication, minimise conflict, share risk management, maximise knowledge	cost-efficiency	greater control over outputs	n/a
agency goals	leverage resources or investment	transfer of administrative control	greater control over outputs of related agencies	n/a

Includes activities, relationship between inputs and outputs.

At the outputs level one would try, for example, to bring together all those involved in providing or regulating a particular service. At the throughputs level, the aim would be to integrate all the relevant activities that involve processing payments to and from citizens; and finally, at the lowest level, the project would be to bring together all those using certain types of inputs, such as the consolidation of a data system.

Measuring the depth of integration

Another useful way to look at holistic ways of working is to look at how to measure the depth of integrated working. There are four component measures: intensity, scope, breadth and exposure.

- *Intensity* is the measure of the resources to be shared between the integrated activities – for example, labour-time involved or frequency of contact. This does not always have to be very great. An Area Child Protection Committee system can be run without the need for the police, NHS psychologists, health visitors, social services or education welfare services committing huge amounts of time or money. In contrast, joint commissioning between health and social services typically requires the NHS and local authority social services to allocate significant slices of their geriatric services budgets.
- *Scope* is the measure of the number of agencies involved in the collaboration.
- *Breadth* is the measure of the relevant range of activities to be brought together (this measure is often cross-disciplinary and cross-functional).
- *Exposure* is the degree to which integration will disturb the core business of each of the agencies involved; or the extent to which central activities, budgets, professional priorities and/or political credibility are exposed to risk in the course of integration.

In general, the greater the intensity of integration, the greater the sovereignty pooled, the autonomy surrendered and the tighter the linkages. This is not necessarily true: there are cases of long term intensive collaboration between agencies where each retains considerable decision-making autonomy. But typically, as resource exchange and resource dependency theory would predict, intensity of resource integration tends to produce situations in which organisations are willing to trade-off autonomy for other benefits (Pfeffer and Salancik, 1978; Emerson, 1962).

Intensity, scope, breadth and exposure do not necessarily rise and fall together. Some low-intensity integrative efforts can be surprisingly highly exposed, because even though few budgets are pooled, or only modest amounts of labour time needed to sustain the partnership, the nature of the integration has significant financial or political consequences. An example would be a major shift by a police force or a health authority towards more preventive working. In the case of the police, the work of crime prevention – long-term, small-scale and collaborative with many other agencies – is often viewed as a low-status, low-value activity, compared to the 'real work' of detection, or even pounding the beat (this perception holds equally true for officers and public alike). Chief Constables intent on pushing preventive work up the agenda at the expence of patrol and detection run a risk of suddenly finding themselves in the firing line politically. The same holds true for health authorities, which have to beware of sharp adverse public reaction to the idea of putting resources into preventive health care rather than directing them towards nurses, doctors or hospitals.

Mechanisms, or what gets done

By this point we can start to identify the specific integration activities to be carried out. *One cannot simply read off the appropriate mechanisms from the goals.* Within relationships as different as mergers and joint projects, the same kinds of integrative activities may be appropriate. Figure 2.5 is an extension of Figure 2.4 and shows how specific mechanisms support goals at each level of integration. The figure synthesises some of the arguments in the service integration literature (especially Kagan and Neville, 1993 and Kagan *et al.*, 1995) with our own findings and analyses.

It is important to recognise that the columns represent goals of integration at the four levels, and therefore, for example, a mechanism that is itself an input can appear as supporting a goal of integration at the outcome level. There is no necessary one-size-fits-all relationship between mechanisms. Most integrative strategies require the use of several or many mechanisms. Conversely, most mechanisms can be used to support more than one kind of goal, and so many appear in several different places in the table.

Setting goals, fixing the dimensions of integration and the appropriate mechanisms for pursuing it: these elements comprise the framework for joined-up government. Without a clear perspective on this big picture, an effective strategy cannot be developed.

Types of holistic governance

We are now in a position to offer our typology of holistic governance drawing on the range of arguments presented above. Figure 2.6 sets out the choices (for alternative classifications see Daines, Lyon and Parsloe, 1990; Scott 1992, chapter 8, especially Figure 8.1; and Koebel *et al.*, 1992, especially Figure 1). Like most spectra offered in the literature, ours is ranked by intensity of mutual involvement as defined above (but in this case, the ranking runs downward from low to high.

Conclusion

In this chapter, we set out the conceptual framework that informs the argument of this book as a whole. We have argued that holism must be

Figure 2.5 *Mechanisms to support goals at different levels of integration*

Focus	Inputs	Throughputs	Outputs	Outcomes
Policy goals	*Policy coherence*	*Better policy management*	*Better quality of service delivery*	*More effective cure, palliation, or prevention/greater control over clientele or public*
Policy mechanisms	• intergovernmental or departmental policy groups • refinancing, grant aid • cross-departmental spending review • regulation waivers • legislative mandates • technical assistance • reclassified funds • policy coordination units	• intergovernmental forums • integration of policy data capture and management	• intergovernmental or departmental audit, performance monitoring	• policy coordination units • interdisciplinary research
Client goals	*encourage citizens' or users' views and/or involvement*	*greater acceptance by clients of service process*	*comprehensive service-delivery/more accessible services*	*greater public legitimacy, community building*

			services tailored to community needs	*enhanced human and/or environmental well-being problem prevention*
Client mechanisms	• joint consultation, surveys	• joint citizens' charters • joint user-feedback system	• one-stop shops/co-location • case conferences • case management • centralised client information • flexibly decentralised funding	• joint measurement of outcomes • joint evaluation of each partner's contributions to single set of outcomes • case management • case conferences • centralised client information
Organisational goals	*avoid duplication, minimise conflict, promote collaboration, share risk management, maximise knowledge*	*cost-efficiency resource-efficiency transfer of administrative control*	*greater control over outputs*	*n/a*
Organisational mechanisms	• interorganisational information systems • cross-training	• creation of new coordinating bodies • pooled budgets	• integrated audit, benchmarking and performance	

Figure 2.5 continued

Focus	Inputs	Throughputs	Outputs	Outcomes
	• joint planning • reorganisation • open planning	• joint staffing • integrated information systems • reorganisation	• monitoring • consolidated personnel management	*n/a*
Agency goals	*leverage resources or investment, avoid duplication, minimise conflict/ promote collaboration, share risk management, maximise knowledge*	*transfer of administrative control*	*greater control over outputs of related agencies*	
Agency mechanisms	• co-location • inter organisational information systems • joint planning • joint staffing • joint training • joint commissioning • joint funding • consolidated personnel management	• out-station staff	• joint inspection • joint monitoring • inter-agency agreements • joint planning • joint staffing • joint training	

Figure 2.6   *The spectrum of possible relationships in holistic governance*

Category of relationship	Type of relationship between entities	Definition
coordination	*taking into account*	strategy development considers the impact of/on others
	dialogue	exchange of information
	joint planning	temporary joint planning or joint working
integration	*joint working*	temporary collaboration
	joint venture	long-term joint planning and joint working on major project core to the mission of at least one participating entity
	satellite	separate entity, jointly owned, created to serve as integrative mechanism
	strategic alliance	long-term joint planning and working on issues core to the mission of at least one participating entity
	union	formal administrative unification, maintaining some distinct identities
	merger	fusion to create a new structure with a single new identity

understood by contrasting it with the merely joined-up, the fragmented, the outright conflictual and the merely muddling along, the distinct but independently important activities of coordination and integration must be distinguished, and the scope of linkages between tiers, sectors and functions must be appreciated. The problems to which holistic governance is intended to be the solution are the 'wicked' problems which are the key priorities of voters, and which cross all the functional boundaries. At the organisational and interorganisational level, the problem is not specialism and the division of labour in governance, which continue to develop apace as they have for centuries. Rather the key problems concern the relationship between specialities, and – following the 'reinvention' era – the most urgent and widespread of those problems is that of fragmented government. Fragmentation is a complex problem with multiple roots and all must be addressed in welldesigned programmes of holistic working. Holism represents an optimistic faith in organisational design: much recent political science is written in a pessimistic vein. The first stage towards a serious assessment of how far we ought to be pessimistic consists in the development of rigorous taxonomies of what actually can be done, and in this chapter we have offered a rich tool kit with which to think about the mechanisms and activities available for both joined-up and holistic governance, and we have summarised these in the form of a spectrum of relationships. These tools will be used and referred back to at every stage of the argument of the book, as we make greater use of the cases of the previous chapter to develop an answer to the key question, 'how far can holism be institutionalised?'

3 The Case For and Against Holistic Governance

In this chapter we draw upon the conceptual framework developed in previous chapters in order to further consider the case both for and against holistic governance. For the organisational achievements that we can observe at national, local, state, province, federal and commonwealth level across the world must be evaluated first against the standards in the arguments of the advocates, and secondly against other criteria. Our argument must also address the arguments of the sceptics about the possibility of coordination and integration.

The chapter begins with a discussion of the trade-off(s) that are involved in the selection of any preference for a model of appropriate interorganisational relationships. Then we consider in detail the case that can be and has been made against coordination and integration. In order to show how these arguments can be answered, we present the case for holistic government, presenting the central claim and citing the main texts in the empirical literature that support it. Then we show how this enables specific replies to the critics.

Trade-off(s)

Any serious consideration of the case for and against a model of interorganisational relationships must begin with accepting the possibility of trade-off(s) having to be struck, of opportunity costs having to be recognised. Nothing comes free, and there is no guarantee that all good things go together. Too many advocates of holistic government have tended to present *trite* 'virtuous cycles' in which all the benefits reinforce each other, and 'vicious cycles' in which all the problems and risks reinforce each other. They then go on to suggest that 'all we have to do is' find ways to 'break out' of the vicious cycle, and we shall find ourselves on the virtuous one (an example of this kind of thinking in an otherwise helpful and thoughtful report can be found in Department of the Environment, Transport and the

Regions, 1999). Nothing in organisational life is as simple as this, and holistic governance is no exception. There are trade-off(s) between holistic effectiveness and short-run economy as well as trade-off(s) between integrating one set of programmes with another. The limited resource of attention to problems means that there are also trade-off(s) between priorities. Finally, holistic governing results in trade-off(s) between curative and palliative interventions on the one hand, and preventive ones on the other.

Holistic governance is far from easy or cheap to achieve. It demands, as our cases show clearly, a great deal of time and effort from public managers. As we shall show in later chapters, it requires the investment of many kinds of resources, including new kinds of information systems, new forms of budget design, new plant and buildings, training programmes, reorganisation of organisations, re-negotiation of relationships with regulators and auditors. Apart from all these tangible resources, holistic working also makes major demands upon that scarcest resource in any governmental organisation, the attention of politicians and senior manages to problems. Moreover, the intelligent allocation of attention is also the most difficult skill to cultivate and train (March and Olsen, 1975, 1976). Devoting the attention of the brightest senior managers or politicians to furthering coordination and integration requires depriving other problems of their attention. If public officials are going to put integration above 'minding the shop' or focusing on 'business as usual' in their list of priorities, then they need to be able to justify that shift in priorities.

In this section, we consider first the range of possible trade-off(s), and reactions of both advocates and critics, before moving on to consider the merits of specific arguments for and against holistic governance. On the one hand, proponents of holistic governance argue that the costs of integration are not significant or that within a typical range the price paid for coordination is acceptable. On the other hand, the critics argue either that nothing is gained and the trade-off represents a zero-sum, or else that the benefits do not outweigh the costs. We group the principal trade-off(s) into two categories.

The first and most obvious trade-off follows from the point emphasised in Chapter 2, that holistic governance does not mean 'one big lump' government. Holistic governance does not abolish boundaries, but proposes to put at least some of them in other places. Indeed, this approach does not even necessarily remove existing functional boundaries. It may, for example, overlay functional line management boundaries with accountability, financial incentive, performance measurement and audit boundaries defined around problems, to create matrix structures. The issue therefore, is not how to abolish boundaries, but where it is most intelligent to put them at any given time. Certainly, by moving the boundaries of accountability, measurement, and management focus at least partly away from functional ones, one pays a price in terms of the loss of coordination and integration within those functions. That is to say, there can be trade-off(s) between the benefits of vertical and of horizontal integration (Morgan *et al.*, 1999). Despite the shortcomings of functional organisation, this approach was institutionalised for perfectly understandable reasons. Therefore, efforts to correct the fragmentation that arises from this vertical model would involve inevitable costs. There are indeed some benefits to functional integration. These include the following:

- the mutual support for sustaining motivation, including through career progression within functionally defined professions, that professionals of the same functional kind can provide each other even though they are applying their skills to different social problems (Bilton and Jones, 1994);
- the ease with which, given the fact of the institutional legacy as starting point, people can now recognise, understand, move around functional systems of organisation;
- the ease with which performance measures defined functionally can be collected, analysed and compared; and
- the ease with which, again given the fact of the institutional legacy as starting point, existing accountability systems for functions can be understood and made to work.

Further, there are trade-off(s) to be struck *within* different levels and foci of holistic governance:

- between integration around the individual client (and her or his multiple needs), integration nationally focused upon a particular 'wicked' problem, integration within a particular locality (Burns *et al.*, 1994), and integration between localities across geographical borders; and
- between internal integration within public sector and external integration with private and voluntary sectors: one reading of the 'reinvention' era reforms would be precisely that they sought better external integration with private and non-profit contractors at the expense of internal coordination within the public sector (Nicol, 1998).

The case against integration

The critics of holistic governance pursue three basic lines of argument. These arguments can best be thought of by imagining trade-off(s) as represented by curves on a graph. The critics argue that the curves are very steep, representing high costs for modest gains. Given where the critics think that governments are starting on these trade-off curves, they argue, it would be better to pursue improvements in functionally organised government instead. The three lines of argument have already been outlined in Chapter 2, using Hirschman's distinction between objections of futility, jeopardy and perversity, and can be broken down into a dozen claims which the advocates of holism must rebut.

Futility

Futility arguments claim that the trade-off(s) between holistic and functionally organied governance are zero-sum. Specifically, they argue that the losses are likely to be at least as great as the gains:

1. The first argument to this effect is that holistic governance is not feasible. The argument is that the obstacles to overcoming institutionalised functionally fragmented governance are so powerful and so strong that efforts in holism cannot realistically hope to dislodge them. A variant of this argument is to admit that it is feasible to initiate holistic governance on an experimental, or a temporary basis, but not to institutionalise it. The success of holistic working, according to many sceptics, is dependent entirely on particular personalities who will move on to other jobs and the holistic initiative will then wither (Challis *et al.*, 1988; Smith, Marsh and Richards, 2000).
2. The second and supporting futility argument is that because holistic governance is infeasible, the trade off is really between the continuation of the present functionally organised system, warts and all, and either failed or expensive efforts in holistic governance, undertaken by a rapid succession of advocates of holistic working who will quickly burn out and give up. Worse still would be to end up with the empty symbolism and pretence of holism (Weiss, 1981) with little achieved by way of coordination and integration.

Jeopardy

The argument here is that the trade-off(s) between integration and dominant functional organisation or different forms of integration are actually negative sum games, at least in the longer run, because the gains from efforts towards coordination or integration are outweighed by the resulting costs or damage. Therefore, the sceptic argues, efforts in pursuit of integration are undesirable. The following are the main examples of this kind of argument in the literature:

3. By comparison with functionally organised governance, holistic governance is less democratic, more statist, more technocratic (Rhodes, 2000). For whether or not it is more effective or cost-effective in tackling wicked social problems, it represents a greater accumulation of state power because it brings together previously fragmented public power. Functional fragmentation may indeed be less effective in tackling wicked social issues, but precisely because it hobbles the capacity of the state for effective intervention, and because we have learned how to hold it accountable, it is less likely to violate liberty.

4. Functionally divided and separated governance may be less effective in solving problems, but it respects privacy in precisely the way that holistic governance violates it. Citizens and service users disclose personal information to providers of public services for purposes that are defined functionally, that they recognise in functional terms. Therefore, the argument runs, there are good reasons for preventing injustice, indignity and abuse to want to limit the disclosure of personal information across functional boundaries.

5. One way to achieve integration at local levels is to create flexibility and allow local public managers to integrate services and policies in ways that make most sense to them, and more importantly, to the consumer. They would do so on the basis of their understanding of the nature of the wicked problems faced in their community. However, the variation created across the country in what gets integrated and how it is integrated can undermine territorial integration. In other words, it can lead to the erosion of policy, client and organisation level integration across territorial boundaries. This in turn creates unacceptable, because inequitable, outcomes for service users in different localities. (Altman, 1991; Weiss, 1981.)

6. The basis, as we shall see, of the case for holistic governance is that it provides a greater chance of developing effective solutions. Where solutions exist, advocates of holism argue, integration can produce effective responses and strategies for tackling wicked problems that are beyond the reach of individual departments, or specialisms. Critics, however, sometimes contend that effectiveness, or at any rate cost-effectiveness, has not been proven for holistic working, and is probably impossible anyway (a futility argument). Therefore, it makes sense to

concentrate on the goals of efficiency and economy instead. Efficiency, they point out, is much easier to achieve in fragmented functional models of governance, and therefore the pursuit of efficiency within functional systems of organisation is both more important and practical than pursuing effectiveness, since the effectiveness of integration is at best unproven (Altman, 1991).

7. Contrary to the claims of the advocates of holistic governance, most people don't have joined-up problems (Burchardt *et al.*, 1998), and the pursuit of holism represents a disproportionate effort for the small clientele who do have multiple forms of disadvantage.

8. When integration becomes 'the order of the day' in national political priorities, then attention to organisational issues becomes the priority and integration and reorganisation tend to become 'an end in itself' (Edelman and Radin, 1991; Golden, 1991; Challis *et al.*, 1988). This takes attention away from much more important political issues about levels of funding for services and equity between rich and poor and between different groups of service users (Altman, 1991; Weiss, 1981; Geddes, 1999, p. 130).

9. In practice, integration leads to poor targeting of services for the disadvantaged. This is because integration is so expensive of resources, that it can only be achieved by using intensive efforts in a small number of local geographical areas (e.g., New Labour's zones or target neighbourhoods). While these areas may contain high concentrations of disadvantaged people as residents or works, most disadvantaged people don't live in such areas (except perhaps in the USA, where ghettoisation may make this more effective, but at very high cost).

10. Incentives for integration inevitably create inequity, because the systems of incentives reward those who are already 'network rich' and able easily to formalise existing arrangements, or – for example, simply redescribe existing forms of coordination or integration as forms that are higher up the spectrum (6 *et al.*, 1999).

11. Integration in practice undermines specialisation, even if it is not intended to. For example, one-stop shops for public service users tend to hire generalist staff. This puts in an additional layer of bureaucracy before service users can reach the specialist, and generalists may also make mistakes that a specialist would not. Concerns have been expressed about 'mission drift', or the failure of inter-agency collaborations to target scarce resources on strategies that are most likely to impact the desired outcomes (Kalafat *et al.*, undated). Moreover, this creates inequity, because middle class people can opt out of public services, pay to use specialists and provide whatever integration they

want for themselves. By contrast, advocates of integration want to pre-design holistic services for the poor, who cannot afford to opt out, pay for specialists and integrate services for themselves (Altman, 1991).

Perversity

12. These arguments focus on the claim that integration exacerbates the very problems of fragmented governance and wicked social problems that it is supposed to solve. The key argument here is that the political agenda that lies behind holistic governance is inevitably centralising (OECD, 1996, p. 41). This governmental centralisation is not only hostile to pluralism at the local level (Chandler, 2000; Rhodes, 2000). It also undermines the organisational capability for integration at the level at which it is often only possible to integrate meaningfully, namely, the level of local governance. This, it is argued, arises as a result of the inevitable tension between policy coordination and operational coordination (Devons, 1950 cited in Challis *et al.*, 1988, p. 11). In sum, perversity arises out of futility.

What are we to make of these arguments? Certainly, there are empirical cases discussed in the literature from which the criticisms are drawn. But the literature does not contain any rigorous test of these claims conducted on a consistent basis, across a substantial sample of different levels, types and foci of coordination integration initiatives. Nevertheless, it has to be acknowledged that the advocates of holistic governance cannot point to any such test either. When all we have are heaps of anecdotal evidence collected on very different bases, it seems a rather desperate way in which to conduct a policy debate about where the onus of proof should lie. However, it seems fair to say that, in order to be conclusive, the critics' arguments need to establish more than the proposition that there are cases where these vices are clearly evident. Specifically, they need to be able to show that integration efforts *must* face these problems, and that there are no safeguards, guidelines, additional measures, side-constraints or smart practices (Bardach, 1998) that minimise these risks at acceptable cost.

The case for holistic governance

We now present the case for holistic governance, and the case in reply to the critics' arguments of futility, jeopardy and perversity.

The central proposition of the case for holistic governance can be stated very simply as follows:

A. *Holistic governance is more effective, and, indeed, cost-effective, in tackling wicked social problems than is purely functionally organised governance.* Naturally, what is claimed is at most that holism is necessary, not that it alone is sufficient for effectiveness. Fairly obviously, effective services must also be financed at an adequate level (that is, there is a trade-off, beyond a certain point, between economy and effectiveness that must be well led and managed, must represent well-designed interventions based on sound causal assumptions, and so on. However, for social problems of any complexity, the argument is that holism at some level is necessary. Given the range of interorganisational relationships at the coordination end of the spectrum in Figure 2.6 in chapter 2 this may not seem to be a very demanding or restrictive claim, and in one sense it is not. However, it represents only a framework claim. A stronger proposition, to which most holists would assent, is that

B. *There are cases where quite high levels of integration (in terms of the spectrum given in Figure 2.6) are necessary for effectiveness, and that*

C. *In the course of strategy development, astute practitioners have the means to identify which those cases are, and to identify at least roughly the relevant and appropriate range of choice for integration strategies.*

The ancillary proposition to these central ones is that

D. *If costs are correctly measured, integration is typically, more efficient for a given standard of service intervention or policy set than functional organisation, because there are costs of fragmentation that are often hidden.*

The evidence for these central propositions consists, firstly, in evaluative studies of functionally organised policy-making and functionally organised services that come to negative conclusions about both effectiveness and cost-effectiveness in terms of outcomes for target clients and service users or environmental quality (as opposed to studies focusing on administrative process achievements, which are more numerous), both more frequently than they come to positive conclusions and to a greater degree. Secondly, there are a smaller number of evaluative studies of coordination, integration for which claims of being joined-up or of being holistic have been argued, and where positive findings on effectiveness and cost-effectiveness are more common and more heavily weighted than negative ones.

The principal (by 'principal' here, we mean simply those that have been widely cited with favourable comment in the literature, if we take citation with favourable comment to be a coarse indicator of academic respect) recent empirical evaluative studies of functional governance, in the fields of interventions for children, offenders, young people at risk, mental health services, job training, and environmental protection or regeneration are to be found in the following texts: Audit Commission, 1994, 1996, 1999; Daines *et al.*, 1990; HM Chief Inspector of Prisons, 1997; Joseph Rowntree Foundation, 1998; Murray, 1998, 1999; Pugh and McQuail, 1995; Utting, 1998.

The main empirical evaluative studies of holistic working examining and finding positive outcomes for target clients and service users are to be found in the following texts: Both and Copple, 1991; Bardach, 1996, 1998; Bergeson *et al.*, 1999; Borins, 1998; California State Department of Education, 1999; Crane, 1998; Garrity and Moore, 1999; Greene *et al.*, 1998; Holman, 1999; Kagan and Neville, 1993; Kagan *et al.*, 1995; McGuire, 1995; United States General Accounting Office, 1992; Philliber Research Associates, 1999; Provan and Milward, 1995; Goldman *et al.*, 1994; Lehman *et al.*, 1994; Morrissey *et al.*, 1994; Jennings and Ewalt, 1998; Veale and Morely, 1999; United States Department of Justice, 1997; Walsh, undated.

Certainly, many of these studies found that coordination and integration were not *sufficient* to achieve the best feasible outcomes for their target clienteles. Good intervention design, well motivated professionals with high morale, work to improve 'social capital', work on wider social change to combat discrimination, a great deal of time and many other things are also necessary. But all found that coordination and integration between services is either necessary or highly valuable. Some (especially the major study by Walsh, undated) found that coordination and integration must be sustained over a period of several years before results can be observed. The earlier report of that study (Annie E. Casey Foundation, 1995) had found that, in working with the poorest communities to improve outcomes for at-risk children, a mere five years was often not enough to produce measurable changes.

The main evaluative studies that focus on outcomes for target clienteles and that are critical of integration are the ones already cited above: Provan and Milward, 1995; Goldman *et al.*, 1994; Lehman *et al.*, 1994; Morrissey *et al.*, 1994; Jennings and Ewalt, 1998.

There are, of course, many, many more evaluative studies of coordination, but most focus on organisational outcomes, practitioner satisfaction, and other internal variables (e.g., Holman, 1999; Geddes, 1999; White,

1999). However, these are often not good proxies for impact on social problems (Jennings and Ewalt, 1998 show just how widely the two groups of variables can diverge).

The defences offered by advocates of holistic governance to the charges of futility, jeopardy and perversity generally are as follows:

1. *Infeasible, can't be institutionalized?* The argument for feasibility consists first in the claim that a credible story can now be told about what a *strategy* for designing, initiating and institutionalising holistic governance looks like. The elements of that strategic approach are set out in part in the conceptual framework in Chapter 2, in part in the theoretical discussion in Chapter 4, and in part in the chapters to follow on management, finance, information and accountability. Secondly, empirical argument shows that efforts to institutionalise holistic governance are being made that at least reflect what is understood about institutionalisation in general on theoretical grounds.

2. *Merely symbolic?* That there are cases of pretended holism and empty symbolism can not be denied. However, advocates of holistic governance point to some of the initiatives discussed in chapter 1 and in the introduction as evidence that the scale of effort, levels of expenditure and the salience of political priority and personal reputations of senior politicians being on the line represent a more than 'merely' symbolic programme.

3. *Statism?* The main line of defence offered here is not to deny that the holistic governance agenda does indeed entail an activist view of government, but rather to argue that functionally organised government is, if anything, more statist, more technocratic and less democratic. Indeed, by comparison with some vision of the nightwatchman state, the holistic governance agenda looks bulky and expensive. However, at least in Europe, that is not realistically on offer. By comparison with the relevant alternative, if the cost-effectiveness argument can be made out, then it may be possible to suggest that the long run expenditure liabilities are much lower than might be thought, and may even be lower than those of less effective functionally organised governance. The advocates of holistic governance argue that by focusing accountability, priority, attention and funding flows around the wicked issues that principally concern the public, they offer a more responsive, more democratic model of governance than the functionally organised system.

4. *Violation of privacy?* Advocates of holistic governance have generally argued that in this respect, there are indeed difficult issues to be worked out, but they insist that it will be possible to reconcile privacy with

holistic governance through the development of new detailed codes of practice governing the flows of personal information (6, 1998c). More boldly, they have also argued that privacy is in fact one of the goals of holism, and not principally a constraint upon it (Prime Minister and Minister for the Cabinet Office, 1999, p. 51). However, they do acknowledge that the appropriate conception of the purposes for which some categories of information are collected may have to be renegotiated with the public, subject to the development of detailed new codes, and with the offer of more privacy-enhancing technologies that will enable citizens to know more about what is held on them and to require the correction of errors and deletion of irrelevant material (6, 1998c). Finally, advocates of holistic government sometimes argue that the performance of functionally organised government in protecting privacy has been much less impressive than its defenders admit. In fact, disclosures across functional frontiers have been made, often without adequate safeguards, and privacy has too often been given too low a priority. The claim that functional boundaries are the appropriate privacy protection is largely only true by definitional fiat, because that was the only available way to imagine controls upon disclosures within the public sector. One promise of holistic governance would be that it could offer more intelligent and more appropriate ways in which to think about where such informational boundaries ought to lie.

5. *Undermines territorial equity?* It ought first to be acknowledged that there is clear tension, if not indeed an outright contradiction between this criticism and that offered in (12) below. Most advocates of holistic government would in general prefer to pursue a more decentralising strategy, although certainly there are centralist holists. For those who believe in radical decentralisation, the defence here would generally take the form of a robust acceptance that the importance of devolution of governance for their conception of justice is greater than the importance of territorial uniformity in provision. This tends to be the view of many US-based advocates of holistic governance. Other more moderate decentralist holists would want to temper this with some national minimum standards or guarantees of service provision that local authorities would not be able to opt out from, whatever integration or other public management strategy they chose. Conversely, the centralist holists do not, by and large, defend their centralism on grounds of territorial equity, but more on the grounds of ensuring that priority social problems are effectively tackled.

6. *Efficiency more important?* The argument that there is a simple trade-off between cost-effectiveness and efficiency would be resisted by most

advocates of holistic governance. In general, they would argue, efficiency can only be measured for some defined benchmark of service quality, or outcome level for target clients or feature of the environment. If this can be specified, and if all the costs are properly measured for both integrated and functionally fragmented strategies, advocates of holistic governance would usually argue that cost effectiveness and productive efficiency measures are simply different ways of calculating the same thing. However, where integration produces – as it often does – a quite different service or intervention with different and more ambitious goals from those available under functionally fragmented governance, then there is no rigorous cost-effectiveness or efficiency comparison, only a comparison of economy.

7. *Most people don't have joined-up problems?* The discussion of this issue in Chapter 2 (see section headed 'Wicked problems') gives the line of argument in reply that would be offered by most advocates of holistic governance.

8. *Becomes an end in itself, takes attention away from justice issues?* That there is a danger of means becoming ends, no one need deny. Advocates of holistic governance would, however, challenge the claim that there is any necessity about this, and would suggest a variety of ways of designing accountability systems to minimise the risk. They would also want to turn the argument around, and suggest that the vice is much more serious in the case of functionally fragmented governance. They also flatly deny that a focus on key wicked social problems can be a distraction from justice issues. If there are problems of underfunding, or poor service quality, then the measurement and accountability systems proposed by holists should, they would argue, show these failings up even more clearly than do those for functionally organised governance.

9. *Poor targeting?* Dilemmas of targeting – choosing between strategies directed to whole populations, geographically targeted groups, groups targeted by income, or by any other proxy variable – are endemic in all public management and social policy models, and are not unique to holistic strategies. Any form of targeting will, unfortunately, miss some people. It may well be that focusing on multiple deprivation neighbourhoods is not the best distributional strategy with which to tackle many issues, or at least it should be supplemented with other strategies. However, nothing about the merits of coordination or integration hangs on any particular way of deciding these issues, since all solutions involve trade-off(s) irrespective of the form of organisation.

10. *Rewards only the already network rich?* That many incentive pro-grammes for partnership and joint working have exhibited this failing should not be denied. However, advocates of holistic working gener-ally argue that this is not an intrinsic problem, but the product of poorly designed systems of competition. Of course, there are both understandable political reasons why politicians want to be able to show quick wins, and why the coping strategies of public managers lead to this kind of outcome (cf. Lipsky, 1980). However, if holistic governance can be institutionalised, then there should be both time and political space to experiment with incentive systems that reward demonstrated new linkages rather than established ones.

11. *Undermines service quality by undermining specialism?* In consumer-focused services, at the point of first contact in a call centre or shop-front one-stop shop, there may indeed be a simple choice between putting in a generalist or a specialist filter. However, when the issues of service design are seen in the round, the challenge is to deepen inte-gration between specialists and generalists, to equip those generalists that are used with sufficient knowledge of the range of specialisms necessary in order to identify which kind of specialist colleague is needed, and to improve the quality, speed and contract involved in referral procedures to ensure that disadvantaged people, in particular, do not fall through the linnet. That there are managerial challenges here can not be denied. But advocates of holistic working would deny that the functional alternative is better for first contact frontline ser-vice, by which citizens have to work out for themselves which kinds of specialists they need to by understand the ways in which public authorities divide up services. On the contrary, they would argue that outcomes from functional designs are typically much worse.

12. *Centralising undermines local integration as well as pluralism?* The defence given to (5) above will serve here as well. In general, most holists want to see some kind of balance between centrally set basic standards and goals about tackling national public priorities in a holis-tic manner, but would want to encourage local diversity in ways to achieve this, and they can point to some institutional means for achieving this, including, in the UK, a range of competitive bidding schemes, such as Best Value, the Beacon Council scheme, and so on.

We turn now to considering the defence offered by advocates of holistic governance to the critics' argument that the trade-off(s) between different foci *within* holistic governance are unacceptable or represent insoluble dilemmas. Indeed, there are choices to be made about how far to integrate at the client level, how far at agency level, policy level, and also choices about priorities in any given period for integration between different kinds of agency. One cannot pursue every kind of coordination and integration and both joined-up and holistic levels with every other agency. That would be both impossible and meaningless.

But this is neither necessary, advocates of holistic governance would reply, nor is it implied by the case for holism. The basis of appropriate holistic governance strategy emerges from reflection on the spectrum of interorganisational relationships described in the spectrum set out in Figure 2.6. Indeed, an agency cannot pursue merger or create even jointly owned satellite agencies with every other agency relevant to the key social problems to which its efforts should be dedicated. However, with those potential partners where relationships at the high end of the spectrum are not appropriate or not selected, there is a range of low end options which are very important, and which can be spread more widely. It is possible, for example, to take a wide range of others' strategies into account. One can engage quite widely in a variety of kinds of dialogue. It is possible and, on holistic governance principles, necessary, to engage widely in dialogue at the policy level. In general, multi-level integration (Kagan *et al.*, 1995) is possible provided that the full range of relationships is used carefully. Further, it is both possible and typically desirable to make changes from time to time in the kinds of relationships pursued with different agencies. What is appropriate to integrate today may be more appropriate for coordination tomorrow, and *vice versa*. Integration in public management is not like a lifelong monogamous marriage, but can be more like a life of promiscuity!

Finally, we turn to the ways in which advocates of holistic governance might answer the argument of the fatalists that holistic working cannot be achieved or at least not institutionalised, because the strength and durability of fragmented governance are too deep to uproot effectively. In Chapter 2 the discussion of the roots of fragmented governance identified eight factors that have led to its rise and institutionalisation, and we distinguished between two categories – the 'benign' which arise from unintended consequences of basically desirable activities, and the 'malign' which arise from the self-interested actions of stakeholders in governance.

The case for the feasibility of progress towards more holistic working in governance rests on the claim that holism can not only be compatible with the 'benign' forces, but can reinforce what is valuable in them without incurring the costs of fragmentation. More specifically, the following eight claims are made by the advocates of holistic governance in reply to those who would conclude from these explanations of the rise of functional fragmentation, that the prospects for coordination are bleak. At this stage, most of these arguments have been offered at the level of domestic governance, but it may be that there are possibilities for applications to transnational systems of governance and regulation of at least some of them:

a. There have been innovations in the measurement of outputs and outcomes that make holistic management feasible in a way that it was not until recently, and when combined with input and throughput based measurement, these would enhance management capabilities.
b. Innovations could be made in the ways in which public services and programmes are held to account that would both support holism and would actually enhance accountability and focus its efforts in the right place.
c. Consumers' best interests are typically served by holistic solutions, and their sometimes observed preferences for vertical over horizontal integration is principally a function of distrust, which would be addressed in some measure by holistic styles of management accountability, and is in part a function of professional capture of consumer opinion, which can legitimately be challenged.
d. These strategic decisions can be overturned, and in many countries, as chapter 1 showed, decisions of equally great strategic importance have been taken recently which at least could begin a process of institutionalisation of holistic working.
e. Holistic working and holistic measurement of impact upon real cross-cutting problems will enhance democracy by enabling citizens to measure the impact of government on the things they fundamentally care about, rather than having to rely on proxies that work mainly at the level of inputs and throughputs.
f. The consequence of (a), (b) and (d) could be that appropriate levels of political control – that is, control by politicians for the right reasons and within the right framework of discipline – can be achieved and even enhanced by holistic measurement, design of interventions.
g. Professional autonomy has its place in public services, but within a broader framework that should be designed around the key problems, and that should limit, insofar as possible, the prospects for professional capture. Holistic measurement, accountability and intervention design can serve this goal.
h. Sometimes, and subject to clear constitutional rules and political accountability, greater span of control for senior civil servants may be appropriate, and sometimes not. In general, span of control should follow the task, rather than the other way around. Holistic working offers

very wide task definition, but also requires pooled or shared control in matrix management styles. Therefore, it can preserve what is valuable in the imperial ambitions of senior civil servants while disciplining any tendencies for this to lead to officer capture. The same claim can be offered about street level bureaucrats. Advocates of holistic governance would argue that it is possible to design systems of incentive that would make various kinds of joint working their preferred solution to work-load coping problems and rationing choices. Indeed, in many cases, studies of particular initiatives have found front line staff to be the ones who initiate and sustain holistic working, for their own reasons and sometimes in the teeth of opposition from senior management.

If the case for holism is accepted, when and where is it appropriate?

There remains one final issue to be dealt with before the case for holism can be considered to have been fully stated. Suppose for the sake of argument that the general case for holism made so far were accepted. Politicians and public managers often ask: 'Where do we need to be doing joined-up working and where does it make more sense to organise by traditional function?' The reply offered by advocates of holistic governance would run along the following lines: The choice is not a simple either/or between doing holistic working or managing on a functional basis. Rather, the choice is about the level at which different kinds of integration might be appropriate for particular purposes.

In hardly any activity of government it is appropriate not to take into account a very wide range of other programmes; there are few instances in which extensive dialogue with adjacent services and programmes is not useful. But there is no general answer that makes the same sense in Gateshead as it does in Guildford to a question such as: 'which services should develop strategic alliances and which should merge?' Local prob-lems and priorities differ; local capabilities differ. The costs and benefits of pooling budgets on elderly care between health and social services will look very different in Bexhill or Lyme Regis than in central Manchester. The costs and benefits of creating a one-stop shop for young people in an area of declining population will be very different from those in, say, the suburban south-east.

Another version of the question goes like this: 'surely we don't need to be working holistically just to deliver basic services like emptying the bins properly and on time?' But this also misses the point. Holistic working is not an addition, nor applicable only to special cases, nor a kind of career move that agencies adopt once they have proved themselves 'successful' in delivering the 'basics' in the traditional way.

Even 'basic' services have to be connected up at some point. Emptying the bins is a good example, for *policy* integration between waste collection and community development, environmental strategy and crime prevention makes perfect sense. Collaboration between waste management, transport planning, development control, environmental health and the public-health functions of the health authorities can be very important in co-ordinating targets and identifying areas where one might be dumping costs and problems on others. It is not sensible, however, to have multi-disciplinary teams co-ordinating everything. They are a scarce resource to be deployed with care.

The first issue is what the goals are. That settled, the levels, focus and depth of working will follow.

Conclusion

This, then, is the case for holistic governance and its defence against its various critics. What are we to make of it? Indeed, the advocates of holistic governance make strong and bold claims, and many political scientists and practitioners are understandably sceptical. We cannot offer a conclusive examination here of the validity of every claim, although in the chapters that follow we offer some considerations that bear on how they should be appraised.

Certainly, it is not possible for the advocates to point to any rigorous, consistent large-scale cross-national, cross-policy-field evaluation study designed specifically to compare the performance under controlled conditions, of various types of functionally organised and holistic governance. In that sense, the empirical base on which the advocates rest is slender. On the other hand, as we have noted, nor is the empirical base for the defenders of the functional model, when restricted to evaluations of cost-effectiveness for outcomes, impressive.

There are a number of not-yet redeemed promises in the holists' case. Specifically, the models of strategy, management, outcome measurement, accountability, privacy codes all require more development. In the remaining chapters of this book we offer some more detailed consideration of these issues. We begin with a consideration of the theoretical background against which we can assess the possibility of aligning all these models.

4 Lessons from Theory: How Coordination Can Work

In this chapter we bring together and deepen the argument about the possibility of holistic governance by situating the debate in its larger theoretical context. We begin by analysing the range of standard images of interorganisational coordination that can be found both in the discourse of practitioners and in the academic literature.

We call these 'tropes' because they are standard, even archetypical, ideas which shape thinking and writing in exactly the way that linguists and literary scholars see stock tropes of speech and writing as shaping thought and writing.

We then identify the tradition of theory in social science that best explains the characteristics of this limited plurality. This is a theory that shows that ideas emerge from experience of actual social organisation. We then use that body of theory to draw some conclusions about how best to develop the central theoretical argument of the whole book. In particular, we argue that the most viable forms of organisation are those that give some recognition to each of the tropes, but without conceding wholly to any of them.

The argument that little can be expected from holistic governance strategies reflects one of these tropes. We suggest both that there can and should be limits to the claims for fatalism about the prospects for holistic governance, and also show how to take seriously the empirical findings about failures of holistic governance which the fatalist theories have emphasised. From this we set out some conclusions about the tool kit which governments can use to pursue holistic governance.

The tropes of interorganisational coordination: commonsense responses?

Sometimes academic literature and the conversations of practitioners are strangely convergent. In our review of both the literature and our interview data with practitioners, we found the same four tropes recurring. Not surprisingly, they are special cases of four basic syndromes that occur almost anywhere.

The first trope, which is strongest in academic political science, decision theory, and organisational sociology, is the trope of the impossibility of effective strategy. The argument is developed in its most extreme form in the work of the Carnegie School (March, 1988; Brunssen and Olsen, 1993), but it also runs through sociological institutionalist theories of organisations (Meyer and Rowan, 1977; DiMaggio and Powell, 1983; Scott and Meyer, 1994; Scott and Christensen, 1995), and the 'empty symbolics' view of politics (Edelman, 1985 [1964]). It can also be found in some centre–right writings on government that stress the peculiarly gridlocked and burdensome character of anything within the public sector by contrast with the private sector (within this genre, the most sophisticated argument is offered by Wilson, 1989).

One overarching version is the trope of the 'unending cycle of reorganisation'. This trope identifies the eternal recurrence of a small number of basic models of public management, each of which has its defining failures and weaknesses that lead people to cycle back through the others, or to try to produce hybrids, but without ever really achieving substantive improvement (Hood, 1998; Hood and Jackson, 1991). Whereas Edelman (1985 [1964]) allows for reform efforts as cynical manipulation of empty symbol and tawdry ceremonial in which some individuals are cheats and others dupes, Meyer and Rowan (1977) and Brunssen and Olsen (1993) tend to regard them as more often innocently futile processes in which everyone dupes themselves and each other. The basic idea here is that the power of institutions, scripts, short-term selfish political interests all block any possibility of developing strategies in government that are – at least in the medium term – rational or effective for problem-solving. The conditions for effective coordination between agencies of governance are just not achievable.

Although practitioners obviously cannot afford to believe in this trope for very long without losing all motivation, most have their moments of fatalism, and we picked up some evidence in our interviews that the fatalistic view can offer a kind of short-term solace in the event of the failure of a particular initiative, by allowing the practitioner temporarily to believe that whatever they did, there was little hope of achieving their imagined goal, because neither they nor anyone else could have achieved the requisite control over circumstance. For example, one senior officer in Beltham who was in general rather optimistic spoke of the feeling that 'People are using the words "partnership", "consultation", "dialogue" … but it doesn't mean anything.' This was not her considered view, but its availability played an important role in helping her cope and muddle through during the most difficult periods.

The second trope is that of the heroic individual public manager, the noble policy entrepreneur or good governor, whose steely determination, clarity of vision, leadership capabilities, grasp of the policy issues, flair for persuasion and powerful oratory bring about coordination. While respectable academics have long since discarded Carlyle's 'great man theory of history', the basic trope can often be found in the references to the importance of individual public managers. The key is having managers who can identify opportunities and risks and calibrate their actions to the crises they face. Such concerns are reflected in work on the role of key personality traits in enabling individual public officials to convert a crisis into an opportunity and in the studies on 'public sector entrepreneurs' (Leadbeater and Goss, 1998, and, with more theoretical qualifications, Moore, 1995).

In conversations with practitioners, for obvious reasons, the trope of the heroic individual recurs frequently. For example, the visionary Director of Early Years and Play in Mixborough spoke of herself in this vein. Strategy is possible, but emergent, in this trope. The hero does not plan to the last detail in advance, but through an iterative process of using uncommon abilities to spot niches, exercise political and policy arbitrage, gradually shapes a strategy implicitly and without necessarily meaning to. Within the academic tradition of organisational sociology, one version of the holistic is that smooth operator, the 'boundary spanner', the person who occupies a key role in making linkages between organisations (Mulford, 1984; Alexander, 1995). Such people were known in the managerial argot of Southbrookborough as 'boundroids' – people 'who have the capacity to live between two warring states and sleep easily on the border', as one senior manager there put it. In this trope, despite the best efforts of hierarchical institutions, networks are loosely tied, and it is this breadth of weak ties (Granovetter, 1973; Burt, 1992; 6, 1997c) that individual entrepreneurial public managers can exploit.

The third trope is of rational planning by objectives which are then cascaded down through the interorganisational structure, or what Mintzberg calls 'deliberate' strategy (Mintzberg and Waters, 1994). Performance-based budgeting is undertaken using sophisticated software analysis of large quantities of verified quantitative cost and benefit data under the leadership of chief executives and governors or mayors or prime ministers or presidents. In these, budgets, aims and objectives are set in holistic problem-and-outcome terms; steering agencies are created to coordinate the range of agencies to be redirected towards more holistic working on the agreed planned outcomes and outputs, and the elected bodies create holistic accountability structures. The hierarchy of mission statement, aims and objective, performance budgets, measurement, reporting is reviewed after agreed periods have elapsed.

Whilst academic political scientists have largely abandoned the idea of the rational synoptic planning and decision-making agency, the trope recurs continually in the public management literature intended for practitioners: the recent detailed model for 'reinvention' towards holistic and anticipatory policy work by Osborne and Plastrik (2000, chapter 1) is only the most recent example. For the trope of hierarchy, institutions ensure that networks are tightly connected and disciplined for rational organisation. In the implementation studies on interorganisational coordination, there are several that conclude quite generally – often based on studies of quite limited samples of organisations working on a single social problem – that hierarchical coordination with centralised structure among providers and a single funding source, is generally more effective than other formations, save in special circumstances where 'second best' (Lipsey and Lancaster, 1956) considerations for solution design begin cut in (e.g., Provan and Milward, 1995). In one moment during an interview, one Beltham senior management slipped neatly into the hierarchical mind-set when she said, as if reciting the creed of working by the rules, 'Organisation development has got to be in synch with budget development'; later on, she remarked 'the key principle has to be movement through the system'.

Fourth is the trope of holistic strategy that emerges organically from the reasonable interests, institutional arrangements and ideas of the loose network of frontline agencies that find reasons to work together. There is a strong tradition of this in organisational sociology. For example, in the classic studies from the 1960s and 1970s in interorganisational coordination, there is found the image of bodies increasing their coordination as they find the need to exchange resources or depend upon one another (resource dependency theory: Pfeffer and Salancik, 1978), or as the density of their ties within a network increases (population ecology models: Hannan and Freeman, 1989) or as they find the other organisations increasingly structure their environment (Lawrence and Lorsch, 1967; Thompson, 1967). In the same period of the 1970s, political science began to borrow these ideas in order to examine experiments in what would today be called holistic working, but were then more often called coordination. Hanf and Scharpf's (1978) collection represents an important convergence between the communitarian models of voluntary coordination then coming from organisation studies with the 'bottom up' perspective on policy implementation (Porter and Hjern, 1981) which took a view of inter-agency relationships in policy programme execution that looked for emergent harmonies, not necessarily the ones that hierarchical elected policy-makers wanted, but ones that nevertheless produced new voluntarily chosen and constructed order (Sabatier, 1986).

In the 1980s and 1990s generally, a common theme in organisational studies was to argue from the limits of hierarchical coordination (Miller, 1992) to the possibility – indeed, likelihood – that mutual adjustment from the bottom up would typically produce coordination and better outcomes (Chisholm, 1989), whether for reasons of transactions costs, resource dependency or network dynamics. In the imagination of individualism, the happy outcome of order and effectiveness would be achieved by the invisible hand. By contrast in communitarian thought, that desired state of affairs would be brought about just as automatically by partisan mutual adjustment. In either case, history had every chance of being efficient (North, 1990). (Even the present authors succumbed to this view at times: 6 and Randon, 1995!) For example, a major statement in organisation studies of this perspective was that by Alter and Hage (1993). They emphasised what they called 'co-prosperity', rather than competition, and 'co-responsibility' rather than hierarchical accountability.

Within political science, the appeal of the theoretical work of Rhodes (1997) is precisely that his conception of public management as loosely connected agencies that voluntarily and collectively form self-organising networks is a re-working of this trope. What this trope has in common with the second is that strategy is emergent on voluntarily chosen actions, but what it has in common with the third is that the conditions in which strategy emerges are essentially collective, and therefore there are at least some occasions on which key aspects of the environment in which choices are made that are given. In this tradition, the role of institutions is fully admitted, but for coordination, care must be taken to ensure that the right institutions are encouraged, to ensure growing mutuality of resource dependence, rather than conflict within networks.

Institutions in this trope enable loose networks to become tight. In Southbrookborough, perhaps precisely because legal and budgetary obstacles had been so difficult to overcome, the picture painted by one of our interviewees of the origins of the partnership was one in which there was a basic and 'strong drive' in both health and local authority to 'join up', because the possibility of benefits was, in her account, basically obvious to both sides; this had principally been slowed, blocked and diverted by the legal, audit and financial structures. At one point in an interview, one Beltham manager declared that 'good dialogue spills over into other areas', summarising neatly the trope of voluntary coordination.

Explaining the dominance of tropes

When we hear the same tropes so frequently, and in such stylised form, the appropriate social scientist's suspicion is that we are hearing the voices of institutions speaking. Tropes are the spoors of institutional forces that, often without writers, scholars and commentators being aware of exactly where and how, shape and channel their understandings.

The relationship between these tropes, and the fact that they or variants of them recur in many areas of life, is – we consider – best explained by the work of Douglas (1970, 1982, 1986, 1992, 1996; Douglas and Ney, 1998) and her colleagues (Schwarz and Thompson, 1990; Thompson *et al.*, 1990; Coyle and Ellis, 1993; Ellis and Thompson, 1997; Adams, 1995; Rayner, 1992; Gross and Rayner, 1985; Mars, 1982) in the neo-Durkheimian tradition of the sociology of knowledge. This approach has been used in the field of public management models recently by Hood (1998), although to argue to rather different conclusions.

Douglas argues, following Durkheim (1995; Durkheim and Mauss 1902), Mannheim (1936), Schutz (1967) and Berger and Luckmann (1966) that the ideas, basic myths and tropes by which people classify their environments and organisational processes are driven not so much by accurate or distorted perceptions, as by the basic forms of social organisation, or what Durkheim (1984) called the 'solidarities' (6, 1999a). The tropes to which we cleave are the product of where we sit in particular structures of social organisation, of our prior commitments to certain kinds of social organisation, of analogies and metaphors from social organisation in one context borrowed in another. In short, each of the tropes is the achievement of an institutional form of *solidarity*, or a style of social organisation (Douglas, 1966, 1970, 1982, 1986, 1992, 1994, 1996a,b).

Douglas goes on to offer a heuristic device for classifying the basic commitments or forms of social organisation or solidarities that produce these tropes, and that device explains very well why the four tropes of interorganisational coordination constantly recur.

Take first the dimension that arises clearly in the four tropes of inter-organisational coordination of the degree to which the emergence of coordination depends fundamentally on circumstances that are imposed either unavoidably or deliberately, on the one hand, or to which it depends fundamentally on emerging from basically voluntary choices of individuals or groups. For present purposes, it might most simply be described as 'constraint'. This is the same thing as Douglas' dimension of 'grid', or, to take the factor back to its most important source in social science, Durkheim's (1951) concept of the degree of social regulation.

Next consider the dimension that also arises in our four tropes, the degree to which the processes which determine whether coordination arises from action (or its impossibility) or from structure or collective processes. For present purposes, it is perhaps easiest to summarise this dimension as being concerned with the extent of bonding between people. This is Douglas' 'group' dimension, and Durkheim's (1951) dimension of the degree of 'social integration'.

This yields for Douglas the now well-known and controversial matrix, which helpfully structures the relationships between the four tropes of interorganisational coordination (Figure 4.1). The figure clearly shows the similarities between the tropes horizontally, vertically and diagonally.

The high constraint, low bonding quadrant is the one in which, logically, little coordination can be achieved, in which efforts in coordination reappear and cycle randomly but can secure little grip on the situation. The constraint is provided by institutions that limit what can be tried or achieved. In this situation, the networks that link individuals to each other tend be experienced as tight because of the institutional constraints, but they are in fact loose because of the weakness of the bonds. Individuals are relatively isolated from one another.

Consider the quadrant defined by low constraint and low bonding, this is the world of the political or policy entrepreneur, the heroic individual politician or public manager whose driven opportunism creates a certain kind of voluntary coordination. Organisational reform is not orderly, but is rather the consequence of the opportunistic behaviour of these entrepreneurs, who are but loosely networked with each other.

The world of at least boundedly rational planning, of management by objectives, of the authoritative subordination of organisational means to defined goals in order to achieve coordination from the top down is, of course, the world of the highly constrained, highly bonded quadrant. Here networks are tight, reform of public management is a progressive, orderly affair, and, if properly managed, can be designed to produce gains for all.

Finally, the loose network governance trope, and the world of co-responsibility and self-organisation, is that which emerges in the quadrant defined by weak constrained and strong bonds. Here institutions are weak and therefore coordination is fragile, because they are dependent upon voluntary mutuality; so institutions of coordination require the constant effort and vigilance of the movements, networks and clans to sustain them. Reform, when it can be achieved, is a progressive affair, in which loose community emerges through determined but shared voluntary effort.

Now, of course, actual situations of these kinds can be found at every level in politics and in public management. These situations are the institutional

forms of social organisation or solidarity, which are reproduced by themselves producing these four tropes as their governing myths, which provide
the motivations for politicians and public managers to make these four
types at least provisionally stable and viable, in their niche. Each has the
strengths and the fatal weaknesses characteristic of its style of coordination.
Any real system of public management and governance must, however, find
space for each of these. The conflict between them must be, to some
degree, contained, but cannot be avoided altogether if that overarching
system of public management is to maintain itself.

Developing the framework: is reconciliation possible?

Of course, the same four – or at least three 'active' – basic syndromes
(hierarchy, individualism, communitarianism) can find their reasons for
opposing coordination and integration in public management. Radical
individualists who want less government certainly have reasons to welcome less effective government and are deeply suspicious of coordination
as a route to tyranny; radical communitarians, or enclavists, are generally
suspicious of government coordination as threatening the vibrancy of community; radical hierarchists see in coordination a series of blockages upon
the means of controlling government that functional fragmentation has
afforded. Coordination in public management is simply one issue on
which at least less extreme forms of these institutional solidarities can
express their rival and underlying commitments.

There are basically two ways to think about the two dimensions in this
heuristic device (Coyle, 1993, pp. 220–2). The first is to think of the two
dimensions of the heuristic as being essentially dichotomous (Thompson,
1982), so that the four tropes and the underlying social realities that produce them are the stable elements. The other is to think of the two dimensions as continually differentiable (Gross and Rayner, 1985, pp. 112–14).
The 'continuist' view allows for the possibility of extremity and moderation of each of the main positions. This makes it easier for settlements to
be struck between the basic biases in thinking about coordination, by
pitching an appeal to moderation in each quadrant. Implicitly, the continuist allows for the possibility of making an appeal to constituencies
nearer the centre of the matrix. The 'discontinuist' interpretation, conversely, renders settlement-making more difficult because it imagines itself
dealing with solidarities that are, taken separately, necessarily extreme for-
mulations: in this interpretation, the centre of the heuristic matrix has no
special status. Indeed, discontinuists more recently have adopted a form of

Figure 4.1 *The tropes of interorganisational coordination as the product of types of social organisation*

High constraint
Coordination/integration or the lack of it
arises from *imposed* circumstances
– rule, role given fact
⇧

	Fatalism – *the trope of imposed (in)action*	**Hierarchy** - *the trope of imposed structure*	
	Strategy: The impossibility of strategy	*Strategy*: Rational planning as deliberate strategy, beginning with objectives at the centre, determining function, means and relationships	
	Institutions: Institutions preclude rationality	*Institutions*: Institutional capacity for change	
	Reforms: Reform as an unending cycle of over-correction of substitution of one flawed model for another; reform efforts as largely pointless, sometimes empty pretences, sometimes cynical manipulation of symbols, sometimes innocently futile	*Reforms*: Reforms as a progressive sequence Institutions enable and constitute rationality	
Low bonding: Coordination/ integration or lack of it results from *action* ⇦ (or the impossibility of action)	*Game model*: Efforts in coordination are a zero-sum game	*Game model*: Efforts in coordination are a positive sum game provided these efforts are managed and structured properly	*High bonding*: Coordination/ integration or the lack of ⇨ it results from *structure*
	Networks: Tight becoming loose	*Networks*: Tight	
	Individualism – *the trope of voluntary action*	**Communitarianism** – *the trope of voluntary structure*	
	Strategy: Strategy emerges from the astute seizing of niched opportunities by smart public managers and boundary spanners	*Strategy*: Strategy emerges from the interaction and interdependence of organisations in a loose network that become a tighter community through growing density of mutuality of exchange, resource dependency, etc.	
	Institutions: Institutions are never so tight that loose ties cannot be exploited by public entrepreneurs.		

Institutions afford a cornucopia of opportunities for coordination to those astute enough to spot and exploit them

Reforms: Reforms are an unstructured sequence of opportunistic acts of arbitrage for temporary coordination

Game model: Efforts in coordination are a positive sum game

Networks: Loose

Institutions: Institutions of the right kind for loose-to-tight coordination are fragile, and they must be nurtured to ensure that community emerges

Reforms: Reform as a progressive process of growing mutual interdependence and coordination, and nurturing of institutional conditions

Game model: Efforts in coordination are a positive sum game in specially cultivated institutions circumstances, otherwise quickly turn zero-sum

Networks: Loose becoming tight

⇩

Low constraint

Coordination / integration or the lack of it arises from the consequences of structure and action that is or can be largely under the control or at least influence of *voluntary* behaviour of individuals or groups three-dimensional non-matrix graphical representation of the relationship between the solidarities in which there is no centre ground to look for (Thompson and Tayler, forthcoming). However, as will be clear from the previous paragraph, the present argument leans towards the continuist interpretation.

How does this mapping of tropes onto basic commitments of social organisation help us? Other writers have used this neo-Durkheimian theory to argue for the correctness of just one of the tropes. For example, Hood (1998) uses it to argue for a fatalism only briefly and perhaps half-heart-edly qualified at the very end of his book where he flirts with the idea that hybrids between tropes might be worth exploring; Adams (1995) has no such qualifications to his case for fatalism; while the late Aaron Wildavsky (1988) used the theory to propose a full-blooded individualism. The previous work of the authors of this book has sometimes perhaps veered towards one or other of these tropes. It was a criticism of 6 (1997a) that the argument there took a too hierarchical view of interorganisational coordination. However, this is a misuse: each of the tropes has its place.

For in this way the approach developed here helps us to understand the nature of the apparent cycles in the rise and fall of public management interest in holistic working. The neo-Durkheimian approach predicts that, if pressed disproportionately far without compensating development of other solidarities, each of the solidarities will undermine its own viability through the working out of its own inherent organisational weaknesses. The information weaknesses of hierarchy, individualism's difficulty in sustaining the production of common and public goods, the fissiparous character of communitarianism, the incapacity of fatalism to motivate, all undermine public management reform strategies that are based upon a single trope and its underlying form of social organisation. Where holistic working has in the past been developed with a highly hierarchical bias, it is particularly vulnerable to this: hierarchy is not, we have argued in this and previous chapters, the only moment in holism, but it has some role, and it can too easily become dominant. Secondly, the assertion of any of the solidarities will provoke backlashes from the others. The theory does not suggest that there is any necessary trajectory that will be followed: it is contingent on many factors whether shifts made from hierarchy will towards individualism, as in the late 1970s, or towards communitarianism, as in the 1990s (Thompson *et al.*, 1990, chapter 4).

However, the theoretically sound way in which to use the heuristic is to recognise, as Durkheim argued at length in his lectures on *Pragmatism and sociology* (1983), that *each* of these four tropes describe, albeit in ideal–typical, extreme form, *real* organisational processes, that *none* describes the whole organisational reality, that organisational reality like social reality generally, may not be capable of any single comprehensive self-consistent representation, but it does *not* follow from this, that representations are not representations of the real. That is, the sociology of knowledge may lead to social constructivism about concepts of the social, but not relativism or anti-realism (Meštrović, 1993), and one that recognises that construction requires *real* raw materials.

This theory underlying the heuristic suggests that 'taking sides' between these tropes is a poor way to proceed in a serious attempt to understand the totality (Meštrović, 1993, p. 85). Certainly, one implication of the argument from the sociology of knowledge is that these tropes cannot be intellectually made consistent in a once-for-all valid synthesis. For they arise from the basic rivalrous and incompatible practices of social organisation that structure conflict in societies generally.

For the underlying argument in Durkheim (1984) and the neo-Durkheimians (Thompson, 1997a,b,c; 6, 1998c, 1999a) is that social viability, or functioning, is achieved by finding ways of organising that are reasonably robust against shocks from each of the solidarities, with their insistence on their peculiar tropes of coordination. The concept of viability is the linkage between the positive analytical moment of the theory, and the more normative moment. For it suggests that those who want deliberately to go about fostering viable coordination should try to find ways of organising that give at least some recognition and institutionalisation to at least some of the practices represented by these tropes.

Correlatively, the most sensible intellectual and practical strategy for coping with irreducible pluralism, as Durkheim argued and as the neo-Durkheimians have developed his thought, is to identify settlements between these basic rival solidarities and their conceptions of how organisational relationships work, that acknowledge something of what each offers and claims, while recognising that none holds more than a portion of truth, and any settlement can only be temporary. At the social and political level of strategy, Durkheim (1984 [1893]) called this 'organic solidarity' or a practical settlement between the mechanical solidarities that each produce their own tropes with which to model the world, and Thompson (1997a,b,c) has developed this into a theory of 'clumsy institutions'. At the intellectual level, the argument proposes an approach of trying to build modest syntheses of all the tropes, recognising that all such modest syntheses cannot eliminate conflict, make consistent an organisational reality that is not itself consistent, and recognising that syntheses that are accepted at one time and place may not be later or elsewhere.

It is this approach which underpins the general argument of this book. We argue that while the academic fatalists, like those who cleave to each of the other tropes, do indeed have some evidence to which they can point, of institutionalised blockages to rationality, and to the recurrence of break-downs and failures, they have no automatic monopoly upon or claim to greater 'fundamentality' of truth. If the social fact to which they point – empty pretence (Edelman, 1985 [1964], 1988), 'garbage can' decision-making (Cohen *et al.*, 1972; Kingdon, 1995), following of scripts, and so forth – well up in any organisational setting, then so too do the phenomena to which the tropes of hierarchy, individualism and communitarianism point. No one solidarity – not even that of fatalism – can claim greater access to or authority over fundamental truth.

This describes at a very high level of generality the approach that we take in the argument of this book. We try to set out a conception of strat-egy, interorganisational coordination, the roles available to managers and of the tools of governance available to coordinators and coordinated, that reflects our concern to give at least some recognition to all these tropes, without surrendering the entire argument to any one of them. This is a dif-ficult tightrope to walk, but, if the theory on which we work is accepted, then it is necessary to understand how different patterns of interorganisa-tional coordination and non-coordination can be viable or vulnerable. Moreover, this theory provides a central theoretical underpinning for our general argument in the book that the fatalism about holistic governance that is so widespread in political science should not be allowed to crowd out approaches that allow for greater optimism, albeit properly qualified, for at least some kinds of coordination and holistic working. For the theory shows why both coordination failure and coordination optimism both spring up afresh, in reaction to each other, without privileging failure in the automatic way that the fatalist arguments do.

Tropes of coordination and the deployment of tools for holistic governance

Perhaps the most important implication for strategy that emerges from our consideration of these tropes is in the vexed debate about what tools are most effective, appropriate, even available, for public managers – whether they are elected national politicians at the most senior level or frontline managers of local agencies – to use to pursue coordination.

For this purpose, we may temporarily focus on the arguments between the three 'active' solidarities of hierarchy, individualism and communitari-anism, for the fatalist solidarity with its trope of the impossibility of coordination contributes to this debate only by insisting upon the null hypothesis that nothing will work, that all tools are blunt and that the debate is largely pointless.

In general terms, however, the institutions of hierarchy are committed to the idea that it is the *strong* tools of governance that make for coordination. By strength and weakness here, we mean the degree to which the tools leave choice, discretion, and freedom for voluntary choice to those at whom the tools are targeted – that is to say, the degree of their coerciveness. Where hierarchy believes in the power of strong tools, individualism and communitarianism believe in the power of weak tools.

For the hierarchical view of the world, the centre must impose, direct, manage, regulate, mandate, prohibit and use powerful financial incentives to purchase and sanction behaviour. Not surprisingly, then, for this view, holistic budgeting or designing budgets around outcomes or at least problems, rather than around line items for inputs, is a key tool (Osborne and Plastrik, 2000, pp. 43–56; 6, 1997a). By contrast, the low constraint solidarities of individualism and communitarianism are committed to the view that by and large, these strong tools tend to be rather blunt, and that it is the weak tools of governance that matter. For them the key tools are: persuasion, training, provision of information, openness, supporting front line and local agencies to learn, to develop joined-up bodies of knowledge and to carefully nurture the cultures that support either the emergence of individual public entrepreneurs or voluntary mutual adjustment by agencies (6, 1997b, 6 *et al.*, 1999).

It is helpful at this stage to present a full classification of the tools of governance in order to state more exactly the nature of the problem. The following table (Figure 4.2) presents our synthesis of the canonical taxonomy offered by Hood (1983), as supplemented by Salamon (1989) and Bemelmans-Videc *et al.* (1998), and reorganised in 6 (1997b) and 6 *et al.*, (1999). From this figure, it can be seen that the are gradations of strength within each of Hood's 1983 categories of *effectors*, or tools intended to change the behaviour of others, detectors, or tools intended to gather intelligence, collectors, which gather material resources, and selectors (6, 1997c) which organise, manage and analyse information to frame, to understand, to model, to generate the mental maps on which policy-makers work.

In our own previous work, we have tried at different times, and perhaps not entirely consistently, to recognise both the power of strong (6, 1997a) and weak (6, 1997c, 6 *et al.*, 1999) tools. From the interview research conducted, it became clear that we could draw upon the evidence of public managers at the centre to help make out the case for strong tools, and from evidence of public managers in localities and in subaltern agencies to help make out the case for weak tools as being the key to coordination and holism.

The theoretical approach that we have developed in this chapter, however, points in the direction of approaches that acknowledge 'both ... and'

Figure 4.2   *The power tools of government, after Hood and others*

Types of power tool	*Tools, ranked strong to weak*

Effectors
(for producing changes in
culture or behaviour)
	direct government provision
	government-owned corporations
	regulation, mandation, permission,
	    prohibition
	rights and systems of redress
	contract purchasing
	loan guarantees
	grants-in-aid, matching grants
	tax expenditures
	information delivery: persuasion,
	    propaganda example, demonstration
	    projects, education, training

Collectors (for obtaining money and other resources)	taxation, direct or indirect levies service fees and charges appeals
Detectors (for acquiring information)	requisition inspection purchasing, barter appeals (including rewards for information)
Selectors (for managing, selecting, analysing, presenting information)	audit cost-benefit analysis performance indicators and measurement cost measurement, resource budgeting management review scenario-building, risk assessment

rather than 'either... or'. However, it also suggests that we cannot automatically expect any particular synthesis to be free from tensions and fully consistent. Ultimately, the relationship between tropes is grounded in *political settlements* rather than intellectual and theoretical reconciliations. Therefore, we can hope at most that settlements can be appropriately balanced for particular but perhaps evanescent institutional conditions, insofar as those conditions can be appreciated (Vickers, 1995) with the limited cognitive capacities of institutionally filtered, solidarity-governed and trope-impregnated appreciative systems. For each of these four 'mechanical' solidarities, as Durkheim (1984) called them, that insist on the internal 'similarity' or 'purity' of its form of organisation and coordination, constitutes a bias, a set of filters, but also a learning and recognition capability that combines searching and framing tools for observations – what Vickers (1995) calls the 'reality judgment' – with a set of presumptions about normative commitments – what Vickers (1995) called 'valuation'. That is, Durkheimian solidarities produce Vickersian appreciative systems. Vickers also gave great emphasis in his account of judgment as a social process in policy-making, to what he called the 'instrumental judgment', which consists in the balancing of rivalrous forces in ingenious and novel ways to reach settlements between the norms: this is what Durkheim called 'organic solidarity' and the neo-Durkheimians call striking settlements (6, 1998c) or developing 'clumsy institutions' (Thompson, 1997a,b,c).

How are we then to move beyond the tyranny of single tropes, single mechanical solidarities, single biases, and to make the most intelligent use of the tools of government? The general argument of this book is that we need to recognise, first, that none of the tropes alone is sufficient for coordination, secondly, that exclusive reliance on either weak or strong tools is inadequate. Third, we shall argue that what is to be looked for in coordination and integration is to find ways, as far as possible, of balancing – in creative tension, rather than complete harmony, which is not available – these tools of governance. The purpose of this creative tension is to stimulate forms of coordination using each of the mechanisms which is given near-mythical status by the tropes. The result will not necessarily be logically consistent, but at least the solidarities will tolerate each other as long as possible. This is indeed, as Thompson (1997a,b,c) says, clumsy. But the wider theoretical argument is that reliance on sleek mechanisms and institutions is much worse. Strong and weak tools need to provide contexts for each other, need to supplement each other without ever being wholly complementary.

We can immediately draw out one crucially important practical implication of this neo-Durkheimian argument. It is a common misunderstanding, which we have criticised at several points in the course of this book, that holistic governance is an agenda of hierarchical rationalism in public policy, and that this is its central weakness. From the work of Lindblom and others in the 1950s onwards, it has been accepted that there are profound political limits to the degree to which government policies can ever be consistent with each other. Interests have to be conciliated; important groups of voters must be kept broadly content; policies must be got through legislatures and concessions granted; media pressures must often be accommodated, at least in part. If our argument in this chapter is accepted, then none of this presents a problem of the holistic governance agenda as we understand it. Holistic government is not about perfect intellectual consistency in politics, but about developing practices by which the inconsistencies that just have to be lived with are, firstly, recognised, understood and selected with as much astuteness as the time and resources available for political judgment permit, and secondly, *managing* as well as possible the conflicts between the inconsistencies that are accepted.

Conclusion

In this chapter we have argued that there is a limited plurality of ways of conceiving organisational structures and processes, and this limited variety reflects the limited plurality of basic imperatives that shape what kind of organisation is possible. Each way of thinking reflects a kind of bias. Viability in organisational and interorganisational systems depends on finding institutions that give some recognition to each of these biases, and on containing the conflict between them. Holistic working in governance, then, must not articulate only one of these impulses. It must give due weight to each. The aim is not and cannot be for perfect consistency in policy, but for creative rather than destructive forms of tension. Nor can the aim of holism be that the most authoritative be used to specify how coordination shall be done throughout the system of public management: there must be some rough and ready balance between strong and weak tools, between centre and periphery, and so on. While the fatalists may be right that a stable utopia is not possible, it cannot follow that fatalism can have its own way completely, any more than may any other basic bias in organising. In the next chapter, we give a concrete example of how this argument works, by showing that reform strategies must give due weight to both top down and bottom up imperatives, to both anticipation and resilience in managing the risks of failure.

5 Designing a Reform Strategy

It is worth thinking about ways in which initiatives in holistic working might not get off the ground, might fail to achieve their goals, or might have undesirable side-effects, as essentially a risk management problem. That is, the central question can be understood as one of whether there are things that politicians and public managers can do to reduce either the probabilities of failure or unwanted consequences, or to reduce their severity, either in advance of their occurrence or as they occur.

Any strategy for reform of government in the direction of more holistic working must at the same time be directed to creating certain pre-conditions for reform and to the management of risks associated with reform. Too often politicians and public managers have tended to think of these as separate activities, and even to talk of managing risk as something that is done later in the sequence of reform. What is now clear from the international experience generally and from the history of British government reform, both during the reinvention era and now in the programme of reform for holistic government, is that this separation of the two leads to serious problems, to the mis-design of reform strategy and even to failures. Rather, pre-conditions need to be thought of as the converse of risks, and other risks need to be thought about in the earliest stages of planning reform.

In this chapter we explore the ways in which well designed reform strategies need to work upon both risk and conditions together. There is only a small number of basic ways in which risks can be managed, and in which conditions can be focused on in order to put them in place. In the first section of the chapter, we set out a framework for thinking about how this can be done. In this section, for the sake of simplicity, we describe this framework in terms of risks, but the reader should always bear in mind that this term encompasses conditions.

In the next section of the chapter, we give concrete examples of the ways in which, in the British case, the reform strategy lacked an adequate recognition of the necessity for the management of risk, which led to a number of serious weaknesses in the programme.

In the third and final section, we situate the management of risk within an understanding of the management of innovation, based on the wider literature in political science and in organisational studies.

A framework for thinking about integration risk

In the literature on the management of risk there is a valuable and fundamental distinction between two styles of risk management, which are commonly termed *anticipation* and *resilience* (Hood and Jones, 1996; Wildavsky, 1988).

Anticipationist styles of managing risk place particular emphasis on institutionalising cultures to look forward, and on investment in instruments that will help policy-makers and front line officials detect signs and clues of potential future difficulties. Moreover, anticipationism is committed to taking early and preventive action. This can, for at least some kinds of risks, be entirely reasonable. There are of course risks that can be prevented and others that cannot, because they appear as shocks, even may be anticipated. But there are many areas where greater preventive activity is justifiable. However, there is also an extreme form of anticipation, which is usually known as the *precautionary principle*. This states that one should act to prevent problems even before one is sure that there is a problem, and even before one has confidence that the technology of prevention will work, on the grounds that many problems anticipated are likely to be so severe that any preventive action will typically prove better than none (For discussion, see 6, 2000a and see also the special issue of *Journal of risk research*, 4,2). The argument for the precautionary principle is often grounded in the idea that one should analyse problems and make decisions on the basis of considering the worst case scenario, so as to be able to plan to prevent it. Those who think the precautionary principle too extreme, too pessimistic (or even incoherent and self-defeating: 6, 2000a) can remain committed to prevention (let us therefore call this variant of the style simply 'preventionist'), if we consider that it is more important to be reasonably confident of the scale, likelihood and severity of the problem, and the affordability and efficacy of the technique to be used for prevention, before taking precipitate action. However, believers in precaution and prevention alike share the optimistic belief that in principle we can have sufficient causal knowledge of how risks and problems arise, then we can devise some kind of preventive technique with which to reduce those risks.

By contrast, the resilience style of risk management starts from the more pessimistic assumption that most risks and failures are probably unpredictable even in principle, and that even if they are predictable, we lack the causal knowledge to design effective strategies to control these risks, and that even if we know something about how to reduce risks, those strategies will typically have side-effects that may be as bad as or even worse than the harms they are supposed to prevent (Wildavsky, 1988, p. 77 ff); indeed, they may even be iatrogenic. By contrast, the resilience style of risk management argues that the scarce resources of money, managers' time and attention should be put into coping with problems as they actually occur – in other words, palliation and cure. These unwanted side-effects can include the accumulation of more government power than would be acceptable – for example, disproportionately intrusive regulation or inspection for the magnitude of the harm in question, or investment in particular activities that has the effect of producing other distortions in the economy or in the priorities of public management.

This distinction can be mapped onto the classification of the tropes of interorganisational coordination introduced in Chapter 4. Hierarchy is committed to anticipation; communitarianism is also, and indeed, in its extreme form, cleaves to precaution; by contrast, individualism requires resilience; fatalism resorts to the most minimal resilience. The general argument of this book has been that in public management, as more generally, what is typically most appropriate in public management is to look for some institutionalised way of enabling people to balance all four, and the same general principle should apply to managing risks of failure as well. Clearly, many risks of failure themselves arise from imbalances in the mix of styles of public management – excessively hierarchical approaches, excessively fatalistic demobilisation – and so they are likely to be best tackled, not by more of the same skew, but by some correction in each of the other three directions.

There are, then, likely to be limits both to anticipation and to resilience. Wildavsky, in general an opponent of anticipation, argued (1988) that its use should be restricted to those situations where the probabilities of particular risks occurring within a given time frame are known with reasonable confidence, and where actors possess a large amount of relevant, well-grounded causal knowledge about what techniques and approaches might work in advance to effectively reduce those probabilities, or failing that to reduce the severity of the harms or failures if and when they should occur, whilst also controlling any unwanted side-effects of the deployment of those techniques. He was pessimistic that these conditions could ever be met, at least for the range of environmental, technological, public health, consumer product safety and work safety risks with which he was concerned. On this basis, he justified his argument for a mix of individualistic and – although Wildavsky was coy about acknowledging this dimension of his thought – also fatalistic institutions with which to manage risk. Should we be similarly pessimistic about our knowledge of the probability, severity and reducibility of the risks of failure in holistic government?

Let us begin by granting the argument for resilience its due in the context of public management. Just as in the field of risk that Wildavsky was concerned with, it is important to avoid the pretence that life can ever be perfectly safe – after all, we all have to die of something – so in public management it is impossible to get the ordinary, dirty, untidy, rough and ready, populist or self-serving practice of politics out of governance, and if, for no other reason, smoothly integrated administration cannot be achieved. Politicians will always want, at least from time to time, to micromanage, to insist on goals expressed in input or activity terms because of their particular importance to some important interest group, and because of their symbolic importance to sections of the public, even though these measures may well, and often do, conflict with goals of integration, effectiveness and even with the officially declared priorities of the very same politicians. This is as it should be in a democratic system, for which the goal is as much responsive governance as it is effective and problem-solving governance. Having imposed them upon public officials, if ever politicians accept performance measurement and performance-related pay for themselves, the performance measures they will accept will surely have more to do with responsiveness and leadership and coalition building, than they will have to do with administrative efficacy. Unlike directors of business corporations, ministers are not elected only to govern well and to solve problems, but also to govern in ways that reflect the preferences of their constituencies, parties and key interest groups.

Moving to the level of executive operations, administration and professional structures, perfect foresight is clearly impossible, and no one can credibly claim to be able to foresee all the possible risks of failure in integration, their probability, timing, severity, and to identify effective strategies to reduce or prevent them. Administrative science is ever likely to achieve that degree of certitude, not least because of the rapid pace of external shocks upon systems of governance from the business cycle and changing patterns of social policy problems from technological change, political mobilisation, and so on.

Therefore, there is no doubt that resilience and indeed a measure of humility about what is achievable must play an important role in any strategy for holistic governance.

However, it does not follow from the fact that one cannot anticipate or prevent everything, that one cannot anticipate anything. If the argument of this book is accepted, then there is a modest but important basis for causal knowledge about the kinds of risks that integration initiatives face, and some information about what is being tried by public managers in a variety of settings who must tackle these challenges. Without doubt, the body of evaluative work on which this causal knowledge rests is often slender, and its mining and use is less systematic than it might be. However, the fatalist interpretation of the case for resilience essentially has to give a firmly negative answer to the question 'can governments learn from their experience, learn from the experience of others, draw upon existing knowledge bases?' While certainly it is easier for public managers to learn in areas that are at any given time less politically contested, to the extent that there has been empirical work done on this question, it tends to suggest that the fatalist answer is greatly over-stated. A recent cross-national collection of essays on the question of governmental learning found that there is a perhaps surprisingly high degree of investment by governments in both policy and programme evaluation and that more of it is actually used and can be used than the fatalist argument seems to allow for (Leeuw *et al.*, 2000).

It is always possible for the fatalist, of course, to reply that the particular case studies selected are unrepresentative, that investment in evaluation and learning is a sham, that what is claimed as learning is really *ex post facto* rationalisation of policy preference change, and so on. But this only reveals the nature of the argument between the four basic biases and tropes. Ultimately, this debate is not one that is amenable to definitive empirical test; any piece of evidence can be used or re-interpreted by any of the biases. The only sensible strategy therefore is to consider how far one can grant a reasonable measure of recognition to each.

One way to begin to do that is to recognise the sources of many of the risks of failure in holistic working that arise from excessive focus on any one of the four basic biases. Figure 5.1 presents a classification of some of the most salient and important risks and weaknesses that have been diagnosed in Chapter 4, and set out in Figure 4.1, and which will be further explored in Chapters 6, 7, 8, 9 and 10, according to the bias in organisation (cf. Hood, 1998).

In general, we can say from the argument of this book, that in response to holistic initiatives exhibiting the characteristic weaknesses of any one of these styles of organisation, practising public managers at local level or in more junior positions in central departments may move towards responses in any of the others, depending on their particular circumstances, or they may produce responses within the same bias or trope. The decision to respond with fatalistic resignation or entrepreneurial behaviour, with the formation of cosy and supportive cliques or with mechanical following of narrow and safe interpretations of rules, reflects as much the particular situation in which the public manager finds herself, as it does her personal psychological characteristics. In highly rigid and rule-bound settings, we would expect junior public managers to exhibit less frequent signs of

Figure 5.1 *Sources of risk, failures and weaknesses in holistic governance by bias*

Failures in holistic working
arise from imposed circumstances
–rule, role, given fact
– strong constraint
⇧

Fatalism Not taking initiatives, due to absence of opportunity or belief (correct or otherwise in given setting) that opportunities are not real, or that nothing can be achieved, or just 'minding the shop' takes priority Initiativitis producing coping and survivalist styles rather than strategic holism Re-describing existing silo-based initiatives as holistic in order to secure funds	**Hierarchy, central community, regulation** Legal, budget, professional structures as obstacles to integration Excessive central control and direction Excessive focus on budget and accountability structures Insufficient focus on knowledge Insufficient devolution of learning Insufficient tolerance for 'managing out of control'
Individualism, markets Insufficient cohesion about objectives to coordinate the work of entrepreneurial public managers Insufficient effort on measurement and research base Insufficient focus on sharing learning between innovators	**Sect, egalitarianism, communitarianism** Excessive focus on knowledge and informal networks, and on securing consensus Insufficient focus on budget and accountability structures More attention to process than outcomes

Failures in holistic working ⇦ *result from weak bonds*

Failures in holistic working ⇨ *result from strong structure of bonds*

⇩
Failures in holistic working
arise from the consequences of structure and action that
are or can be largely under the control or at least influence
of *voluntary* behaviour of individuals or groups –
weak constraint

sectarian or individualist responses, except when – as De Tocqueville famously suggested in explaining the timing of the French Revolution – the system is beginning to break down, the situation is moving to weakly constrained settings but when expectations of change are outstripping the actual rate of change (de Tocqueville, 1988 [1856]; Elster, 1993). Conversely, when the 'tyranny of structurelessness' becomes unbearable within sects. Likewise frustration with lack of coordination makes even individualistic behaviour very difficult to sustain. This is because the costs of finding information about opportunities start to rise as the public good of cheap information provided by coordination and shared learning is under-provided. This explain why we can expect that subaltern officials may respond with biases in behaviour other than the prevailing one. Whatever their personal psychological characteristics, these structural and institutional positions in the trajectory of organisational change are likely to be the most important determinant of their decisions about how and indeed whether they pursue forms of holistic working.

Failures in practice: key lessons for national government – the British case

In the second half of this chapter we consider which of these weaknesses and risks are being run by the present British government programmes for more holistic working. This discussion is based on our interviews in the local case studies and on a wide range of other conversations held with public managers, as well as on consultancy work with local authorities, central departments and other agencies.

Our central finding is that in the British case, the principal imbalance has been an excessively hierarchical bias to the design of the programme for holistic governance. Despite the public support for individualistic public managers as entrepreneurs (e.g., the endorsements by Prime Minister Tony Blair and senior minister Peter Mandelson for the arguments of Leadbeater on the dustjacket of his 1999 book, in which he amplifies the argument for supporting public sector entrepreneurs made in Leadbeater and Goss, 1998), in practice, the great weight of effort has been on the use of central accountability. In response, there is a real danger in the British case of more fatalistic strategies among junior public managers emerging.

The energy and pace with which New Labour has developed initiatives in holistic government are impressive. Almost every department has produced important new programmes. A great deal of senior civil service time and effort, prime ministerial backing and a fair amount of junior ministerial time have been committed. The theme runs through the work of the Social Exclusion Unit, the Modernising Government and Modernising Local Government white papers, the public-health agenda, the reorganisation of the Cabinet Office and several strands of the Comprehensive Spending Review (see, for example, Utting, 1998; Department of Health, 1998; HM Treasury, 1998; London Housing Unit, 1998; Social Exclusion Unit, 1998; Department of the Environment, Transport and the Regions, 1998; Cabinet Office, 1998). However, our study has shown clear tensions between the aspiration for successful integration and some of the ways in which New Labour is pursuing its goals.

Key problems

The key problems are the following:

Impatience.   Holistic initiatives do not take root overnight. Too often the politicians' demands for 'quick wins' can stifle integration, because it takes time to build trust between agencies, identify the correct focus and outcome measures, and develop the right strategy.

Initiativitis.   This is the syndrome in which public managers end up swamped by the volume of special projects, discretionary funds and demands to produce plans. Some local authorities report having filed fully seventy-five plans, each for some holistic programme, with central government in a single year. In the attempt to develop a hierarchy out of many cross-cutting issues, social exclusion can often end up at the top of the local agenda, while sustainability, regeneration, community safety and disaffected youth all find themselves 'jockeying for positions' (Holman, 1999, p. 75). This may end up making a nonsense out of integration.

Fragmented holism.   This is the problem of integration without coordination, which can lead to messy and time-wasting duplications of effort, and can end up reproducing the problems of fragmentation at a higher level. Fragmented holism has been the besetting vice of the New Labour style of integration, with each department generating its own proliferation of special initiatives to join up particular activities, but between which there remains very little coordination.

Thus, for example, in cities which have several special action zones, coordinating bodies have had to be set up to sort out relationships between them. One interviewee said to us: 'Pieces of the jigsaw of Health Action

Zones, Drug Action Teams, and Crime and Disorder Bill arrangements overlap all over the place.' Managers begin to feel that they are discussing the same issues in different forums: 'a waste of their increasingly hard-pressed time'. Some of our local case study interviewees reported feeling completely overwhelmed because officers did not have the time to pursue the range of new initiatives. In Redbrickham there were sometimes difficulties in getting voluntary-sector bodies involved because they did not have the time and resources to cover the range of partnership initiatives to which they were invited.

Eventually the failure to coordinate can undermine integration. One central government civil servant conceded to us that even if you pool funds and decide how much money is spent by each department on an integration initiative, 'the silos come back'.

Badly designed bidding competitions   This can quickly lead to shallow and fragile integration, to the distraction and loss of focus of the brightest managers and the erosion of important continuities in policy (Harries *et al.*, 1998). Our respondents often talked of the 'bidding game', the 'fantasy' involved in bidding for special central funds, and of the ways in which spurious partnerships come together to make a bid, later dissolving when the money is not granted – or even when it is, so shallow are their roots. As one senior officer in Beltham observed: 'You get seven days to come up with some fantasy numbers, and then you have to spend seven years pretending to live up to them.'

Partnerships motivated solely by securing money do not often achieve genuine integration. In Beltham a bid for discretionary regeneration money was successful, but only half the requested sum was awarded. Predictably there were difficulties. As one interviewee there explained: 'a lot of people still have expectations way above the money.' The promise or implication of money in this case had been a means of persuading agencies to sign up to the bid. But this led to overly high expectations which then had to be talked down; this did little to increase trust and damaged working relationships at the point when they needed to be strongest.

Over-hasty measurement of the wrong things.   While it is vital that holistic working be focused on improving outcomes, there is some skill required in working out how and when to measure these. As one Midcaster interviewee put it, 'If we were starting out now the requirements would probably be a lot clearer.' In Beltham, we were told, performance measures of output and outcome had been 'constructed for the funding application, but it was a bit of constructive grantsmanship'. Hastily set measuring systems can either quickly become irrelevant in practice as the project acquires its natural focus (causing problems later with accountability), or can from the outset skew and distort the initiative. Central government does not need to design its systems of accountability for discretionary budgets in this way, so it shouldn't.

Intolerance of failure. We found many examples of managers in pilot projects being firmly told that the project had too high a political profile to be allowed to fail. The effect of this message is that managers become unwilling to innovate or undertake risky initiatives. A system that cannot allow for failure cannot learn.

Hogging the lessons at the centre. The main sources of intelligence about what works in holistic government and what does not are highly centralised. The National Audit Office and the Audit Commission collect some of the information. The most politically influential agents of learning about holistic experiments are central government units, such as the Social Exclusion Unit, the Performance and Innovation Unit and the Centre for Management and Policy Studies in the Cabinet Office, plus departmental task forces set up by ministers dealing with specific pilots. All are accountable centrally. Also collecting intelligence, but of more peripheral use, are national umbrella bodies such as the NHS Confederation, the Local Government Association, national support agencies such as the Centre for Management and Policy Studies in the Cabinet Office and the Improvement and Development Agency for Local Government, and private agencies working nationally such as the Office for Public Management.

The distribution of best practice and learning is also highly centralised, through national policy publications, guidance documents, and so on. This may seem natural and efficient, but it has real costs. Because these same politically charged, powerful bodies tie learning closely to accountability and the threat of centrally imposed sanctions, they undermine the possibility of a more open kind of learning. Public managers in fear of central sanctions will, understandably, be more concerned to cover up failures than to discuss the lessons learned frankly with colleagues. Moreover, many findings from holistic experiments will have highly specific local value: what makes sense in rural areas may not work in conurbations; what makes sense in comparatively prosperous areas with tightly concentrated pockets of poverty will be different from the needs of extensive urban areas with dense mixes of classes. Although there was some hope that the creation of Government Offices for the Regions and the Regional Development Agencies would aid this level of learning, the development priorities of GORs and RDAs have prevented them from playing this role.

Finally, the centre is not putting enough effort into adopting the lessons learned from the most innovative local initiatives and applying these to the great departments of state and non-departmental public bodies. The Centre for Management and Policy Studies ought to be a key locus for bringing coherence to Whitehall's learning from the best of the town halls, as well as from national initiatives.

Conflicting policy priorities. Very often policy priorities for individual services, such as cutting waiting lists or reducing class sizes, come into conflict with integration. Many interviewees told us how the pressures to achieve government manifesto commitments reduced the time available for integrative activities and undermined the motivation to integrate, because it meant putting effort into things that may not benefit the real outcomes of health, learning, employability or community safety.

Each of the pitfalls identified above is understandable, and none is unique to New Labour. They reflect three kinds of impatience which have deep roots in our system of government. The first is the peculiar pressure that national government politicians feel themselves to be under. They believe they must be seen to deliver certain things in order to secure their licence to govern from a sceptical public. What those things are might not be the priority goals one would deduce from a rational analysis of public policy, yet to fail to deliver them threatens unacceptably high political and electoral costs. In our interviews with national policymakers, it became clear that some ministers – of all parties – believe they can tell a different story from each side of their mouths. With one side they can address the popular press, and indicate their toughness in line with perceived 'popular demands'. With the other side they speak more softly to public managers and the clients of public services, assuring them that these 'popular demands' need not disturb the commitment to well-managed reform of services. Unfortunately each audience is present when the message is addressed to the other.

A second source of political impatience is the short-term pressure of elections or reshuffles, before which ministers' imprints must be securely stamped upon their bit of the body administrative. Many senior politicians are haunted by the sense that the political – indeed, the historic – window of opportunity never remains open for long.

The third source of impatience derives from a disdain of local politicians and managers. The view from the centre is that these people lack the passion to transform, are less competent, less accountable, more prone to take the line of least resistance and to relax into the comfortable sofas of administrative routine. Hence only the most relentless regime of inspection, incentive, sanction and discipline will produce effective action. This type of impatience results from a lack of trust. Any call for a longer timescale in which to take on reform is interpreted as the excuse of the idle, the unwilling, or the vested interest. A minister with a zeal for reform will brush aside such calls, reminding her colleagues expansively that she will brook no undermining of her goal.

However understandable, all the pitfalls we have identified here are serious because they all act as forces for short-termism, and have the capacity to undermine New Labour's commitment to governing for the long term.

Pitfalls are not the same as excuses

It is important to be clear about what we are *not* arguing here. We are absolutely not suggesting that:

- taking any amount of time is acceptable;
- ministers should not set timetables;
- central initiatives are not valuable or that all initiatives should begin locally;
- one cannot work on more than a few fronts at once;
- 'early wins' are never valuable;
- a single overarching holistic goal should be set, under which all others can be ordered hierarchically;
- competitive-funding programmes are a bad thing or should be abandoned;
- any partnership that springs up in response to a funding competition will be shallowly rooted;
- low standards, low achievement, long-term failure are acceptable;
- failure is the only way to learn; or that
- the policy priorities of any government can ever be made wholly consistent and mutually reinforcing.

The danger is that, when criticisms are voiced, they are mistaken by ministers and their advisers for complacency, challenges to the right of ministers to govern, or excessive rationalism. This produces a polarised debate in which no one listens and no one learns. While central government has the right and the duty to set the direction and the goals, it is at the front-line of executive agencies operating locally that the knowledge, the capability and the practical networks necessary for successful reform will be found. The centre needs to learn from the local level about implementation, just as the local level needs to learn from the centre about commitment to the goals of reform.

Consideration of these failures in risk management leads inexorably to the view that the source of the failures in the British experience has been too hierarchical a style of managing risk. The centralism, initiativitis, tendency to hog lessons learning at the centre, impatience with local variation and local learning are all the hallmarks of the peculiar blinkers of hierarchical systems. Hierarchy is indeed committed, explicitly, to anticipation and foresight. However, like any institutional style, it is unable to inculcate the capacity to anticipate failures that arise from *its own* organisational weaknesses. For the very features of an institution that enable it to motivate people and to create and sustain interests are the same ones that produce blinkers (see Chapter 10 for more discussion of this). The sources of their strengths are also the sources of their weaknesses. It is for this reason that good risk management needs to institutionalise some, but necessarily qualified, recognition of the concerns of all the institutional styles.

'Top-down or bottom-up'?

The commonest way in which political scientists discuss the origins of initiatives of this kind is to ask 'what are the consequences of ministerial decision made at the centre, which are then implemented by the deployment of the tools of government?' These tools include mandation, prohibition and regulation; incentive and disincentive; persuasion and mobilisation. In short are the initiatives top-down in nature?

The main alternative to be considered is whether they are bottom–up in nature. Projects may be the outcome of the collectively self-organising behaviour of networks of practitioners among public managers, agency heads, locally elected or appointed politicians. These actors develop initiatives either of their own or else so adapt central initiatives in the course of implementation that the goals shift to those voluntarily chosen by subordinate public officials or which are emergent on their actions. There is a large literature in implementation studies which normatively prefers the latter route, either on grounds such as a dislike for central interventions or for reasons of doubt about the feasibility centrally-driven initiatives because of the unavoidability of mutual adjustment (Lindblom, 1959) and bargaining within networks without overarching goals (Porter and Hjern, 1981; Rhodes, 1997).

In fact, initiatives in holistic working, much like every previous programme in public management reform, reflect both kinds of pressures. The centre is indeed often unable to direct all organisational change across the public sector, as successive Prime Ministers have lamented (cf. Mr Blair's famous statement in a press conference in 1998 about 'bearing the scars on [his] back' from efforts to direct major change in public management). However, there are ways in which the centre can elicit semi-voluntary, semi-induced innovation from public managers, which are broadly within the parameters of its preferred model of public management change. This was indeed the general story of the introduction of many of the reforms of the 1980s such as the development of agency status: offers of 'opt-out' or 'fund-holding' status were made, subject to general approval from the centre, or purchasing systems were put in place that empowered some groups of public managers, within constraints, to pursue strategies that fitted with the overall direction of centrally set policy. In the UK, this has been true of both Conservative and Labour initiatives in holistic working. For example, the Heseltine initiative for the Single Regeneration Budget was a good example of using the tool of financial incentive or 'treasure' (Hood, 1983) to elicit innovation in integration from the middle tier of public management. In the same way, many of the New Labour discretionary competitive bidding schemes such as New Deal for Communities and Surestart, or the style with which the Best Value programme has been designed, and even those with little or no central money attached such as Better Government for Older People, have all used the same principle.

Therefore, it makes more sense to move beyond the idea of a simple dichotomy between 'imposition' and 'organic growth' of innovation in styles of public management, and to consider ways in which centrally created initiatives constitute changes in the environment for organisations to which they may respond either as threats or opportunities or both combined ('throffers', combined threats and offers: Dowding, 1991, p. 68 ff).

Organisational innovation in general: a game of two halves with compulsory extra time

We need to situate the triggers for holistic working in the wider context of the body of theoretical innovation in interorganisational systems.

In general, organisational innovation is found to be, to draw an analogy with football, a game of two halves with compulsory extra time. That is, it results from a particular combination of *crises* – the depressing half – and *opportunities* – the cheerful half – to be followed by a process of *learning*, evaluating change, disseminating and diffusing ideas and lessons, benchmarking, getting support, and so on.

The depressing half is that necessity is still the mother of invention. Crises, cuts, dramatic changeover of top personnel, new duties in legislation that put strains on resources and skills, conflict with popular critical movements, and generally being in a mess, recognising it and feeling you need to do something about it, are typically the main sources of innovation in both the public sector and in business (for public sector cases, see Clark, 1994, chapter 1; Borins, 1998, chapter 3; for private sector examples, see Grønhaug and Kaufmann, 1988). Indeed, much of the innovation in British local government in the 1980s and early 1990s emerged in response to crises brought about by the actions of central government – cuts in grant support and powers to raise rates, the challenge to legitimacy, the Widdecombe limits upon officers' political roles, and so on (Stoker, 1999). In the same way, in the USA much of the innovation in local government in the 1980s and 1990s was a response to austerity (Clark, 1994). Being forced to do things in the public eye, and justify them in public is a powerful discipline on any level of government (Drèze and Sen, 1989; Luban, 1996; Rawls, 1993, Lecture VI; Kant, 1983). Ironically, greater publicity and freedom of information is required of local government than of central government. However, the role of central government (the 'top') in eliciting innovation in public management is often to generate crises or at any rate find ways to pass on crises it faces to other tiers ('the bottom'), which then innovate in their style of management, interorganisational relationships, and so on in, ways that either do or do not fit with the overall direction of central policy, depending on the balance of incentives, the quality of the design of central incentive-shaping, institutional constraints, interests, world-views and so on. In more theoretical terms, crises can arise from one or more of the following 'push factors':

- *Changes in the environment of immediate material inputs or the resource base*: In this case, an organisation experiences reduced levels of income or capital, staff, information of or other key inputs. It is crises of this kind that are given particular emphasis in the resource dependency theory tradition (Thompson, 1967). In our case studies, cuts in budget allocations from central government proved to be a common crisis trigger for holistic working, as Clark (1994) found they were for the last generation of public management reforms. In Riverborough, for example, budget problems in 1994 led to a longer-term financial review which revealed a projected deficit of £25 million in the coming three years if radical steps were not taken. This led to investment in information and communications technologies for the network of one-stop shops beginning with Alberton.
- *Changes in the wider environment*: Crises of this type arise because of the arrival of new entrants into a field in competition with existing organisations or incumbents, which are then faced with increased competition. This

creates new selection pressures, to which they must adapt. In the population ecology models (Hannan and Freeman, 1989; Baum and Singh, 1993),
this process is given particular emphasis, and feedback is posited between
adaptation and selection. With the growth of competition within the public
sector for contracts for provision, in regulatory competition, and in other
ways, this type of crisis has become more important in political science
than it once was. However, institutionalist theories also predict that
changes in forms of regulation or bodies of formal or informal rules, or
other institutional constraints creating legitimacy and 'license to operate',
can create crises for organisations (Scott and Meyer, 1994), to which
organisations may have to respond with innovation, the course of which in
turn may be guided by the nature of the new institutional arrangements, if
they are successfully institutionalised. In our case studies, changes in territorial boundaries of legal jurisdiction were one kind of institutional change
that caused a crisis which served as a trigger for innovation towards holistic working. The perception of publics or central politicians that an organisation is under-performing, whether or not this triggers specific threats to
its resource base, can be an wider environmental change that causes a crisis internally, which in turn leads to innovation (cf. Bovens *et al.*, 1999).
In one of our case studies, a very public scandal over the state of a nationally known beach was a trigger for a crisis that led to innovation towards
holistic working in the environmental field.

• *Internal structural change*: While organisational sociology, in contrast with business and management studies, has rightly tended to down-
play the importance of leadership as automatically effective authority, it is
recognised that key personnel can represent important resources, and
important catalysts in cognitive and cultural change, albeit within wider
systems (Martin, 1992). Changes of control within the organisation such as
the arrival of a new chief executive or other chief officer, a new leader, the
coming to power locally of a new party or coalition, can all be important
catalysts for innovation in the direction of more holistic working. In
Midcaster much of the drive for change was attributed to a change in
council leader. In Redbrickham a dynamic and charismatic deputy chief
executive was the trigger for the council to develop a programme of partnership building and integration.

• *Cognitive problems and failures*: In these types of case, the crisis
arises as a result of failure in capability of the formal or informal knowledge or beliefs in the organisation's culture or worldview to cope with
environmental or internal change. Understandings of the institutional contexts, the resource-based or the nature of competition can all prove inadequate, causing problems that call for adaptation and innovation, which

may take the form of collaboration and integration (Brown and Duguid, 1994, pp. 179–83). Also under this rubric belong mismatches of expectations and outturn, decision overreach, miscalculations, adherence to scripts that are no longer appropriate (Wilson *et al.*, 1999).

• *Failure to reach critical thresholds*: In these cases, the crisis arises from failure to achieve one of the quantum leaps that mark stability in a particular environment. Most organisations fail when they are new – the so-called 'liability of newness' hypothesis, which is now well confirmed in the population ecology studies (Hannan and Freeman, 1989; Baum and Singh, 1983) and in other kinds of research (Hager *et al.*, 1999). Similarly, failure to reach critical mass or a threshold in size can cause a crisis. In either case, collaboration and integration can become a rational strategy, if other incentives, institutional pressures and so on, are also in place.

The more cheerful half of the game of achieving organisational innovation is that good management is both possible and a necessary condition of stimulating change. More specifically the following are key 'pull factors' in being able to recognise, construct, frame, understand and seize opportunities:

• *Leadership*: Good leadership matters in mobilising commitment to organisational innovations (Eccles and Nohria, 1992, p. 196 ff; Moore, 1995). However, as Weber was at pains to argue throughout his major works, the key challenge in organisational innovation is that of institutionalising the organisational commitments – such as holistic working – that charismatic leaders can, at least initially, stimulate (Weber, 1968). Weber stressed, and social science has found nothing to contradict him although it has often rejected his explanations (cf. Douglas, 1986, chapter 8), the importance for the institutionalisation of an organisational change after the decline of charismatic leadership, of such things as the introduction of systems of information generation, flow, storage and analysis; of legitimate systems of sanctions and rewards; of systems of social status and of career progression; of wider systems of law for environmental stabilisation and governance.

• *Institutionalising creativity*: Attempts to institutionalise creativity can help in securing innovation – for example, within cells dedicated to innovation (Fairtlough, 1994). In our case studies, the allocation of time and high calibre staff to identifying organisational innovations proved to be critical in developing partnerships and other forms of holistic working.

• *Whole systems thinking*: The importance of analysing whole systems in the causation of wicked problems is useful not only in general management (Senge, 1990), but specifically for innovation toward holistic working

(Wilkinson and Applebee, 1999; Osborne and Plastrik, 2000). This is because it enables leaders to identify the range of organisations, causal forces and institutions that need to be connected in an effective joint intervention. Techniques such as strategy mapping are of particular value here (Osborne and Plastrik, 2000, chapter 1). This argument about both coordination and integration across whole systems has recently been developed most fully in the field of environmental policy, and specifically with reference to holistic working arrangements in the field of waste management (Murray, 1998, 1999); rather few whole system analyses of the same depth have been conducted for many fields of social policy.

Indeed, in political science and political thought there are plenty of sceptics about both the possibility and the desirability of whole systems thinking. Popper (1949) famously argued that attempts, failed or successful, at whole systems thinking could only be tyrannical, and that only piecemeal social engineering could respect liberty and democracy. Nevertheless, his examples hardly sufficed to support the generality of his claim. Indeed, there are many more examples of dictators and tyrants engaging in the modest and piecemeal social engineering than there are of them attempting systems analysis and whole systems change: Franco was a more typical dictator, even when Popper was writing, than Hitler or Stalin. Most commentators on the aspirations of van Bertalanffy's aspirations for general systems theory acknowledge that the programme could not be implemented. However, systems thinking in general does not depend on the validity of such general models. In political science, textbook criticisms of the possibility of policy analysts achieving 'synoptic' rationality for decision-making (Hogwood and Gunn, 1984; Ham and Hill, 1993) are often regarded as damning of all attempts at systems thinking, even on particular problems. But this is muddled. Systems thinking does not necessarily lead to wholesale attempts to change everything, nor does it require synoptic understanding or complete information. Rather, it calls for diligence in tracking the full range of causal flows relevant to the production of particular social problems, and requires iterative learning and development of those models through experience. There is nothing here that is incompatible with the general finding of the impossibility of synoptic rationality. The use of the word 'holism' in holistic governance might seem to fly in the face of the strictures of analysts who revive Popper's arguments, such as Lindblom (1990), concerning the importance of humility about the limits of our understanding. But it does not. Holism in the sense used here privileges no élite of technocratic analysts, privileges no particular model, but is a tool for directing that scarce resource, attention to problems, towards a particular style of thought that recognises the breadth of causation – even, if necessary, at the expense of depth in the analysis of particular strands that have been the focus of professions and functions. Moreover, it calls initially for the juxtaposition and only if possible the integration of wide ranges of indicators. The decision-making that flows from this will no doubt be as modest as the theories of incrementalism, partisan mutual adjustment or mixed scanning permit. Rather, the argument behind the case for holistic governance is that there can be – to put the point no more strongly than possibility – differences of quality between decisions made on the basis of professionally and functionally defined incremental change and adjustment, and those based upon partnership and coordination (if not always integration), albeit that partnership and coordination may often be experimental and limited in the quality of its capability for systems thinking and for explicit modelling.

Within the traditions of twentieth-century political science, perhaps the most respected advocate of the position that systems thinking is normatively essential in governance, that it should focus on human systems rather than the deterministic systems that obsessed the general systems thinkers, and that it is possible and need not conflict with the unavoidable limitations on the rationality of human decision makers, was the late Sir Geoffrey Vickers (1973, 1995; Blunden and Dando, 1994). Such cognitive approaches as soft systems methodology (Checkland, 1989; Checkland and Scholes 1990) were developed directly under his inspiration (Checkland, 1994).

● *Culture matters*: Innovation is always a risk, and experimenting with holistic working was, our case studies showed us, typically seen as a major risk for many public managers. In terms of the conceptual framework set out in chapter 2, exposure is often seen as high. One widely accepted characterisation of culture is that it consists of shared cognitive resources, which are the product of institutions, through which the world is perceived as risk and opportunity (Douglas, 1966, 1970, 1986, 1992). Organisational innovation of some kind is selected by almost every kind of organisational culture. To be risk averse towards one kind of risk is, *ipso facto*, to be neutral or positive towards taking other risks – or rather to accepting decisions that one probably does not even regard as risks – that are more consonant with the prevailing organisational culture. For example, the more hierarchical the institutional foundations of the culture, the more open are members to risks that might reinforce the authority of hierarchy; the more egalitarian, the more open are members to risks that seem to reinforce community, and so on (Douglas, 1986, p. 92). The simple idea that culture is merely a constraint, a blockage, a force to be invoked in explanation when risk-taking or willingness to accept risks is observed, is quite misguided.

Our case studies were not sufficiently detailed or numerous to enable us to distinguish the features of organisational cultures that selected acceptance of the risks involved in high rather than low exposure in integration or coordination, by comparison with the features of those that resist coordination altogether. However, on wider theoretical grounds there are good reasons for thinking that commitment to closure around organisational boundaries, to attempting to keep rigid the systems of classification that distinguish one organisation from another, and so would be least willing to contemplate coordination and integration, is characteristic of the cultural (institutional) form known in the neo-Durkheimian tradition as 'enclave' or 'sect'.

This tradition, which draws on the work of Douglas (1966, 1970, 1986, 1992; Fardon, 1999) has recently had more influence in public management studies since the publication of Hood's (1998) recent work using the theory (see also 6, 1999a).

The enclave or sectarian form is characterised by high levels of mutual supervision both giving rise to and sustained by egalitarian internal structure, commitment to charismatic leadership, a tendency to fission and schism, a commitment to sustaining zeal and ideological rectitude, a commitment to keeping categories rigidly apart (Douglas, 1972, 1993). The enclave or sect form is one of what Durkheim 1984 [1893] called 'mechanical solidarities', or institutional imperatives that seek, unless tempered, to impose their model of social organisation universally, in search of what Durkheim called 'similarity' and Douglas (1966) called 'purity'.

By contrast, cultures that exhibit willingness to accept blurring of categories are more likely to exhibit the characteristics that Durkheim (1984 [1893]) described as belonging to 'organic solidarity' or to settlements, compromises, coalitions between at least moderate forms of each of the mechanical solidarities that make up any network of organisations (or for that matter, a whole society) (6, 1998c, 1999a). For this is only possible in a culture that will accept fudging of categories and what Thompson (1997a,b,c) calls 'clumsy institutions' will manage implicit or explicit dialogue between solidarities. Therefore, we would expect to see organisational cultures that are committed to some form of organic solidarity – and the forms differ widely between contexts – to be more likely to demonstrate openness to holistic working than those disproportionately skewed towards one of the mechanical solidarities.

Some critics might argue that there may be a tension here between factors for holistic working, if it is thought that the cultural form that would be most open to whole systems thinking tends to be the mechanical solidarity of the hierarchical form, as alleged by many of those who see in holistic governance a tendency towards centralisation and hubristic technocratic decision-making. However, as we argued above and throughout this study, there is nothing necessary about the linkage between centralism or technocracy and either whole systems thinking or holistic working, although it is certainly true that the holistic governance agenda does give due weight to the legitimacy of the centre and to the supporting and ancillary role of technical policy analysis in democratic governance.

• *Legitimacy*: Skills in securing legitimacy for experiments are crucial in public sector innovation and learning (Moore, 1995). Our own case studies showed that key staff who act as boundary spanners (Scott, 1992; Williams and Williams, n.d.) between organisations often put most of their effort into securing legitimacy from central government, from local elected politicians or power brokers within the officer cadre, for their programmes of holistic working. In Southbrookborough, one public manager graphically described this to us as 'steering through the maze of unspoken accountabilities'. This was often regarded as the most stressful, and most difficult, challenge. If the theoretical argument offered in respect of culture is broadly correct, then we would expect the characteristics of organisational cultures most open to holistic working also to be the ones in which legitimacy would most readily be secured by boundary spanners for their work.

• *Techniques, systems of measurement*: If opportunities for holistic working are to be available, then there have to be techniques within the grasp of practitioners by which they can pursue these goals. In Figure 2.5 in Chapter 2, we presented a taxonomy of mechanisms. However, the key issue in explaining when these techniques and systems of mechanisms function as opportunities in helping to trigger initiatives in holistic working, is to understand when they seem to make themselves obvious or salient, in what circumstances they feel available, usable, affordable to practitioners. The cultural variables and issues of legitimacy and the support given to the use of particular techniques by central authorities all play key roles here. However, the dissemination of information about innovation in techniques is a basic resource. Cultural variations in institutional capacity to construct risk and opportunity in techniques will explain much about the organisations that will express more interest in a technique if it is framed as wholly new, and those that will be more likely to adopt if it is framed as tried and tested.

The compulsory extra time in the game of stimulating organisational change, including change for more holistic working, is concerned with *institutionalisation through diffused learning*. On theoretical grounds, there are good reasons to expect that institutionalisation depends on networks for learning. For example, the literature on policy networks (Marsh and Rhodes, 1992; Marsh, 1998) taken together with the well-known work on the advocacy coalition model of policy network interaction in the policy process (Sabatier and Jenkins-Smith, 1993; Sabatier, 1999) and the Dutch work on network steering (Kickert *et al.*, 1997) show not only rich models with which to explain mobilisation, influence, flows of information, but also illuminate the centrality of institutionalisation of network structures in learning. Again, even the slightly more idealist literature on argument, advocacy and rhetoric in the policy process stresses the importance of friendship networks of politicians, practitioners and professionals in making persuasion possible and in institutionalising it (Forester, 1993). 'Learning' here does not necessarily mean the acquisition and full acceptance of indisputable truths followed by behavioural change towards an universally agreed consensually correct decision. Rather, 'learning' means the acceptance of propositions, correct or otherwise, which may not have immediate consequences for behavioural change, and that behavioural change like those propositions may be highly controversial. For organisations, given their existing commitments, institutional constraints and cultural formations, learn only those things that they can learn, receive the messages that threaten least their existing ways of working (Douglas, 1982; Sabatier and Jenkins-Smith, 1993; March and Olsen, 1975, 1976). While some cultures are, as we have seen, more resistant than others to learning that sustains holistic working, there are also possibilities for cultural change, if institutional systems that support particular patterns of cognition can be changed. As John (1998, chapter 4) argues, network structures and change are not typically fundamental causal drivers of policy change such as changes in basic paradigms of public management, but they can play an important role in diffusion and institutionalisation.

In the course of our case studies we encountered a number of British initiatives that showed promise in creating networks through which ideas, techniques, and indeed commitment might be diffused. While few if any of these networks might themselves become institutionalised as long-term durable features of the interorganisational landscape, however the general commitment to the practice of networking through supportive communities for learning could become institutionalisation through a range of

- informal networks of individuals, such as those supported by the University of Warwick and other research centres;
- formally organised networks of individual public managers such as the New Local Government Network;
- professional institutes, such as those for social work, the medical professions, environmental health, land use planning, policing, and so on;

- inter-professional bodies, such as the various networks involved in the promotion of integrated public sector information systems such as FIT-LOG for local government;
- partisan networks, principally of elected local politicians and appointed politicians in agencies;
- networks supported by public sector management consultancy firms and agencies, including the Office for Public Management, specialist firms such as Newchurch operating in the health care management field, or Kable in the field of public sector information systems;
- local and health authority and representation bodies, such as the Local Government Association and the NHS Confederation and the various regional bodies;
- training and management development bodies, such as IDeA and the Civil Service College; and
- networks supported by central government agencies dedicated to the promotion of the holistic governance agenda such as the Centre for Management and Policy Studies in the Cabinet Office, with its direct involvement with both the Civil Service College and IDeA.

Specific lessons

Derived from this analysis of risks and problems, we can offer some general thoughts on the best way to change public organisations in a holistic direction. They are outlined below and we hope they will provide some guidance to practitioners and policy makers.

Lead public opinion, but don't run too far ahead of it

The public has been taught by professionals and politicians over several decades to believe in government organised by functions rather than holistically. Most people, asked what they want done about crime, demand 'more resources' (longer sentences, more police officers on the beat, secure accommodation for young offenders), and similarly for ill health and medicine, learning and schooling and many other areas of public policy.

Government must bring public opinion with it in pursuing more joined-up solutions. This represents a difficult balance. On the one hand a democratic government must be accountable to the values, attitudes, commitments and cultures of the sovereign people. On the other hand, it must influence those same cultures. Persuasion is not necessarily illegitimate, but in a democratic system innovations that challenge popular attitudes require special effort in legitimation. Only politicians can shoulder the responsibility for explaining the agenda and showing how it can more effectively meet the public's underlying concerns with outcomes.

The holistic government agenda is therefore much, much more than simply rearranging the furniture within the executive. It will have to become a core programme of democratic re-engagement. Dialogue between agencies is not enough; there must be dialogue with the public about some of integration's big dilemmas:

- the priority problems for integration to address;
- the ethics of holistic handling of personal information;
- the legitimacy of increasing the power of boundary-crossing managers; and
- the ease of comprehension of new systems of accountability.

Politicians locally and nationally need to take responsibility for this commitment to a new dialogue. In the UK context it could become a key role for backbenchers in the Westminster, Edinburgh and Cardiff parliaments and assemblies to promote exactly this dialogue, and to involve taxpayers and service-users alike in constructing local priorities for integration.

Be patient: allow managers to learn how best to integrate

Senior politicians – engaged with the public – should set goals for holistic initiatives, ideally by specifying outcomes and achievable timetables. Those targets should reflect what we already know about the efficacy of public interventions to tackle community safety and crime, health, learning and employability. But they should also permit public managers enough freedom to develop the appropriate partnerships locally and should allow local initiatives to develop their own goals, interpretations of outcomes and legitimacy.

There is a positive role for impatience. Shocks can sometimes be useful. Major budget cuts, territorial boundary changes, legitimacy crises such as the exposure of scandalous environmental conditions on many beaches, have all served as triggers for reform. But no system can develop and sustain reform if continually shocked. After a shock, a period of patience is needed for the forces of reform to learn to work together, to develop their own culture, trust, local goals and organisational structures.

Value the early stages, build bridgeheads for later integration

Impatience can lead policy-makers to devalue the early stages of integration. For example, dialogue and taking into account other agencies' work may seem humdrum, a 'mere talking shop'. But no effective partnership, strategic alliance, joint working or satellite agency can be built without dialogue. The fashionable form of impatience is to say: 'there's no point in talking until we have some concrete, practical proposal for joint working to talk about.' This, we found in our fieldwork, is usually not true. Dialogue can provide a bridgehead, gaining legitimacy for more ambitious programmes. Where there is powerful opposition, mutual suspicion, or other serious obstacle, dialogue can be used as a 'Trojan horse' for subsequent deeper integration.

Bring holism into the mainstream; don't consign it to special initiatives

Special initiatives can be valuable in helping people to find new ways to work together, and in supporting experimentation. But when a plethora of special initiatives and competitions for small chunks of discretionary funding dominate the landscape, problems are readily created for the overall integration programme. At a local level the big budgets are those drawn from councils' general grant and council tax revenues, or health authorities' main resource allocation. It is here that departmental boundaries need to be broken down and integration developed. When managers who are highly committed to integration and reform become preoccupied with small initiatives and discretionary slivers of money, it is easy for them to lose sight of the main issues.

Central government in the UK has been particularly prone to launching initiative after initiative. We identify the problem of initiativitis as a particular difficulty of the New Labour first term. There is always a need for special programmes but what is needed is more effort at ensuring that holistic working is institutionalised across the public sector. This has only recently begun to be understood better at the centre at the UK (Performance and Innovation Unit, 2001).

Design bidding systems with greater care

The purpose behind competitive funding systems was to create incentives for public managers to work together. Yet our fieldwork revealed that creating incentives is slipperier than that: public managers were able to secure cash on the shallowest promise of integration. Competitive funding systems also risk rewarding those who would have integrated anyway, but at extra cost and with no necessary additional benefit. The key here, as with overcoming 'initiativitis', is that competitive funds for small discretionary projects should not be the main instrument for integration, because they can distract managers from innovating within mainstream budgets.

These bidding processes can be better designed. For example, we distinguish between programmes where the aim is to achieve deeper integration among prior enthusiasts, in order to create and spread learning, and those programmes where the goal is to encourage the sceptical or the fearful to adopt tried-and-tested integration methods. Budgets, selection criteria and evaluation systems can be designed to reflect these priorities.

Fail well: if you're not failing, you're not learning

This argument is prone to misunderstanding, unless one makes the crucial distinction between chronic and acute failure. Chronic failure in the public services typically occurs where managers do not learn from initial failure. Something has gone wrong with the learning process: signals are not being received; incentives are lacking; or a culture has developed in which mangers do not respond to problems imaginatively. In such cases, an external shock – budget cuts, new conditions and duties, task forces, commissioners, inspectors – is likely to be appropriate, provided there is a clear strategy for follow-up with support.

By contrast, acute failure need not get shock treatment. Often the real value of a special initiative is only yielded when it fails, because the lessons can be learned and disseminated. When the managers of a special initiative – a pilot project, an experimental budget, a risky partnership that goes far beyond traditional professional expectations – are told that the project is 'too important to fail', they know immediately that they are being asked to 'play it safe', and therefore to take an approach from which less may be learned.

What can be learned from failure? There is no general answer to this (Anheier, 1999). Most lessons will be specific to a particular experiment, initiative, situation, partnership, network or locality. Nor is there necessarily always a single correct interpretation of what went wrong. Most of our learning from failure is left implicit, tacit, in the heads of individuals who often carry the blame and therefore have little incentive to discuss what they have learned. The challenge is to design incentives and cultures in the public service that capture this tacit knowledge and subject it to the discipline of debate and further trial.

Much of what is to be learned is in fact *unlearning*: the shedding of assumptions inherited from now-inappropriate institutional contexts

(Leadbeater, 1999). Unlearning is particularly challenging, and requires a climate and a culture in which public managers can make honest appraisals, be self-critical and critical of the inheritance of their organisations. The public sector has been rather bad at doing this, mainly because of its commitment to accountability and propriety in the use of public money, leading it to establish systems of sanctions that focus on blame.

Resolve conflicting policy priorities, and do it gently

Complete coherence in policy is indeed impossible. However, there is scope for reducing conflicts between priorities, for making clearer trade-off(s). We have noted that when it comes to such conflict resolution central government tends to reach instinctively for the strong tools of pooled budget incentives, regulation, inspection and sanctions. But these tools are not always the best. What really needs to be joined-up is bodies of knowledge, and it is here that the weak tools of government – persuasion, information, systems of learning, training, building networks, setting or borrowing examples, evaluation, and changing cultures through the delicate evolution of expectations, aspirations, motivations and commitments – really come into their own. The machismo of strong tools can too easily be part of the problem, not part of the solution.

Promote pinball careers

Public sector career paths for front-line managers remain firmly locked within functional models in the UK and in most other countries (Williams and Williams, n.d.). Many managers we interviewed were making considerable sacrifices to pursue holistic working: they risked losing out in promotion, status, managerial and peer support, pay and training to colleagues who remained within functional career silos. There are too few reward systems for cross-boundary working and too many penalties.

Governments should cajole, encourage, persuade and negotiate with the professional institutes and training colleges of housing managers, police officers, probation officers, social workers, town and country planners, transport managers, leisure services managers, the plethora of medical tribes, health-service managers and the like, to experiment with common foundation courses and cross-disciplinary mid-career training programmes. Only government can persuade these bodies to develop systems of professional recognition and status for those who take up 'pinball careers', moving between professions as appropriate in order to pursue joined-up working.

Drive budgetary change from the heart of the Exchequer

Although we have reservations about the efficacy of pooled budgets, there is nevertheless plenty of potential for encouraging holism from innovation design and use of budgets. Locally and centrally it will be important to design outcome-based spending and performance reviews, to attach mainstream budgets to priority outcomes for policy goals, and to give 'accounting officers' the freedom to purchase as they see fit in pursuit of those outcomes. It is not hard to appreciate the dilemma faced by those who control the purse strings: new holistic systems of accountability should greatly strengthen their capacity to direct public spending effectively, but in the short term the systems and skills for delivering this do not exist; thus change feels risky. Yet outcome-based change will only happen by devolving decision-making powers for the holistic pursuit of goals to permanent secretaries and senior officials, agency chief executives, local and health authorities.

Benchmark the best; manage expectations

Elected and appointed politicians and chief officers are responsible for building a climate of legitimacy for holistic working, recognising and encouraging innovators and pioneers and recognising the learning value of bold failure. In this, benchmarking against best-known practice is more valuable than 'naming and shaming'. It is important to combine an inspirational approach that encourages and rewards holistic effort with an open and measured account of progress both for practitioners and the wider public. This process is the opposite of every quick-fix ever dreamt up by an opportunist politician in power.

Let us state immediately that we recognise the scale of the challenge posed by the changes outlined above. For governments to go about their business in the manner we propose will require some significant shifts from current practice.

Conclusion

Following the principle of requisite variety laid down in the previous chapter, we have shown here that strategies for the reform of public management systems are like strategies in any organisation. They need to exhibit some combination of foresight and 'emergent' responses to events, unanticipated and indeed unforeseeable risks and opportunities (Mintzberg and Waters, 1994). Moreover, strategies must be a combination of setting directions, putting in place systems of encouragement and sanction, but also allowing people to find their own way and to innovate within the overall direction. Over-planning is as misguided as under-planning; over-centralisation and excessive micro-management is as likely to fail as lack of strategic direction.

The experience of New Labour in office in Britain shows some of the problems that can occur when there is an excessive bias towards central control. For better strategy, a more reflective account is required of how innovation of any kind takes place within organisations and systems of interorganisational relationships. In this chapter, we have tried to present some of the basic elements of such an account. We propose that successful innovation involves creating conditions under which innovation is the only sensible thing to do, followed by institutionalising the cultures and commitment to carry that through, but this needs to be followed by a period of reflection, learning and dissemination. Without due weight being given to each of these stages, reform strategies that seek to elicit innovation in public services are likely to fail. This puts a peculiar premium on getting a sensible relationship between policy and management. Having considered the overall policy issues at some length already, in the next chapter we turn to the management challenges, tactics and tools that are most appropriate for intelligent work towards holistic governance.

6 Interorganisational Relations and Practice

In the previous chapters we argued that it is important to balance strong and weak tools of governance. This is a daily challenge for public managers and officials, for whom a central problem is to find appropriate, effective and acceptable ways in which to gain leverage over interorganisational relations.

In this chapter we offer a theoretically informed account of the practical challenges in building workable interorganisational relations necessary for sustainable and holistic working. The first part of the chapter draws principally on the sociology of organisations and in particular on the study of interorganisational relations. However, later sections become progressively more management oriented, and draw more on management theory about both the public and the private sectors.

First, we begin by exploring the critical issue of how trust can be built between practitioners working in different functional organisational structures, for without trust the shared culture and knowledge on which effective holistic working depends cannot be built. Next, we review the principal barriers to building robust interorganisational structures for holistic working in the public sector. Finally, we consider the tactics and management styles that are being deployed by practitioners to develop sufficient trust to overcome some of these barriers. Here we draw heavily upon the interviews conducted in our local case studies, as summarised briefly in the introduction.

Building trust: a key ingredient for holism

That any credible account of what is possible in coordination and integration requires – as a priority – an understanding of how trust is developed between organisations, has been understood for some time. Indeed, this seemed to be one of the lessons learned by many of those who had worked within government and been leading commentators upon some of the British experiments of the 1970s and early 1990s (see Webb, 1991).

Trust is what keeps any society going: Durkheim (1984) famously described it as the precontractual condition of contract. Trust is an agency relationship, in which principals act in ways that put themselves or their interests at some risk. They do so in the belief, held with varying degrees of confidence above some threshold, that the agent, who has some discretion, will act, subject to incentives or rules that the principal invokes. Trust exists where it makes sense for the principal to rely, with varying degrees of confidence, upon the agent in respect of the expected behaviour and the principal's interests. (Cf. Zucker, 1986; Sztompka, 1999; Barber, 1983; Fox, 1976; Sako, 1992; Gambetta, 1988; Eisenstadt and Roninger, 1984; Elster, 1989; Hardin, 1993; Coulson, 1998; Kramer and Tyler, 1996; Lane and Bachman, 1998; Govier 1998; Fukuyama, 1995; Seligman, 1997; Misztal, 1996; Bianco, 1994; Hollis, 1998; 6, 1998d).

This means that typically we trust people or organisations for given reasons to carry out particular tasks. Therefore, trust is quite distinct from esteem, in which no tasks are required, and from respect, where even clear and distinct reasons may be absent. It is an empirical question whether someone will only trust the people or organisations that she holds in high esteem or respects, and *vice versa*, and if so, whether esteem or trust comes first.

We classify the reasons why anyone might trust anyone else ('reasons'), and what they might trust them to do ('tasks'), in the following way. We begin with reasons.

First, we might trust on the basis of past *experience* of dealing with the person or organisations, that they have proven reliable.

Second, we might trust on the basis that the person or organisation has a *reputation*, in either of two ways. We might take evidence of that reputation as a kind of reference, trusting on the basis of the reported experience of others. Or we might infer that the person or organisation will value that reputation and behave in a trustworthy way, in order not to damage it: in this case, a reputation acts like a kind of hostage (like an institutional reason) although one built up from experience.

Thirdly, we might trust on the basis of *shared characteristics* or *shared identity* – for example, because we share the same nationality or local roots as the person or organisation, or in some cases, simply the same sex, we might decide that they are trustworthy; alternatively, if we believe someone to be reliable on the basis of an eyeball-to-eyeball judgement, we are ascribing a characteristic that is, for us, a reason for trust. In some cases, this may be a special kind of reputation-based trust, if we think that reputation in the community of shared identity is valued. Alternatively, if we think that the person or organisation may feel some sense of obligation to us because of that shared identity or some other characteristic, the role of the community of identity is more to do with moral scope of duty.

Fourthly, we might trust on the basis of various *institutional* factors. *Generic institutional factors* include the availability of legal redress in the event of default, while specific *institutional factors* include the warranties and guarantees or other 'hostages' that the person or organisation may offer us.

Broadly, we then classify the tasks as follows.

First, the *minimal* or merely *prudential* level of trust is the case where we trust that a person's statements of intent can be believed. Promises, threats and other indications of intention to do or not to do a certain thing can be believed, whether or not they are welcome.

Secondly, we may trust the person or organisation to carry out the *contract* that we have with them – explicitly or implicitly by virtue of some legal rule – and, presumably, to do so to the threshold level of *competence* required, explicitly or implicitly – by the terms of contract.

Thirdly, we may trust the person or organisation to exercise *goodwill*. That is, we trust them to put our interests first, and use their discretion in the agency relationship to promote our interests. If the terms of the contract turn out not to be in our interest, then one who exercises goodwill trustworthiness will set them aside. If they are in our interests, they may do a little more for us than the contract requires.

There is a fourth category of trust, which we might call *absolute* or *moral* trust, in which we no longer trust the person to do anything in particular, but trust them, *tout court*. Organisations are not normally eligible for this category, and it will be ignored henceforth.

Cross-tabulating these categories yields the matrix demonstrated in Figure 6.1.

In most situations, if we trust at all, we will not trust for just one reason, but for a combination of reasons. Moreover, if we have reached goodwill trust, then implicitly we have already achieved contract trust, and likewise one cannot place contractual trust without first placing minimal trust. Therefore, we should think of any particular trust relationship as being represented, not by occupying a cell in the matrix, but rather by an area of the matrix covered.

However, experience and reputation typically take some time to build up. Therefore, initially, the only guides for managers on whether and how far to trust people in other organisations are any shared characteristics and institutions. Institutions in this context can include specific legislative obligations on the other party to collaborate, sanctions and rewards for coordination imposed from superior authorities. If the relationship is successfully built and trust develops, then we would expect to see reasons and

Figure 6.1 *The dimensions of trust: reasons and tasks*

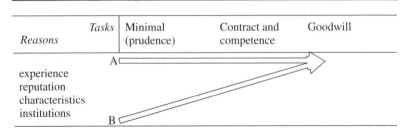

tasks for trust spread like ink on blotting paper out from the bottom left hand cell of the matrix in Figure 6.1, eventually reaching the top right hand cell, as shown in the arrow marked A.

However, with each setback, we would expect to see the ink retreat. It is not, of course, necessarily the case that after any betrayal, trust will disappear altogether. It is not necessarily the case that having forfeited our goodwill trust, the person or organisation will retreat all the way to the left hand border of the matrix, or even back to prudential trust: they may still be trustworthy under contract, provided we retain reasons for trust that lead us to think that breaking a contract would

- be so out of character that even the negative experience of failure to provide goodwill does not lead us to imagine that they would do so;
- damage a valued reputation;
- break some duty owed by virtue of particular characteristics; or
- run risks by way of some institution such as contract law or a prior specific warranty.

Therefore, if goodwill trust is damaged, managers may nevertheless trust those in the other organisation at least to carry out the implicit contract to an adequate level of competence that counts as carrying it out, or minimally to carry out specific statements of intent, threats or promises.

The story of every initiative in holistic working can be described using this analysis. In practice, all four categories of reasons for trust are often necessary for effective collaboration.

Obstacles

There are, of course, many obstacles to holistic working – obstacles to achieving and sustaining trust, obstacles to securing an adequate institutional platform, obstacles to securing willingness to behave in a

Figure 6.2 *Obstacles to holistic working*

Obstacle	Excuse	Examples
authority	mayn't	no legal power; no budgetary provision; violates law e.g., on data protection; different data confidentiality standards; beyond powers of accounting officer; can't re-write existing contracts
legitimacy	shouldn't	other organisation led by non-elected politicians, or self-appointed committee members; outputs aren't immediate, tangible, visible to public
capacity	can't	lack of managerial skills for 'managing out of control'; resource-base isn't large enough
priority	needn't	'minding the shop' comes first; takes too much time; can't plan that far ahead when there are emergencies; central money on offer is too marginal to be worth the effort; can't spare this key individual
inertia, loss of control	won't	political or professional fear of loss of power, control over budget, decision-making; pride in existing services; loss of career opportunities, promotion, rewards, reputation
bargaining	wouldn't unless …	side-deals with 'barons' required but can't be afforded or struck
jeopardy	mustn't	threatens stability, survival, public acceptability; first setback taken as evidence of misconceived objective; would undermine our existing accountability or expenditure control system
perversity, futility	won't work anyway	integration irrelevant to policy objectives, or may undermine them
difficulty	can't see how	boundaries are not co-terminous; can't overcome problems in employment law, e.g., transfer of pension rights; can't create appropriate accountability structure; organisations have different cultures, time horizons; incompatible performance indicators; incompatible data systems and data standards

trustworthy fashion, obstacles to creating shared cultures and bodies of shared knowledge.

From our fieldwork, the main types of obstacles are the following (Figure 6.2; For other classifications of obstacles, see, for instance, Parston and Timmins, 1998; Blank and Hoffman, 1994; United States General Accounting Office, 1992).

Issues of professional pride can be as important as those of law. One interviewee in Southbrookborough told us of the enduring disdain of some professions for others. In other cases professional pride is more about asserting a leadership role. 'This is not about money. Doctors are not that interested in managing budgets, but they do want to lead a professional team.'

Career prospects, status and rewards are critically important. These are at the heart of what often appears, when things are going badly, to be a zero-sum relationship between integration in the mainstream and integration on the margin. One respondent in Beltham told us about their efforts to create a successful regeneration partnership: 'If mainstream officers put their hearts into SRB work then they get into trouble for neglecting other work. But if you employ separate staff then it becomes marginalised as a project rather than changing the way in which the whole organisation thinks and works.' If career incentives, rewards and professional status were better aligned to integrated working, this perception of no-win would be far less likely.

The law did cause headaches, though. As one respondent in Southbrookborough said: 'One of the biggest blocks to joint working is employment law. It's so difficult to move people from one organisation to another.' Others had to overcome union opposition both to the movement of staff and to potential redundancies. Pension arrangements were another difficulty: in one Midlands city-centre partnership we studied, all the staff are still technically employed by one agency (the local authority), mainly because of the pension problems, despite agreement among managers that other types of employment arrangement would be more appropriate.

Another kind of legal difficulty arises when geographical boundaries for the different agencies (for example, education, social services, health, police and probation) are not co-terminous. While these obstacles can be overcome, it takes additional effort, cost and political will.

Working beyond the scope of a specific legal duty or power also has consequences, as one interviewee in Norlingshire told us: 'We have to be more political with non-statutory duties. With statutory duties it is clear what departments should do. With non-statutory projects, you are dependent on departments' good will and interest. I suspect this is why things go so slowly and not necessarily how you want.'

Many of the obstacles fall into more than one category. For example, the borders between authority, capacity and difficulty are not always clear in practice. Similarly the line between priority and jeopardy is often fuzzy. Inertia, control and autonomy problems are often fundamental. Few politicians and public managers would put them forward publicly, but they might use them when 'upping the ante' in negotiations.

Obstacles can compound each other. Lack of legitimacy, for instance, can reinforce inertia: if no one in authority is going to make this a priority and specifically give permission, why bother? Those who raise obstacles in the hope of achieving a deal to their own advantage will use almost any kind of argument that comes to mind.

However, it became clear from our case studies that when it is hard to persuade people to do something, it is more usually because they do not want to rather than because they cannot. In every case that we studied, with determination, effort, some guile and ingenuity in securing political clout, each of these could be overcome. That is not to say that where all the obstacles are present, it would be easy to overcome them. However, these obstacles can be interpreted either as objective phenomena, as real conditions of actual interorganisational conditions, or else they can be read as subjective phenomena, as ways of framing the world, as patterns of risk perception, each of which has its elective affinities with a particular bias or trope.

Most of the reasons that make holistic government hard to achieve stem from fear, lack of ambition, risk aversion and the power of incentives to maintain the status quo. However, because it is not generally thought clever to parade one's fears, low aspirations, aversion to risk or vested interests, the arguments that get voiced against innovation tend to focus on institutional blockages. In general, 'can't' turns out to mean 'won't'.

Tactics for overcoming obstacles

The main resources required for integration (as for any substantial change-management programme) include authority to make decisions or confer status; people and their skills; bodies of knowledge; and skills of communication and persuasion. Figure 6.3 summarises the key resources.

Resources are assembled by combining power tools as set out in Figure 4.2. Figure 6.4 summarises this and shows how those resources can help to create various of the necessary conditions.

Only the elected national government has extensive access to a full set of power tools. But many public agencies and organisations have a good proportion of them. Local authorities, police constabularies, government offices of the regions and health authorities between them command a wide range of legal powers (including the power of councils to levy and

Figure 6.3 *Obstacles and resources*

Obstacle	Key resources to overcome obstacle
all	means of communication and persuasion
no authority	legal powers, decision-making authority
no legitimacy	status-defining authority
no capacity	people, skills, money, knowledge
no priority	decision-making power
inertia, loss of control or autonomy	decision-making authority, status-defining authority
bargaining	money, decision-making authority, status-defining authority
jeopardy	knowledge, skills
futility, perversity	knowledge, skills
difficulty	knowledge, skills

Figure 6.4 *Making resources from tools*

Resource	Power tools needed	Helps put in place condition of...
knowledge, information	all detectors	acceptance that gains can be secured, reasons to integrate
means of communication and persuasion	information, persuasion	trust, legitimacy; perseverance
people, skills	all collectors; information and persuasion	leaders, skilled managers at the boundaries
money for investment, incentives	all collectors	reasons to integrate; catalysts
legal powers	regulation	catalyst; legitimacy
decision-making authority	regulation	catalyst; reasons to integrate
status-defining authority	information, persuasion; regulation	legitimacy; reasons to integrate; leaders
accountability	regulation	legitimacy; reasons to integrate

collect taxes), and their political leaders and chief officers have the power to define accountabilities and status within their domains. If the entities seeking integration are very weak, they may need first to engage with others to access the necessary power tools and resources. But many agencies can use their vertical systems of accountability to reach many of the resources they require.

The key weak tools are information and persuasion, but to maintain these takes effort and has costs. An interviewee in Riverborough said: 'Being a product champion takes up an awful lot of time: research, keeping abreast of the issues.' Another in Redbrickborough noted: 'Sharing information and intelligence is a necessary condition for integrated planning and working. That means creating time, space and a place for that.'

The repertoire of tactics

The next stage is to develop a tactical programme to serve the goals and, if necessary, help secure the right conditions. It should enable managers to overcome obstacles, secure access to tools and build some of the principal resources, such as legitimacy. Tactics are not themselves specific integrative activities; they are the micro-political devices that make the integrative activities possible. *Organisational* tactics involve creating or rearranging the structure of entities. *Rhetorical* tactics are deployed to change hearts and minds. Our research demonstrated that both kinds have to be used. Figure 6.5 summarises the most important types and examples.

Events or crises may serve as triggers for intervention. They do not have to be externally generated: some crises can be engineered, or at least exploited. Thus budget approvals can be held up; chief officers can be sacked or suspended, or their resignations quietly procured; committee

Figure 6.5 *Understanding tactics*

Driver	Organisational tactics	Rhetorical tactics
event-driven	engineering a crisis to be a trigger	using a crisis to build legitimacy
knowledge-driven	creating specialist structures for knowledge creation and sharing	advocacy
personnel-driven	creating safe havens	managing expectations
structure-driven	Trojan horse	managing expectations

chairs can be removed or induced to spend more time with their families; cuts can be made without being demanded by central government; activities can be privatised in new ways; regulators can make an example of particular authorities, and so on. We have seen a number of cases where politicians and chief officers have used crises to remove key obstacles or stimulate people to innovate. The really important thing is to use the crisis to build legitimacy for the integrative solution.

This, in turn, calls for knowledge-driven tactics. Public managers pursuing integration engage in careful advocacy to build the culture. They draw on the external expertise of consultants and researchers; they pray-in-aid bodies of research, analogies or benchmarks; they use the wider political environment, such as appealing to central government's commitment to bring down 'Berlin walls' between health and social care, or to Local Agenda 21 or Kyoto targets for reducing emissions. If necessary, they supplement advocacy with study groups, joint or inter-professional working parties, planning cells, scenario-building or community-visioning workshops, consensus conferences, and so on, in order to build and share knowledge between those among whom they seek integration.

Tactics are also needed to secure the commitment of key individuals: for nurturing leaders and boundary-spanning managers, for keeping people on board (see below for the specific case of 'managing out of control').

At the level of structure, or interorganisational relationships, 'Trojan horses' can be a useful tactic. In this case, the lead agency lulls its potential partners into going along with a modest type of relationship, and gently encourages its development into something deeper. When more ambitious relationships or deeper integration are proposed, it is very hard to refuse or to pull out without undoing work that is by then valued on all sides.

Marketing skills are universally important. Powerful rhetoric, imagery and symbolism can persuade the reluctant. One of our respondents in Redbrickham described the way they had secured the participation of other key agencies as 'glitzy packaging'. But the glitz shouldn't be allowed to dominate. Managing expectations is a crucial tactic. On the one hand aspirations need to be raised about how integration will enhance organisational performance, personal work satisfaction, public recognition and plaudits, leveraged resources and learning, and so forth. On the other hand expectations cannot be allowed to soar so high that any setback – and there are usually many – will lead to crushing disappointment. All reporting should be imbued with a sense of realism and robust anticipation of setbacks.

Finally, public managers need occasional relief from the pressure and the exposed nature of their work. This can be very informal, little more than support networks in which leaders and key individuals can share problems and experiences. Equally, though, more formal structures may be appropriate to demonstrate support, such as training in specific skills of public-sector entrepreneurship, boundary-spanning, negotiating complex legal minefields and so on. In Riverborough, frontline and senior staff from across council departments and external agencies were offered training together in joined-up thinking, planning and working. All staff were required to discuss and plan a project focused not on departmental needs, but on customer services.

In the long run, however, support for staff with key responsibilities integration will need to go further. In many of our case studies, to take on the role of cross-boundary working was perceived as carrying a double risk: of being marginalised in today's organisational and professional power structures, and of losing out on future career opportunities. Hence the need for a reappraisal of public-sector and professional career structures and statuses to recognise this new way of working.

Skills for integration

There is a large literature on the practical skills for:

- partnership working, aimed at practitioners (e.g., Holman, 1999; Parston and Timmins, 1998), policy-makers (e.g., Jupp, 2000) and of more academic character (e.g., Bardach, 1998);
- for developing trust in the public sector (e.g., Coulson, 1998) and more widely in organisational and interorganisational contexts, again both for practitioners (e.g., Whitney, 1996; Reynolds, 1997) and for academic readerships (Kramer and Tyler, 1996; Lane and Bachman, 1998); and
- for the management of networks (e.g., Nohria and Eccles, 1992; Kickert *et al.*, 1997).

These bodies of literature are far too large to be reviewed comprehensively, but the works cited here are widely regarded as leading texts or collections. What might be surprising to practitioners looking for new insights is just how few specific and practical 'tricks' are actually offered that are not at some level common sense, or simply applications to the field of trust building, network steering or partnership building of much wider and more general good management practices. It turns out from these bodies of literature that the tricks of the trade are, in essence, the same sound maxims of management that apply to managing any organisation, any project, any initiative, any group. For example, Jupp (2000) stresses clarity of objectives; ensuring that all partners benefit; building in evaluation; introducing fun; and developing understanding. Parston and Timmins call for consultation of users and local communities to identify both boundary problems and priorities, appropriate degrees of involvement of staff at all levels in formulating strategies; clarity about objectives, roles and mutual expectations; development of consensus (they really mean political legitimacy); creation of incentives and sanctions; willingness to accept failure if it can teach; Reynolds (1997) summarises his message with the following maxims: choose the right people; tell them the score; make them accountable; identify their concerns; lead decisively; act with integrity; give feedback; and promote learning. Whitney's (1996) recipe differs principally in his greater insistence on such tools as measurement. Bardach (1998) offers the most sophisticated theoretical analysis of the process of building interorganisational relations and the largest set of specific things to do. But the practical focus of his message about what he calls 'smart practices' is similarly unsurprising. It includes such prescriptions as dialogue to identify common concerns and motivations, teambuilding exercises where useful; devolution of implementation responsibility; lobbying for financial resources and legitimacy or 'licence to operate'; exercising leadership; celebration of early wins; careful calibration of the pace of integration to the willingness of the partners and the state of political legitimacy; using resources to building career opportunities and status. Writers in the Kickert *et al.* (1997) collection stress the importance of such activities as bargaining, identifying areas of compromise; lobbying or cornering superior politicians into providing legitimacy and resources; using lobby power to stress linkages between issues; developing financial instruments such as incentives, pump-priming funds for partnerships and network structures, and so on.

The disappointment of any practitioner reading this literature looking for some tactics and tricks she would not have thought of for herself is understandable. Yet in a way, the authors of these texts are right. There is, for the most part, nothing special about the management skills of holistic working. Managing partnerships and integration initiatives is exactly what one would want – the application of the generic skills of management to a particular problem. It was to test this sobering hypothesis that we asked the managers in our case studies about how they went about their integrative work. Their answers to our questions broadly confirm the hypothesis. However, we did find two important twists. The first concerns the relationship between clarity about objectives and trust. Whereas the conventional management literature calls for clarity and assumes that this will build trust, we found our respondents sometimes more Machiavellian than the management gurus and the public administration scholars. They often ensured that partners in integrative work were unclear about their longer term objectives for the relationship, in the hope of building sufficient joint experience, culture, knowledge and trust to enable them to use the initial period as a Trojan Horse. Secondly, we did identify a set of practices we shall call 'managing out of control', which may be distinctive only to a period in which holistic working is not institutionalised, when only the brave and sometimes even only the heroic will be willing to face the obstacles, but may on the contrary turn out to be an enduring feature of holistic working and perhaps of 'actually existing' matrix management systems. However, in the remainder of this chapter we present the main points that arise from our interviews on the key management challenges and tactics. That many of them are applications of general management good sense is precisely the point. Holistic management is not rocket science: it is the application of sound management practice to a particular problem, not an arcane field of practice with its own laws.

Developing new information bases, categories and systems

Holistic management needs new information categories and systems and holistic managers need to access not only existing information systems but also to ensure that systems meet their data needs. In many cases data for holistic management exists but is not collated and analysed in appropriate ways. Several of our case studies demonstrate the ways in which combining or re-analysing information sets may create invaluable data for holistic management. Such data are of value not only in highlighting the need for and legitimacy of integrated and preventive approaches but also in suggesting new practical programmes and approaches.

One way of encouraging new thinking and concepts is to institute 'strategic conversation' in the 'purple zone' where the 'red of politics' meets the 'blue of administration', as practiced in New Zealand (Boston *et al.*, 1996; Matheson, 1998). This was, in some respects, what the Redbrickham Social Strategy Forum attempted to achieve.

One of the occupational hazards of holistic management is the need for huge amounts of information processing with which formal systems – and, equally significantly, human beings – cannot cope. Many of the managers in our case studies felt increasingly smothered by the requirements of information planning and control systems. In reality, of course, as everyone who has ever worked in an organisation knows, much information exchange and decision-making is carried out via informal channels and relationships – but this is rarely formally admitted, especially in government. In multi-national companies, where information processing needs are at least as high and complex as those in government, senior managers are now trying to use, influence and actively create informal information exchanges by, for example, bringing managers and others together in situations which encourage formation of ongoing relationships.

'Getting space' for cross-boundary working

In our case studies, managers emphasised the need for space for cross-boundary working, and they used the word in several distinct senses.

Space here often meant *time* allocated to joint working and away from day-to-day internal management tasks. They spoke eloquently of the tensions between doing inter-agency working and minding the shop, delivering services and avoiding crises, as the Beltham manager's remark quoted above indicates. Managers emphasised the need for time to develop plans and legal structures, the frequency of setbacks, especially in the very early stages, and acceptance that the end product may be very different from the initial plan.

Space also meant *people* freed up to do integrative work, and with jobs structured in the the right way. Many spoke of the dangers involved in creating space by employing designated inter-agency workers who leave when the 'project' ends, taking their knowledge, contacts and experience with them. Employing 'special' staff or people dedicated solely to holistic initiatives also runs the strong risk of confirming the view that inter-agency working is a stand-alone 'project' with nothing to do with mainstream thinking and work and not critical to the mission of the main sponsoring organisations. But such strategies are difficult to resist because the mainstream is under so much pressure.

Staff talked of the need for *political space* – space to choose partners, make offers, do deals and so on, as well as space to take risks, make mistakes and explore ideas and relationships which may come to nothing. They talked of the need for delegation and a shift in the bases of power – but without 'bearing consequences'. They also talked of the way in which existing committee structures can hamper holistic working, and more generally of the way in which holistic working reverberates through the whole system. One public manager spoke of keeping her several principal sets of elected member authorities informed on a 'need to know basis'.

Space could also mean appropriately flexible systems of *performance measurement* and reward. Managers talked of the need to recognise adding value by brokering with people rather than presiding over departments (and budgets). They complained about the effects of tight and narrow performance measures on flexibility and holistic working, including interim outputs and outcomes; and of the effects of community involvement on achieving performance outputs to time.

Moreover, they also spoke of space as *legitimacy* for integration, which could only be won by careful development and deployment of tactics. They emphasised the need to deliver early wins – short-term tangible benefits buying time to work on strategic longer-term goals. They noted that for boundary spanners success is what one achieves outside the organisation, but this does not fit with internal values, reward and promotion structures.

Finally, space could mean the trust and legitimacy to take risks, to fail in interesting and fruitful ways and to and learn from those failures. Too rarely, at least in the blame-diffusion culture of British administrative politics, was this space readily available.

'Getting talking': opening new channels of communication and influence

The first challenge was to create dialogue between agencies. Often this involved translation between very different professional and organisational languages or at least dialects, in order to enable each side to recognise each other's basic commitments, before hard discussion of how to reconcile conflicting priorities and objectives could begin.

Managers talked of the need for new channels of communication and influence and of the need for relationships of influence to shift from the vertical to the horizontal. They emphasised the new skills required in bargaining, selling and negotiating, rather than issuing or following commands. They emphasised the skills involved in developing influence capacity. Managers highlighted the difficulties of doing inter-agency working via existing hierarchies and channels of communication which depend on x briefing y who briefs z.

Getting to mutual understanding and trust

Managers emphasised the need for understanding where other people are coming from, their language, values, constraints, priorities, what they need/want to get out of the relationship. 'It takes time' was the phrase that recurred in Southbrookborough, Midcaster, Beltham and elsewhere, describing the processes of generating mutual understanding, a measure of respect, trust and willingness to accept the legitimacy of everyone's point of view. 'You've got to be prepared to accept that everyone is right', said one Southbrookborough manager. Managers talked of the need to understand the internal and external implications of cross-boundary alliances and the effects of changes on other people in one's own organisation, not represented at the table.

They asked how to learn enough about other functions and organisations to be credible, let alone influential members of teams or alliances – is a little learning a dangerous thing? Does knowing a little about a lot lead to loss of specialist knowledge and thus loss of credibility? How does one access the information within and across organisations one needs to work credibly and constructively in alliances?

'Trojan horses'

Dialogue and taking into account other agencies' work may seem humdrum, a 'mere talking shop'. But no effective partnership, strategic alliance, joint working or satellite agency can be built without dialogue. A common form of impatience reported to us from many of the boundary spanning public managers we interviewed, on the part of their senior managers and some politicians, was to say: 'There's no point in talking until we have some concrete, practical proposal for joint working to talk about,' or else 'this is just a talking shop: if this network/partnership has not produced deliverable outcomes in terms of practical service changes after three months, then I can't justify its continuation.' In Redbrickham, one chief officer dismissed all the talking as 'girly', a term he certainly thought highly derogatory. This, we found repeatedly in our fieldwork, is not merely (!) sexist, but often counter-productive. Dialogue can take much longer. However, it can also provide a bridgehead, gaining legitimacy for more ambitious programmes. Where there is powerful opposition, mutual suspicion, or other serious obstacle, dialogue can be used as a 'Trojan horse' for subsequent deeper integration. We found cases of integration where one agency persuaded another to become involved on the basis that the goal is modest joint planning or working, but this served as a Trojan horse for a longer-term agenda of, for example, a strategic alliance. As the integration develops the second agency may feel that deepening is a natural process, while the first has intended this all along. Both may have considered it successful, but there is no shared understanding of, or even clarity about, goals. In essence, the lead agency lulls its potential partners into going along with a modest type of relationship, and gently encourages its development into something deeper. When more ambitious relationships or deeper integration are proposed, it is very hard to refuse or to pull out without undoing work that is by then valued on all sides.

Creating new leaders and heroes

Exhortation to 'change the way people think' is unlikely to be enough and, in any case, may run the risk of undermining existing knowledge and skills without putting anything very coherent in their place, as well as creating resistance to change from staff who feel threatened. The challenge in creating more integrated ways of thinking and working is to protect the organisation's existing knowledge base and competencies while establishing new management perspectives and capabilities.

The transition process needs to be undertaken in logical sequence and gradually. The first step is to provide legitimacy for senior managers promoting holistic perspectives. Bartlett and Ghoshal (1989), in a study of multinational businesses implementing change towards a more corporate, integrated approach, suggest that although companies adopted a variety of methods, two common broad characteristics stand out in successful examples: transferring high status managers from the dominant group to the new team, thereby upgrading the latter's perceived legitimacy and allowing it to tap into the contacts and relationships of the former, and aligning the new group's activities with the interests and needs of the dominant group (speaking their language, for example, without being taken over). Our case studies in, for example, Riverborough, Norlingshire and Midcaster support these findings.

The new 'heroes and leaders', managers with responsibility for promoting and implementing holistic approaches, need not only legitimacy but also access to the organisation's information resources and communication channels. This means access not only to existing resources and channels but also the creation of new channels and forums of communication to form linkages across management groups and to encourage information sharing and joint decision-making.

The new 'heroes and leaders' need to both access and influence the organisation's key decision-making channels. This means ensuring that the new management has the organisational clout to influence decisions. Legitimacy and access are not enough for this – these need to be backed by more formal organisational power. According to Bartlett and Ghoshal the two most important elements in being seen to have organisational power are: an allocation of resources and a distribution of responsibilities that empowered the emerging group in its negotiations with more established management groups. Furthermore, they suggest, being held accountable for outcomes brings substantial power and influence in decision-making processes (Bartlett and Ghoshal, 1989).

'Making it up as you go along'

Managers talked at length about the need for high tolerance of uncertainty. In Beltham, one senior officer spoke of the importance of 'getting people to live with a sense of chaos'. In Southbrookborough, one interviewee remarked 'it's very easy to slip back into wanting things to be clear'. There are few rules for inter-agency working/networking, and those that there are probably don't help much. There is no book to follow and no obvious success criteria – how do I know when I'm doing well? Who will be to blame, and who will protect a public manager or an exposed middle-ranking politician if things go wrong?

Cross-boundary working involves taking big risks without being sure where the safety net is, and greater personal exposure for managers. The uncertainties of cross-boundary working links back to the points above concerning channels of communication and sites of action – do I know what's going on elsewhere and do I know what or at least when I don't know?

Managers emphasised the importance of good legal advice for all sides and the need to understand the issues for their organisations. They talked of the need to be adaptive and flexible which in many ways sits uneasily with emphasis on structure and process in the public sector.

'Managing out of control'

Managers engaged in integration often describe what they are doing as managing 'out of control'. This can be both exhilarating and exhausting. In these circumstances, the same interviewee acknowledged, it was not surprising that members and officers 'keep wanting to rediscover security and go back to the old ways to feel safe and in control'.

Managers emphasised the need for political and managerial willingness to lose control. Old hierarchies and formal structures and ranks are no longer relevant in understanding and working in relationships within and across organisations with partners not subordinates. Cross-boundary working means working with people over whom one has no control and in situations where there are no clear rules of engagement.

They talked of loss of accountability, of dependence on others to achieve results, of handling multiple accountabilities in different structures and value systems and of being accountable for things beyond their control. They emphasised that cross-boundary working requires recognition that the job of the public manager is not about gaining control but about letting go of control – a very different mind-set from that with on which they had been brought up. Managers noted that more cross-boundary working means less oversight of what staff are doing out there and more opportunities for people to initiate action, with the increasing possibility of cross-boundary chaos.

They talked of the tensions involved in reconciling accountability to the organisation with accountability to the alliance; and the tensions in managing accountability up to central and regional government and emphasis on accountability to local community and users.

Managing out of control takes particular skills. One interviewee in Eastwoodshire explained: 'The work involves battling all the time and we're asking people to work outside their professional training. They need to learn new skills that they haven't been trained for – persuasion, brokering and so on. You need people who can think outside their box.' Cross-boundary working skills also included handling multiple points of accountability in different structures and value systems, being accountable for things beyond one's control, talking different languages and learning to let go.

It is a demanding role. Our interviewees stressed the importance of personal charisma, managerial and political abilities, as well as expecting the individual to be suitably senior in ranking, to carry clout.

The most basic prerequisite for managers to cope with the risks of managing out of control is explicit support: they must be assured that they will be backed if they run into opposition or criticism. In Redbrickham, our interviewees told us that the council chief executive had given them explicit permission and guidance, and a clear indication that they would be protected. Without this, the council officers involved would not have felt able to proceed as boldly as they did (or even at all, in some instances).

Creating commitment

Changes in incentives and rewards, via valued career paths, is one part of a wider requirement for tomorrow's government: creating commitment. In transnational business management this requirement is well recognised: 'Top management must obtain the personal commitment of every individual in the firm to the overall corporate agenda. We call this process co-option. Its integrative effects often prove to be more powerful than those of any structure or system, however sophisticated' (Bartlett and Goshal, 1989, p. 70).

Three techniques are regarded as particularly important in creating personal commitment: clear, shared understanding of the company's mission and objectives; the visible behaviour of senior management; and the company's personnel policies. Our case studies demonstrate the power of constant re-iteration of integrated, preventive thinking and goals in central government policies and statements as a means of creating a shared understanding of the public sector's mission and objectives. They also demonstrate the importance attached to visible behaviour of senior politicians and management at central and local level, and the damage and confusion caused by visibly inconsistent behaviour (as in silo-based performance measures which stress outputs rather than outcomes and fire-fighting rather than prevention). These need to be accompanied by personnel policies which stress the need for (and the value of) team players rather than soloists; moving managers around to broaden perspectives and knowledge; training and development to reinforce corporate values and foster personal relationships across divisions, performance evaluation considering not only measurable output but cooperation with colleagues and adherence to organisational values (network makers).

Managing professionals and street-level bureaucrats

It is sometimes argued among academic political scientists that there is a tension between the imperative for holistic working on the one hand, and, on the other, the fact that street level bureaucrats – front-line police officers, probation officers, nurses and general medical practitioners, classroom teachers, social workers and so on – unavoidably have great discretion in their work (Lipsky, 1980). The argument is that, as Lipsky argued twenty years ago, street level bureaucrats resort to a variety of coping and rationing mechanisms when their case loads become impossible, or when (most of the time) they find difficult fully to satisfy all of the conflicting pressures they face from different managerial and political imperatives. These rationing and coping mechanisms tend to take the form of finding the line of least resistance, of finding those strategies that maximise their work satisfaction, optimising their preferred work flow and soon. Therefore, Lipsky argued, they tend to focus their energies and their attention on tackling the easiest problems and defer dealing with or referring on, or otherwise disposing of, the more difficult ones. In two ways, it is sometimes argued, holism demands that they work in different ways which they will, on the Lipskian account, be reluctant to adopt. First, the holistic governance agenda calls for them to work on the most complex, multi-dimensional cases, and secondly, it calls for them to make themselves accountable both vertically to their functional line management system and to the horizontal systems of peers in multi-agency networks and partnerships.

That there is a genuine challenge here is certainly true. But it would be wrong to read Lipsky's theory of street level bureaucrat's coping mechanisms as suggesting that there can be no innovations in managerial arrangements that could overcome the problem or at least mitigate it. The challenge for the public manager concerned to promote holistic working is to find ways in which holistic working becomes the line of least resistance for the harried street level bureaucrat. One obvious way to do this is to create separate structures with separate staff teams for dealing with the most disadvantaged people who have the most complex problems. This can work in some areas of the rehabilitative programmes that follow up after the criminal justice system has done its work, but the risks of stigma that arise from these strategies are often no longer acceptable in many fields of secondary education, services for people with disabilities and health care, where integration between client groups is now a major priority as well as integration between professional interventions. Another strategy, following Le Grand's (1989) suggestion of differentially weighted vouchers for the worst off, would be give street level bureaucrats incentives in their compensation to prioritise cases differently. It is possible, conversely, to design penalties, and sanctions can also be used for failure to focus attention on the multi-dimensional aspects of social problems. Naturally, there are stark limits in many countries as to the extent to which subordinate authorities such as local governments can deviate from national compensation and employment conditions. Therefore, local agencies tend to resort to more informal mechanisms to mitigate the effects of the dilemma.

Profession, status and pay

Professional career structures, public sector pay systems and patterns of professional status can all be major obstacles to holistic working. At present, at least in the UK, national structures dominate in these fields across much of the public sector, and the scope for local innovation and variation is limited. Therefore, again, public managers wanting to promote holism have to use more informal systems. They can informally find ways to promote particular individuals who do important boundary spanning work, to indicate to them that their work will be valued in promotion, and they can use informal signalling about what is valued to try to influence local patterns of status.

Training

Training clearly has a key role to play in preparing both staff at all levels in organisations, as well as politicians, for holistic management. Staff training is unlikely to be fully effective unless local and national politicians and other members of boards also understand the implications and requirements of holistic working. Encouraging staff to think and work holistically will only lead to frustration and conflict unless their political bosses are similarly prepared.

Training for holistic working needs to be carefully related to the levels and tasks involved and may be more or less specific depending on the roles of workers. The task is to create a matrix in the minds of staff, but the size, structure and complexity of that matrix will depend on the role of the worker and the task in hand.

At senior management level there is a need for 'integration architects' – people who can see the broader picture and understand the relationships, languages, values, concerns and constraints of different players within and across departments, organisations and sectors. As Jenkins (1998) points out, the old community development projects provided this sort of training. Similarly, there is a strong argument for a re-examination and up-dated revival of the old notion of civil service generalists. Training for integrative work also needs to be given prestige by politicians and senior civil servants and must be backed by a career structure in which such skills are valued.

At all levels in the organisation, training should encourage multi-skilling (as in Riverborough, for example, where staff in the service centre are expected to understand a range of benefit systems, much as Citizens' Advice Bureaux workers have always had to and, indeed, as service users are expected to). Co-location may be one means of encouraging multi-perspectives but if co-location simply means workers working in the same building without sharing ideas, information, skills and work then co-location will not be sufficient. Cross-training, shadowing, coaching and mentoring may be more effective than simple co-location.

Transferring staff between departments and organisations is a powerful method in developing a common definition of the problem and encouraging more complex cognitive structures.

Overcoming obstacles: answering the fatalist

There is no shortage of fatalist arguments to the effect that trust cannot be achieved, that joint cultures and bodies of integrated professional

knowledge cannot sustainably be reproduced and then reproduced elsewhere, that the institutions of functional governance militate so powerfully
against holistic management that nothing can be achieved, that street level
bureaucrats will always have greater incentives to organise their lives in
ways that suit them and that will reinforce functional organisation, that
political 'space' for holistic working will never be available in sufficient
quantities because of the pressures on politicians to micro-manage on
inputs, that public managers cannot learn to 'manage out of control'. But,
when examined, most of these turn out to be essentially *a priori* arguments. They are the very same arguments that were used at the beginning
of the 1980s to argue that reinvention could not be achieved or institutionalised, that public managers could not acquire the skills for it, and so on.

What emerges from our case studies and from many other studies of
network steering, partnership management and joint working, is the fact
that public managers can be remarkably innovative in finding ways to do
joint working, if they are modestly encouraged and given at least some
political support to do so. One reassuring finding here is the general one
that there are few, if any, management skills for holistic working that are
unique to this practice. Most are simply the generic skills of good management applied to a particular style of problem and solution.

Surely, there will be some situations where all the obstacles can be
found together, all highly powerful, and where few of the necessary
resources can be readily created. Complete success over a short period of
time in making a shift to holism from a longstanding base of functional
organisation is not to be expected, nor is this necessary to the argument for
holistic governance.

Finally, in this chapter, we have further developed the argument that
there is a need for both strong and weak tools, for both hierarchical and
more individualistic and communitarians styles of public management, by
showing that the range of management skills and measures involved in
promoting holistic working involves both the strong tools of incentives
through pay structures and the weaker ones of persuasion through training,
lobbying for political legitimacy and a 'licence to operate', both the strong
tools of internal regulation for joint working and the softer culture building
styles involved in dialogue for trust building. Two peculiarities stand out,
which suggest that the weak tools are often wielded most successfully
when managers are prepared to be less than fully candid about goals and
accountability – namely, the importance of the Trojan horse as a tactic and
the skills of 'managing out of control'. Weak tools do not necessarily mean
managerial weakness: they can be deployed with some guile, at least in the
short run.

Conclusion

The debate about the previous upswing in interest in and effort towards holistic working focused on the question of the limits of certain strong tools deployed at the macro-level – namely, those of synoptic rational planning and budgeting (Challis *et al.*, 1988). In the last chapter, we argued that a weakness of the recent wave of holistic governance, at least in the British case, has been the excessive reliance on strong tools deployed from the centre but at the micro-level. In this chapter, we have demonstrated that often the most effective and promising initiatives in holistic working spring from and are sustained neither by grand exercises in synoptic planning and budgeting nor by central micro-management, but, within a centrally set direction (constrained hierarchy) and with suitably modest aspirations (limited fatalism), by much more opportunistic and manipulative processes by which leaders both seize and exploit resources (individualistically), and build horizontal networks (communitarian and egalitarian in nature). It is often in the interstices of the hierarchical order of accountability, although that order is important, that committed managers are able to innovate most effectively, by 'managing out of control'. If this leads, in this chapter, to an account of how this is done that appears to consist principally in maxims, then this reflects the nature of organisational life when viewed from the point of view of the public manager in this situation. In the next chapter we show that fundamentally similar issues arise in connection with the management of formally structured bodies of information that arise in the unstructured process information we have been concerned with here.

7 Information Systems

In this chapter we consider the possible role of information systems in facilitating integration at key levels of government activity. We examine digital systems to support coordination and integration in service provision, and in governance. Then we bring together these arguments in a review of the theories that implicitly run through all the debates about electronic government. Finally, we address one of the central ethical questions about the relationship between information systems and integration that has been the focus of major political conflicts in many countries, namely, whether integrating the information systems of different parts of government involves unacceptable violations of privacy.

The world's largest information technology systems suppliers and information technology consulting groups have invested very large sums in equipping themselves to be capable of offering public authorities information systems that will both support the holistic activities that governments want to undertake, and that will enable citizens as consumers of public services to integrate for themselves the packages of services they need, without necessarily needing to know which agency, department or authority provides which service. Governments at every level around the world have spent very large sums in buying in these systems and this expertise, and in developing their own in-house expertise. The result is that the information technology issues in integration are now perhaps better understood by many policy-makers, and certainly by many contractors to government, than are the issues of, for example, budget design, accountability, personnel management and development or partnership building.

There is now a plethora of vision documents setting out ideals of electronic government (Kable, 1995, 1996, 1997; Gosling, 1997; Moore, 1998). Visions typically offer integrated and seamless services to citizens or consumers and more effective communication between policy-makers and implementers. They diverge only on the question of how far information and communications technologies make it feasible and legitimate for government to cease to use taxpayers' money to finance certain activities altogether. Or, to put it more modestly, the question is whether they make it easier to continue to finance but contract out certain activities, or whether they have no effect upon the questions of what government can and should do, and how it should organise it. Academic commentators, by contrast (Bellamy and Taylor, 1998; Heeks, 1999) have been much more sceptical. The recent history of large-scale project failure in government information systems has also given many reasons for doubt about these visions.

It is helpful to start by distinguishing three broad categories of information-using activities of government.

First, in its *democratic* role, government gathers information from citizens and consumers of public services about what they care about, what they think of what they get, what they would like done not only for themselves but more 'nosily' (Goodin, 1986) for others. It collects summary information in the form of votes for representatives, and in order to facilitate deliberation and reflection from citizens before they offer this information, puts out a variety of types of information about its activities, the options faced, the considerations for and against these options, through a variety of consultation media. We shall not discuss e-democracy initiatives here, because their connections with administrative and policy integration are not well developed (for a review of the key issues in e-democracy, see 6, 2000b).

Secondly, in its *governance* role as maker of policy, maker of decisions and manager of executive and administrative operations to implement those policies and decisions, government generates, circulates internally, manipulates and analyses large quantities of information.

Thirdly, as a provider or at least financier of *services*, government both provides consumers with information about how to consume, where to consume, what choices they can make and how they can express them. Government providers collect and analyse information coming from consumers, and returns information to them in the course of providing those services.

Service provision

The vast bulk of the effort, investment and expertise that has been put into electronic government has been devoted to service provision and the back-office processing required to make it possible (Pratchett, 1999; Bellamy and Taylor, 1998; Heeks, 1999). Because the most visible part of what government does, and the part that most people care about most, at least in the short term, is the service operation, this makes eminent political sense. From the commercial point of view of the supply industry, this also makes sense because there are more interactions in service provision than in democratic and governance activity that call for hardware and software, and which represent profitable opportunities; moreover, the service provision functions are those which are most similar to the operations of the private sector, enabling the supply industry to adapt existing products and expertise more easily. However, because much of the investment and development of systems was made during the 'reinvention' period of the 1980s and early 1990s when functional organisation was being reinforced, the result was that government today has a set of legacy information systems that were designed for functionally organised service provision, not for integration. Because government departments, authorities and agencies do not have the resources to write off legacy systems and replace them with the speed and apparent casualness that large publicly quoted commercial corporations able to raise capital easily on global stock and bond markets can, governments around the world have tried wherever possible to pursue the informational part of the integration agenda by bolting on integration tools over the top of functional systems, but in ways that will allow them gradually to adapt the transaction processing systems as the resources become available to invest in newer, more flexible systems.

A good example of this is the initiative by the British government's Central Information Technology Unit, located in the Cabinet Office at the heart of central government, to develop a tool that will enable citizens to enter a change of address once, but the software will then update all the different departmental databases which hold records on that individual. This is far from a simple tool. For each department records the basic name and address information in different ways. Some use initials for first names, some use initials only for second and third names. Some hold the street and the town in separate fields; others combine them into a single field. Then there are the issues of how persons with similar or even identical names are handled. The updating software has to hold a great deal of information about how different departmental systems work, and needs to hold a large set of rules for the transformation of the information provided in the single format by the citizen into the formats required by each department or agency. Because many government services related to entitlements and many are applied coercively, errors could have vast consequences – the wrong person being charged a sum in tax, the wrong parent's children being taken into care, personal information being inadvertently divulged to someone else of the same name or similar address, and so on. These risks weigh heavily on the minds of the users, and, not surprisingly, of the British Data Protection Commissioner (as the Registrar became on the delayed implementation in 2000 of the 1998 Data Protection Act).

The alternative strategies to this can easily be imagined and described, but much less easily enforced and afforded, or, indeed, made legitimate with the public. In order to avoid the risks of error, one might specify a single set of data standards in great detail to which all central government departmental, agency, local authority, National Health Service and other databases would have to conform. All legacy systems would be redesigned, new fields created and old fields deleted, and each record changed, checked for errors on being changed, and loaded into new systems. Then, the change of address data collected from the single point of access for the public would fit exactly into the centrally defined data structures required of and used by every part of the public sector. If this were feasible at all, it would be prohibitively expensive, would probably tend to create as many new errors as it eliminated old ones, given the error rate of data entry clerks and data checking programmes; it would also take many years. Moreover this would have the effect of requiring many departments and agencies to use a system that was designed, not for their needs, but for an aggregate conception of the needs of a typical public agency. In those cases where the mismatch was greatest would be the ones where there would be the greatest risk that the agency would, in frustration, develop a separate data system that did not conform to the central standards, and gradually the system might begin to be eroded.

An even more extreme alternative might be to construct a single central database on the entire population and on all businesses, and each department, agency or authority would have to use it, rather than create their own. The popular concern about privacy, centralisation and fear of abuse of power this would raise would surely make it politically impossible, whether those popular fears are well grounded or not. Technically, it would also be very difficult to design and use, given that in any one second of time, a great many agencies might be trying to access and add or change data in the very same citizen's or business's record.

Both centralisation of standards and centralisation of data holdings, then, create difficulties, and therefore the overlaying of an integrated public point of access which will then interface, albeit riskily, with the functionally separated systems, represents a reasonable second best solution. Perhaps there is a case for centralisation of standards for at least some simple 'tombstone' data needed in not very differing forms by most if not all service provision agencies, but designed to come into force on a target date some years into the future to enable all agencies to prepare their investment and development programmes in time.

Across most of the world there is now a core vision of where information integrated service provision should be moving. The heart of the vision is the single point of access for the consumer. Instead of having to know how to deal with many local, regional, national, state and federal agencies for each of the many aspects of their problem as they are broken down by

function, the consumer will deal with a one-stop shop, either by voice telephone to an integrated service call centre, or on screen through the tiny
WAP screen on a mobile phone, on the World Wide Web through a personal computer, or on a dedicated channel through a digital television.
Where citizens need to demonstrate their identity, they will be able to do
so securely and instantaneously using a digital signature, perhaps stored on
a smart card (6 *et al.*, 2000). The consumer will, either by speaking or key-
ing plain text, or else by choosing from an intuitively written menu, identify their situation, their problem, the type of person they are, the outcome
they want, the episode in their life that gives rise to a need for contacting
public services – falling ill, being bereaved, giving birth, becoming unemployed, moving house.

The software system will identify, using as few additional questions to
the consumer as possible, the entire range of public services that may be
relevant, including ones that the consumer herself may not have thought of
but may be either required or useful, and will package them together
through a common application, passing information on to each of the back
offices as appropriate. If the consumer needs to make a payment of a tax
bill or a charge, then she can do so either by interfacing with her on-line
bank account and demonstrating that the authorisation has been made
(using a digital signature on a smart card to perform the same job on line
as a cheque offline) by informing the government agency of the authorisation number, or for some small sums, by using digital cash stored in a
smart card. The back office systems of the various departments and agencies will be fully capable of interfacing seamlessly with the single point of
access software, and for many routine matters they will be able to return
information, authorisation, even digital money, immediately to the consumer in the same on-line session. Where claiming or accessing one service affects entitlement or duty to contact another, the software system will
manage this automatically, but giving control to the consumer as far as
possible over how this is done. Where the consumer needs to provide an
agency with a piece of information about herself that is already held by a
different body in order to demonstrate some characteristic necessary for
entitlement, she will be able to give permission for it to be shared.
Passports, driving licences, and other permissions could be downloaded
directly onto a smart card. Money will be downloaded onto another smart
card or directly into a bank account, by enabling interfacing not only
within the public sector, but also with the mainstream commercial banking
transfer, payment and redemption systems. The heart of the vision is that
the software will enable consumers to integrate government for themselves
in a fully personalised manner. It is this aspiration that runs through the

Conservative administration's green paper, *government.direct* (Chancellor of the Duchy of Lancaster, 1996), and the Labour government's white paper, *Modernising government* (Prime Minister and Minister for the Cabinet Office, 1999), a vast plethora of think-tank reports (e.g., Lawson, 1998), many local authority and agency strategy papers, ministerial speeches (e.g., McLeish, 1999) and the strategy documents of many governments around the world, often available on their web sites. At federal level in the US the Vice President's National Partnership for Reinventing Government (formerly the National Performance Review) has produced a series of vision and strategy documents inspired by this commitment, and have developed a number of joint initiatives with state, including those under the Access America and Hassle-free Communities programmes.

Technologically, there is nothing in the vision that requires software solutions which do not yet exist, or basic technological breakthroughs that have not yet been achieved. But of course it does not follow that therefore the vision can be implemented straightforwardly.

Despite the sales pitches of many supplier companies, it is only true to a limited extent that governments can substitute integration at the 'front end' – the face government presents to the consumer of public services – for integration at the 'back end', that is, between agencies, departments and authorities. The choice is a false one: governments have to do both at the same time. There is a long-standing trope in debates about technology by which technologists hope to substitute a technical fix for a social problem: first openly proclaimed by a famous physicist as possible in the immediate post-war years (Weinberg, 1997 [1972])), and often discredited on particular cases, the trope is eternal although today the advocacy of this claim is usually much subtler. But social problems always require renegotiating relationships between human beings, their interests, their institutions, their ways of thinking about the world, and none of these are readily amenable to being passively changed simply in response to the forms of social organisation embedded implicitly in any technology. Rather, technology is shaped, used, selected, undermined by the people who invest in it, use it, refuse to use it in the ways instructed by their superiors, and so on (Schwarz and Thompson, 1990; Bijker and Law, 1992; Mackenzie and Wacjman, 1985).

To see the central importance of this point, consider first the case of the call centre or the physical one-stop shop, both of which may be transitional technologies, but which will remain important for at least a decade and almost certainly much longer. In Riverborough, the Alberton Centre was not a call centre, but a walk in centre, although it also handled a great many telephone enquiries. This was considered by staff, managers and politicians to be a success. Necessarily, however, the front line staff were generalists. Inevitably, their knowledge of any particular service was limited and some consumers who used the one-stop shop and who might well have known which functional specialist service they needed, would find the one-stop shop generalists only an additional hurdle to get over before reaching the expertise they needed. The one-stop shop was created as a local authority operation, but in many cases, staff there found themselves working with respect to their colleagues in the functional departments in ways that were more akin to the ways in which a case worker in a Citizen's Advice Bureau or a law centre would work. That is, they had to work as advocates. Staff in functional departments would not necessarily be helpful. Because departments were not necessarily geared up to coordinate with each other, for example, on the appropriate sequencing of the delivery of their respective services to a particular consumer, the one-stop shop staff had to lobby, cajole, persuade, plead and threaten referral of the client to outside agencies, if departments would not agree to the coordination they proposed. Advocacy work in one-stop shops is not necessarily a bad thing. But it does demonstrate that behind the integration at the front-end, the linkages were difficult fully to organise, both between the integrated point of consumer access and each of the functional departments, as well as between the various back offices.

Moving away from the human generalist staff integrator to the software generalist integrator does not remove all of these problems. On the contrary, it places even more demands upon the integration with and between the 'back offices'. Functional information systems need to interface with the software in a seamless, standardised way. Moreover, there need to be developed protocols that handle mutual recognition when different departments or agencies have stored an individual's name or address differently, and real time common error checking and updating protocols are needed to deal with the situation where one agency holds records with, say, an out-of-date address or a previous name that does not tally with the records of another agency, but where each must coordinate its service with the other. Since a complete set of rules cannot possibly be devised in advance to deal with every eventuality, there must always be the possibility of recourse to a human staff member with authority to unblock a situation, and this requires relationships between agencies to have been developed at some appropriate level, as in the spectrum in Figure 2.6 in Chapter 2, for that staff member to be able to do her work effectively.

The greatest challenge for seamless electronic service delivery remains the division between local and centrally accountable public services. This illustrates well that the problems of electronic integration of government are political, not technological, in nature. Local government is often under-standably nervous of central government's commitment to holism being extended to cover their terrain, for local government officials often fear that seamless integration with the centre will mean a further loss of auton-omy, which would be politically unacceptable even if consumers, who are also voters, do not benefit from that autonomy. In many cases, where gov-ernment has sought access to the data sets held by local authorities – for example, to gather evidence in cases of suspected benefit fraud – they have required changes in primary legislation to do so, including changes to pri-vacy and data protection laws, and there has been resistance to such legis-lation from local authorities as well as from civil liberties groups. The hostile feelings of the locality to the centre are also sometimes returned. Until very recently, central government in Britain was very reluctant to grant local authorities access to the Government Secure Intranet (GSI) sys-tem, which offers a wide range of security and integration features. In gen-eral, conversely, British local authorities have no right of access to data on persons who may be their own clients, where those data are the property of a central government department, although there are some special exemp-tions for fraud control.

Moreover, and fundamentally, the software integrator that sits above the functional systems must be managed by some agency, wholly dedicated or otherwise, who can be held to account for its performance, design and management failings, in which the ownership of the assets is vested. This cannot come about without integration at the back office level, up to and typically including the policy-making level. In this sense, integration at the front end, or the consumer interface is dependent upon at least coordina-tion and in many cases integration at the back end, or in the policy and management systems of all those to be affected by the system (for the dis-tinction between coordination and integration, see Figure 2.6 in Chapter 2).

Nevertheless, as we have argued throughout this book (and see espe-cially Chapter 10), a key issue for the institutionalisation of holistic work-ing remains the commitment of the centre to it. In the field of electronic service provision, this was, at least until recently, clear and palpable in many countries. It was therefore rather surprising when in 2000 Britain's new Labour government took a step that seemed to suggest that their com-mitment to seamless electronic service provision was wavering or even being reduced. In the late autumn of that year, the long range policy research group, the Performance and Innovation Unit, which reports to the Prime Minister, and whose reports reflect centrally agreed policy, pub-lished and secured a great deal of press coverage for its report on electronic service delivery, entitled '*E-gov*' (Performance and Innovation Unit, 2000).

That report announced the creation of an 'incubator' for new electronic service delivery projects, following the current fashionable style of business venture capital financing, start-up support and development in the private sector. However, and despite the rhetoric in the report about the continuing commitment to seamlessness and joined-up government, the report also made it clear that the focus of the incubator would be the encouragement of new initiatives that would be entirely separate from the mainstream programmes of service provision, indeed designed to bypass the mainstream, and the emphasis seemed to be entirely on separate development of these as stand-alone services. The inconsistency with the official commitment to holism is, although denied in government, quite clear. It remains to be seen, therefore, how in practice the incubator will work, and whether other institutional forces for holistic working will be sufficiently strong to outweigh the potentially re-fragmenting effect of such a brief.

Governance

Here we are concerned with policy coordination using digital means at the level of governance, which we can characterise for the present purpose as including digital support for policy-making, decision-making, group work between ministers and their juniors, senior civil servants working on policy formulation, development and management, and with those privileged few policy advisors outside who are contracted to provide confidential policy support, and their equivalents at regional and local levels.

   Much less investment has gone into this area, and academics have also devoted much less study to it (Kraemer and Dedrick, 1997). Yet many of the first applications of information technology in government were in fact to support cross-governmental budget planning, and in the second half of the 1980s the availability of cheap personal computers and spreadsheet software represented a major boost to budgetary coordination across departments at both local and national levels (6, 2000b,c; 2001). In the same period in France, integrated financial tools were in use in many local authorities for policy coordination of a much greater sophistication than anything in use in the UK until recently (Klein, Roux and Villedieu, 1991). In the 1980s most digital support for policy-making, however, was commissioned, designed, used and organised on a functional basis. Expert systems, models and simulations were developed for functionally defined purposes. A partial exception might be the articulation of economic models by the British Treasury and by finance ministries in many countries that could be accessed by government economists working anywhere in the public service; however, there was little effort to coordinate the actual uses of these economic models across government. Similarly, policy tools for document flow analysis in development of policy were typically within departments rather than across departments, although there was nothing in the technology that specifically called for this (Prinz and Syri, 1997). Intranets, which could at least in principle be an important tool for policy integration, came into general government use during the first few years of the 1990s. While take-up was high in some fields of government and especially in local government, actual use was of a limited subset of the features of such systems. In many departments and authorities, intranets were often used as little more than over-engineered internal e-mail systems (Comptroller and Auditor General, 1999). Off-the-peg groupware such as Lotus Notes is used in some parts of government – and is a major commitment in reinvention programmes in states such as Victoria, Australia (see <http://www.mmv.vic.gov.au/>) – but these systems are too often only used for very simple shared data requirements such as external contact management. There is now a wide range of e-governance tools which could be used to support more integration, including group decision support systems, idea generation tools, graphical problem structuring tools, meeting management tools, argumentation and deliberation support tools, neural nets for modelling and simulation of policy problems, expert system tools, knowledge management tools for document profiling and flow tracking, mental map analysis and presentation, organisational memory capture, hypermedia data organisation tools (such as those used for geographical information systems (GIS)) (see 6, 2000b,c; 2001, for a discussion and review of the literature).

Again, it is clear that the key determinants of whether these technologies are used for policy integration or within functional boundaries are political, rather than technological, and that where they are used in integrative ways, the scope for substituting technological fixes for political solutions to the barriers to integration is very limited. Consider, for example, the experience of using the Decision Conferencing method (Phillips, 1990; Wood *et al.*, 1998) using computer based modelling support in British local government budget setting (Morgan, 1993). One leading information systems company in the UK has for some years offered decision conferencing facilitation and software to local authority elected members and senior managers to assist in the budget process and in other forms of strategic decision-making, and has explicitly set out to use the process and the software to help politicians and public managers think more imaginatively about budget options, to identify linkages, to develop whole systems thinking, to clarify trade-off(s) involved in decision-making. The tool – that is, the combination of the group process structure, the facilitation skills and software – could readily be used to enable holistic budgeting by outcomes, or at least to conduct traditional input-based line-item budgeting in ways that support and offer incentives for integration. However, most of the uses reported at least in the UK have been for decision-making within departments, or for functionally structured budget making. This is a choice dictated not by restrictions or implicit judgments in the design of the technique or by the available software, but by the political commitments of most of those local politicians who use it. Decision conferencing is one of the more flexible systems: there are, by contrast, many less flexible tools the design of which does assume completely functional organisation on the part of the user's client organisation.

By contrast with their investment in integrated consumer interface systems for public services, both governments and the information technology industry have devoted rather low levels of resource to developing tools and strategies for holistic policy work. If, however, our argument is accepted, that it is a mistake to imagine that one can substitute joining up at the front end for at least coordination at the back end, then this will be a serious limitation in the development of an electronic government agenda to support holistic governance.

In some measure, as we saw in earlier chapters, behind the agenda for holistic governance is an aspiration to increase the level of coherence in decision-making. It is this that the fatalists regard as futile. We now need to ask whether the trend toward more electronic government at the levels of service provision and of governance, even if information systems are successfully designed to support holism, will in fact support this increased rationality? As we have argued above, of course, the holistic governance agenda does not imply or require any ideal of synoptic rationality, the impossibility of which is one of the most robust findings in the social science of decision-making. What it does require, we argued in Chapter 2, is only the more modest capacity to identify as wide a range of factors influencing and shaping wicked problems as are discernible within the prevailing constraints of knowledge, institutions and networks, and the willingness – if only under the pressure of crises – to exploit this implicit modelling work for some coordination or integration initiative. The planning horizon may be quite short; the decision criteria may, and typically will, exhibit all the signs of satisficing; the process of exercising diplomatic skills in negotiation to build the relationships with other agencies may and typically resemble 'muddling through' and partisan mutual adjustment as described by Lindblom (1959). Yet the aspirations and commitments behind all this may nevertheless reflect an attempt to be, if not ideally or fully rational, at least marginally more policy rational than some of the alternatives – business as usual, cutting deals just to keep agencies alive come what may, empty manipulation of symbols in the pretence of programme delivery. That we know the best to be impossible is undeniable; what does *not* follow from this is the fatalist conclusion that therefore we know in advance that all efforts to be more effective are futile. The question about electronic information systems therefore is, how far does the evidence about their introduction and use in governance suggest that they are capable of being used to support even modest melioration in rationality?

Broadly, there are four types of theory on offer about the potential impact on governance of the use of these systems. Each theory can be treated as one possible future scenario for understanding the potential impact of e-governance.

First, there are those who argue uncompromisingly that the use of these technologies represents a major once-for-all improvement in the capabilities of governance and in at least the possibility of rationality in decision-making (e.g., Tapscott, 1997). The only price that this improvement comes at is in the cost of investment and the running costs. Indeed, from this point of view, these systems reduce the costs of acquiring, ordering, coding, organising, selecting, managing and using information steadily over time. Therefore, the initial investment costs will more than pay for themselves over the life time of the systems (this is argued by, for example, Reschenthaler and Thompson, 1996). This optimistic view is based on the classical cybernetic theory (Wiener, 1948) that information is control, or more exactly, that (borrowing Overman and Loraine's 1994 summary),

- information decreases uncertainty;
- information slows entropy; and
- information increases system control (decrease variance) by feedback and deviation correction, and, in general that more information enables more control (or at least up to a point that we have not yet reached, if the relationship between information and control is conceived as curvilinear).

It is fair to say that, at least in its canonical form, this cybernetic assumption is basically still an article of faith, and all of the rival accounts either qualify it or reject it outright. If such critics of the holistic governance agenda as Challis *et al.* (1988) were correct, that coordination and integration is a hyper-rationalistic project, which requires the possibility of synoptically rational planning, then it would follow that holists would have to be committed to the rationalisation theory of e-governance. However, as we have seen, this is not necessary.

The second group of theories are those that accept at least the possibility of greater control, quality and rationality in decision-making, but insist that this comes at a price. The main theories in this group accept that there will or may be modest increases in policy-maker control and grounded decisions but, at least without a great deal of effort to put safeguards in place, that improvement in decision-making will or may be itself compromised by damage to:

- citizens' individual liberty and privacy;
- citizens' collective (democratic) influence over governmental decisions (Raab, 1997);
- politicians' control over decision-making agenda in favour of civil servants or officers' 'infocracy' (Zuurmond, 1998) or an oligopoly of private contractors (Margetts and Dunleavy, 1995); and/or
- civil servants' capability to exercise constraint upon populism of politicians.

A variant of this tradition acknowledges the possibility of increased short-term technical rationality of decision-making but at the expense of long-term substantive rationality and the humaneness of decision-making that admits a place for affect. On this view, e-governance is the final arrival of Max Weber's 'iron cage of rationality' (Weber, 1958, 1976; van de Donk, 1998). These theories essentially share the cybernetic theorists' conception of information as control, but want to stress the darker sides of control. The most extreme version of this view is perhaps that of the 'governmentality' theorists who follow the thesis of the later Foucault in arguing that government technologies and rationalities – including e-governance – tools have become steadily more invasive through their extension of knowledge and information about populations, and their exercise has produced systems of socialisation that have steadily shaped citizens into ever more docile subjects of authority (Burchell, Gordon and Miller, 1991; Barry, Osborne and Rose, 1996; Dean, 1999).

The third view is the most pessimistic. This argues that e-governance will actually reduce the quality of decision-making. It points to a range of pathologies of excessive demand for policy analysis. These include delaying action or 'paralysis by analysis', the bloating out of the policy advice industries among think-tanks and consultancy firms, the problems of sheer information overload, the allegedly lesser ability of the public sector to manage information as well as private citizens or businesses. This view also emphasizes the dangers of the obsession with the already measured that distracts policy-makers' attention away from tacit, implicit, qualitative, unstructured factors and towards formal, explicit, quantitatively measured, structured factors and information. Finally, and perhaps most crucially, this theory warns that, due to mechanical rule following as suggested by overly simple data interpretations, overly simple modelling, and by overly simple expert system flows from analysis to recommendation, the cultivation and the exercise of judgment in decision-making will be crowded out. This view wholly rejects the cybernetic faith that information is control, and prefers the trope of information as noise.

The fourth and final cluster of theories argue that there will be no very fundamental and independent impact of technology itself on technical or political rationality of decision-making. According to this view, both continuities and changes in governance are driven socially and politically, not by technology itself. Technologies are means by which styles of governance are changed or preserved, in broadly two styles of the social shaping of technology (Mackenzie and Wacjman, 1985; Bijker, 1997; Bijker and Law, 1992):

- *'conservative' social and political shaping*: political systems (decision-making units may be whole national governments, departments, agencies, authorities, and so forth) select technologies, use technologies, innovate with use of technologies, to preserve their existing patterns of governance, leadership and decision-making; and/or
- *'radical' social and political shaping*: political systems (decision-making units may be whole national governments, departments, agencies, authorities, and so on) use the occasion of opportunities for investment in technologies, select technologies, use technologies, innovate with use of technologies, to make changes they would want to make anyway, to their existing patterns of governance, leadership and decision-making.

Figure 7.1 summarises some of the key differences between the theories.

Each theory has some empirical support, although most empirical studies have been of rather limited scope and not in general designed to test, let alone falsify, these rival theories.

Sifting the evidence on the impact of e-governance

It is relatively straightforward to obtain evidence that appears to support the control theory if one limits oneself to asking no-longer-new, now familiarised decision-making users about their satisfaction with a particular technology. For example, a study of the implementation of a system to support Norwegian local politicians, which provided an integrated graphical

Figure 7.1   *Theories of e-governance at a glance*

Theory	Rationalisation	Rationalisation at a price	Loss of rationality	Social shaping
information as	control (positive)	control (negative)	noise	totem
public management style	integration	integration	fragmentation	depends on balance of forces
planning style	anticipation	anticipation	resilience	depends on balance of forces
power shift	to policy-makers	captured by special interests	undermining power	depends on balance of forces

user interface for managing phone calls, conference calls, faxes, e-mails and electronic document interchange (EDI) found that the participating local politicians and policy officers found it useful (Ytterstad and Watson, 1996). However, such findings need to be read with care. As people tend to engage in rationalisation and cognitive dissonance reduction, they will tend to report that the technology provides them with valuable information and with greater control, when infact they have simply adopted their way of working to the design of the technology. (For one of many surveys of this kind, see Hasan and Hasan, 1997: this examined Australian local government officers' use of some e-governance systems.)

We now turn to the evidence for the theory of information as rationalisation but at a price. One price of rationalisation commonly alleged in theoretical writings is that decisions that ought to be the subject of judgment and deliberation are reduced through the use of e-governance tools to the operation of algorithms. There is some evidence that decisions that can be treated in this way are pushed down the hierarchy of decision-makers as soon as they are subjected to automation, and they can cease to be regarded as policy matters at all (Bugler and Bretschneider, 1993). But this is not always the case. For decisions about monetary policy were treated in this way in some countries during the years of high monetarism in the 1980s, but since then most of the automatic correction mechanisms based on available economic indicators have been abandoned, and with the adoption of direct inflation targets, deliberation and judgment has returned to this area of policy-making, even though the responsibility for conducting that deliberation and making those judgments has often been handed from politicians to central bankers.

One variant of the loss of quality theory is the widespread finding in the research on performance management and audit that the focus on quantitatively measurable dimensions leads policy-makers to neglect the less easily measured aspects of public services, public goals and public management (e.g., Power, 1997).

While this first category of rationalisation at a price theory focuses on the loss of quality of decisions, other theories within this category accept that the use of, for example, expert systems, can improve the quality of decision-making. However, they suggest that the decision makers may be less committed to decisions they make when they follow the reasoning and suggestions of such a system. This was the finding of a recent experiment using expert systems (Landbergen *et al.*, 1997). One might argue that use of such systems over time – which no experiment can explore – would increase confidence. However, if as, the experimenters themselves think, the loss of confidence and commitment in decisions made in this way is related to a feeling on the part of decision makers that they have less control and understanding of their decisions, and in part because expert systems offer a wider range of options and alternatives than traditional forms of policy analysis often do, then it could be a more enduring feature of e-governance. The effect can be mitigated by providing decision makers with access to, and explanations of, the workings of the underlying model, and this does seem to increase confidence. However, this is not possible with many neural net based systems, which do not work, as expert systems do, by developing models on the basis of pre-programmed rules, but which work inductively.

Nedovic-Budic and Godschalk (1996) found some evidence for a modest increase in rationality at the price of providing individual decision-makers with more personal benefits than were achieved for the organisation in improved rationality of decision-making (for a similar conclusion, see also Berry, Berry and Foster, 1998). Only a few recent studies have attempted to study perceived benefits and costs of new information systems in the same framework, and have used these data as evidence for the rationalisation at a price theory. One recent sociological review argued that 'virtualisation within organisations can result in the progressive formalisation of social relationships which, while genuinely increasing the levels of participation, can erode the sense of meaningfulness and value of that participation in decision-making' (Wilson, 1999). Sometimes norms, customs, rules, roles, practices that have been used successfully in face-to-face settings or settings where policy-makers principally use the telephone for communication will be carried over into settings where they begin to use computer-supported groupware for making decisions. This was the finding of a study of a network of British general practitioners in the National Health Service who began to exchange information about a range of practice management, prescribing, purchasing and health policy issues in which they were involved (Fox and Roberts, 1999). This finding seems to be explained by the particular institutional setting within which the on-line network was embedded. But it cannot be assumed in advance that this transfer will occur automatically. One study attempted to test for such changes by predicting what roles a group of people in an experiment would play in such a setting, based on how they behaved in face-to-face groupwork, and what roles they would want to delegate to the software, and then compared these predictions with roles observed. The main finding was that people played fewer roles than expected, and that at least some – but, to the surprise of the experiment designers, relatively few – participants described the software as playing the role of recording the group memory and monitoring procedure, and a few saw the software as group facilitator and motivator (Zigurs and Kozar, 1994). It may be that, unlike the medical case, the institutional setting within which the experiment was embedded was simply too thin to provide existing norms that could be carried over. It is very difficult in designing experiments of this kind, and even in designing studies in working organisations, to avoid Hawthorne effects, and so it is hard to know what weight to put on such results.

If there are changes in norms, customs, practices associated with moving to computer supported decision-making among policy-makers, that may at first sight provide evidence for the rationalisation at a price theory, we should be alive to the possibility that what is really taking place is radical social shaping. That is to say, the introduction of new technologies into groups of decision makers is also being used as the occasion and the opportunity for making other changes that superior decision makers want to make. Indeed, the conventional management literature argues that this is exactly what good managers should do with technology, in order to avoid wasting investment on automating bad old ways of doing things (see, for example, Hammer and Champy, 1995). There is an extensive body of work that shows that where superior decision makers use the opportunity to introduce more control, surveillance and accountability upon the work of lower decision makers, the technology is experienced as introducing rationalisation at the price of discretion, autonomy and freedom of action (Overman and Loraine, 1994; Hayes and Walsham, 2000; Shapiro *et al.*, 1991). Academic researchers, being peculiarly sensitive to threats to their own intellectual freedom, may often be more sympathetic to claims to autonomy in decision-making by other groups than, for example, national politicians or national civil servants, and this can lead them to represent social shaping of certain kinds – whether conservative or radical relative to institutional starting points chosen for the period of a study – as rationali-sation at a price. However, many of the findings support the view that pro-jects for radical social shaping of decision systems typically provoke counter-shaping projects of a more conservative or differently radical nature (and *vice versa*), because users are ingenious in using such systems for their own private benefits, subverting the intentions of superior deci-sion makers who may be seen likewise as shaping the technology as much for their private ends as for organisational goals (Shapiro *et al.*, 1991).

In general, the loss of rationality theory seems overstated. The move towards the reduction of arbitrary administrative discretion by street level bureaucrats in public service decision-making about individual entitle-ments such as cash benefits (Snellen, 1998), has not been the thin end of the wedge for the substitution of automated decision-making in policy judgment, or the final coming of Weber's (1958) 'iron cage' of bureau-cratic rationality. Despite the burgeoning investment by governments in the technologies listed above, there is little evidence of policy-makers in finance ministries or land use planning departments following wholesale and mechanically the recommendations that are cranked out casually for them by junior staff from crude software models.

Much of the evidence for the noise theory of information comes not so much from studies of use of computers by policy-makers, as from studies of accountability in public management. Successive studies of the actual use made of performance indicators – which are, of course, now typically collected, coded, submitted, analysed, collated, and now published elec-tronically – have found that much of the information is not read, not used at all, or provides more complex pictures than those who hold public ser-vices to account really want or think-that they need (Carter, Klein and Day, 1993; Grønbjerg, 1993; Heinrich, 1999). But again, this reading of these findings is not uncontested. Many recent commentators looking at audit and accountability mechanisms in the public sector see these as evidence for the totem theory – namely, that rituals of accountability are being per-formed, symbols displayed, without necessarily achieving the substance of control (Hogwood, Judge and McVicar, 1998; Power, 1997). One impor-tant substantive effect of the development of e-governance tools princi-pally to handle quantitative information, these theories would suggest, has been a reallocation of that the scarcest resource in government, namely policy-makers' attention to problems (March and Olsen, 1976), to those problems that lend themselves to highly formal treatment. Had there been, for example, greater development and use in government of charting, creativity and soft systems methodology tools (Checkland and Scholes, 1990; Checkland, 1989; Ballantine and Cunningham, 1999), which have developed some of the ideas of the late great Sir Geoffrey Vickers (Checkland, 1994; Vickers, 1995) attention to problems might be allocated rather differently, but that selection of technologies would only have taken place had the institutional pressures upon policy-makers been rather different.

Again, if a different set of questions is asked than those asked by many studies that find satisfaction with growing control about coping with workload then because of implicit suggestion in the phrasing of a question (for example, using leading phrases that hint at 'information overload'), one typically gets data that can be used to support the noise theory of information.

Historical and ethnographic work on long-run usage by policy-makers of information technologies tends to provide more support for the totem theory (see Nidumolu *et al.*, 1996), as does some survey work with different design (for instance, Overman and Loraine, 1994). Ethnographic research on the use of e-mail provides further good evidence that all projects for social shaping provoke counter projects. Romm (1999) shows that even supposedly 'simple' and 'low bandwidth' technology like e-mail does not greatly constrain its users; Lee (1994) shows that the real 'bandwidth' of information yielded is as much as function of interpretation, implicit and tacit knowledge as of technical characteristics of the medium. For it is used by rival groups, subaltern and superior, and horizontally opposed factions, to their own ends: Romm shows that each exploits certain features of the technology – multiple addressing, recordability, processing and routing – to pursue their own goals. In this sense, e-mail merely reminds us of the longstanding finding in organisation studies that the flows of power, information and knowledge in organisations almost never follow the official organisation chart (see, for instance, Scott, 1992). E-mail does not deepen or exacerbate these informal networks of power and information, but merely provides them with new means to pursue their particular goals. This suggests that the hypothesis that because of e-mail, certain groups of policy-makers will gain power at the expense of others, because they are gaining control (rationalisation, perhaps at a price) – perhaps local chairs at the expense of leaders, or ministers at the expense of premiers, or civil servants at the expense of politicians generally – should be rejected. The technology is almost certainly not responsible. Rather, people use technologies as occasions, foils, symbols, tools, ritual objects, to develop and institutionalise the forms of solidarity they are committed to.

How are these theories to be appraised? Is there a straightforward choice to be made between them to favour one that is correct or at least not yet falsified? Or are they reconcilable – perhaps by allocating them to different domains or else to different levels of explanation?

There are differences between theories in the explanatory level at which they work. Social science distinguishes between variables that are close to the phenomenon they purport to explain – proximate variables – and those which are at some explanatory distance, working at deeper levels, not necessarily observable. For example, the control theory works with proximate variables – individual decision makers' satisfaction, their sense of efficacy and control in their work, collective action capabilities of groups of decision makers. The noise theory is basically the converse of this – focusing on decision makers sense of being overwhelmed. By contrast, the totem theory works with distal variables – institutions, symbols, meanings, ritual formations, group identities and the ways in which they shape group interests. Indeed, the totem or social shaping theory can be used to offer an institutional explanation of the phenomena to which the control, rationalisation at a price and noise theories point, as if they were data rather than explanations. Only in this restricted sense can the theories be reconciled. Correlatively, whereas the control and noise theories can be tested in large part through classical survey, interview and behavioural observation techniques, the totem or social shaping theory calls for quite different kinds of research to test it – it would require ethnographic work of a high degree of sophistication. The rationalisation at a price or dark side of control theories are a mixed bag. Some are social shaping theories *manqué*, because they assert that social shaping by one group will dominate, no matter what counter shaping is provoked. Others – such as governmentality theory or 'iron cage' models that move beyond capture to look at whole society dynamics – are closer to totemic institutionalist theories in their use of distal variables, but close to the control theory in their central claim that technology is itself a major causal force.

The central problem in using empirical studies to test the power of these theories, then, seems to be that if one sets the standards of what counts as 'control', 'noise' and 'totem' sufficiently high or low, then almost any empirical work one could design can be read as confirming any of the theories.

On balance, however, the theories that seem most worth considering seriously are the rationalisation at a price theories, and the social shaping theories, but consideration of the evidence of the former suggests that the two are not necessarily wholly incompatible. The social shaping account may a deeper explanation and a broader context of some of the phenomena given such weight by rationalisation at a price theories.

This is a qualifiedly optimistic conclusion, for it suggests that there is scope for making more intelligent use of e-governance tools to support the kind of 'whole systems' thinking required for holistic policy making. E-governance will not deliver synoptic rationality, of course, but it can be used to support modest initiatives in sustaining political judgement as a style of decision-making that gives some recognition to the full range of biases. Indeed, some tools can be used to model the relationships between the biases for policy-makers engaged in holistic working.

Integration and privacy

Holistic governance or service integration often creates pressures for the sharing of personal information between departments, agencies and authorities that have long been prohibited from sharing such information, on grounds of privacy. Is there then an irreconcilable tension between holistic governance and information privacy? (The following discussion draws upon that in 6, 1998c.)

For much of the post-war era, many people have fondly imagined that the most effective protection for their privacy *vis-à-vis* government was the inefficiency, poor coordination and weak data management of the public sector. Therefore, the hobbling of authorities' data sharing activity by regulation may have reduced efficiency and effectiveness, but this was widely considered in the post-war climate to be an acceptable price to pay for privacy and for reducing the possibilities for the abuse of power by agencies in the welfare state. Today, however, far fewer people are content with this trade-off, and many of us want both effectiveness and privacy. The holistic governance agenda has challenged many of these information 'firewalls' between parts of the public sector. The development of contracting out of services during the 'reinvention' era also raised new questions about how far private commercial and voluntary non-profit agencies should be sharing data with each other, with government bodies, and conversely, how far they should be permitted to access data held by public authorities.

For example, there are growing demands for more matching and mining across departmental boundaries to detect fraud. A number of pieces of recent legislation in the UK have removed firewalls that limited the authority of fraud detection staff from requiring information to be divulged from any part of the public sector. The best known is the 1997 Social Security Administration (Fraud) Act, which explicitly permits data matching and mining that would otherwise be of very doubtful legality. The 2001 Social Security fraud bill extends this approach even further. Indeed, before strenuous lobbying from the Data Protection Commissioner to persuade ministers to amend it, the bill proposed to remove almost all restrictions upon law enforcement bodies, tax and benefit authorities to engage in surveillance of people, simply on the basis that they fall into some category of people who have been found, as a group, to be disproportionately likely to commit benefit fraud. The amended act requires fraud investigators to be satisfied that there are reasonable prouds for thinking that the person to be investigated has committed or intends to commit fraud or is a family member of such a suspect.

The same issue arises in other contexts. For example, in the management of risks presented by convicted persons, joint co-ordinated arrangements between the probation service, relevant local authority departments, the police and others increasingly involve the sharing of 'soft' personal information (see guidance in Home Office *et al.*, 1995). While confidentiality is supposed to be maintained within the group of agencies sharing information and subject access is granted (Home Office *et al.*, 1995, paras 41–3), the kinds of information recorded and shared are very wide indeed, by comparison with the restrictions in data protection law for conventional situations: such official record-keeping on convicted persons is subject to a number of specific exemptions from data protection law.

Data matching is risky, because putting together profiles produced for different purposes can easily produce something which is misleading. For example, the same incident can be described differently for different purposes, and when the data are put together, it may look like two incidents.

In Eastwoodshire, for example, social services, education welfare, the police and later the local health authority agreed to pool data on children and young people at risk. The data were analysed using geo-demographic methods. This was considered a major success by the authority, and there is good reason to think that in terms of holistic governance, it was. It enabled much better targeting; it was linked to the introduction of generic case workers who could put together packages of services from across all the agencies involved in the partnership. However, at the time of our interviews, the managers were in protracted talks with the Data Protection Registrar, as she still was then, and had not secured registration for their database. There were rules in place about who within the partnership could see fully identified data, who could see only anonymised data, and care was being taken in data matching to minimise errors, because managers recognised that these could lead to disastrous outcomes if draconian decisions about care or arrest or other action were taken on the basis of incorrect information from inaccurate matching. A number of reports have been published from the project, some of which present maps of particular districts within the country, which are on a reasonably large scale, showing the location of young people at risk. Although roads and other landmarks are not shown on those maps, it might not be too difficult for someone with both determination and other maps of the districts to re-identify some of these households. Therefore, the Eastwoodshire experiment raises a number of issues of much wider significance.

As local authority social services departments increasingly experiment with matching and pooling data on children at risk in their areas, from sources across the authority and other public bodies such as health authorities, and using geo-demographic profiling methods, there is a real risk that draconian action in individual cases will be taken on the basis of mis-interpretation, simple mis-matching, or excessive reliance on models that predict risk of abuse inaccurately on the basis of apparently correlated characteristics. While many authorities are currently confining the decisions being made on the basis of such modelling exercises to matters of generic priorities in aggregate resource allocation, it is possible to see a natural line of development into decision-making in individual cases. Today, the data resources exist and the data handling techniques are available to local authority social services departments to develop risk indicators on individuals who have not even yet become parents turning into abusers of their own children. Decisions about keeping such persons under surveillance on the basis purely of such modelling exercises would raise privacy concerns about unjust inference as well as unwarranted intrusion and reversal of the presumption of innocence (Thomas, 1995).

Many partnerships and integration initiatives require more inter-professional decision-making. Whereas general medical practitioners have a code of confidentiality of a strictness that makes the consulting surgery the equivalent of the priestly confessional, police officers, social workers, housing managers and teachers have more relaxed principles about the situations in which disclosure of personal information about clients may be acceptable. Much of the information held by the police, social services and housing authorities on individuals takes the form of allegations, hints, suspicions and other 'soft' data. Traditionally, outside the police service which has specific exemptions, these soft data have been kept in manual systems precisely in order to escape the application of the Data Protection Act. The 1998 new legislation extended coverage to manual records. Agencies at the local level have very different codes and principles for the treatment of such data – including matters of recording, disclosures to third parties and subject access. This has been particularly difficult in connection with the recent furore about demands for community disclosure of information about the whereabouts and risk assessments of convicted paedophiles who have served their sentences and been released, or even of persons suspect but never actually convicted of child abuse. Information that was once confidential to a single agency may be kept from the public by that agency, but shared with another in a multi-agency programme, and then disclosed by that second agency which has very different confidentiality rules. The issue is especially sharp in connection with very soft information – unsubstantiated allegations, for example. Some professional bodies have issued guidance (for example, Chartered Institute of Housing, 1998), but there are no over-arching codes that cover all the agencies that might be involved in any holistic initiative. The risk from more holistic strategies of government is that pooled data on individuals who present risks will become subject to the lowest standards of the least self-regulated.

The urgent question in the present context is whether there is an unavoidable conflict between holism and privacy. Certainly, the official view of the British government is that there is no long-term conflict. For example, in the White Paper, *Modernising government* (Prime Minister and Minister for the Cabinet Office, 1999), the bold statement is made that privacy is not an 'obstacle' but an 'objective' of joined-up working, and the government commits itself to careful and detailed scrutiny of the privacy implications of its policies. At the time of writing, the Performance and Innovation Unit (or PIU), a long range policy research group within the Cabinet Office, reporting directly to the Prime Minister, was working on a major project to develop policy options to improve the compatibility between holistic government and privacy and to make recommendations for UK government policy. The report is expected to reaffirm the principle that privacy is fully compatible with holistic governance, and that it is indeed one of the goals. In addition to reaffirming the commitment to existing safeguards in data protection law and calling both for additional clarification of privacy rights and for new procedures to provide reassurance, the report is expected to identify a number of specific areas where further data sharing between agencies would be beneficial, both for mainstream and for socially excluded groups of citizens.

One major part of that study was a small scale piece of research (conducted by the lead author of this volume for the PIU) to examine the attitudes of several categories of people who are, whether they know or it, data subjects – that is to say, government agencies hold personal information about them. That study found that few could see many benefits in the government departments with which they had to deal sharing information about them between those departments, and many did not feel very strongly about those benefits. It is clear from studies of this kind that the public as a whole has not yet been persuaded of the benefits of data sharing. Some groups were very supportive of combating fraud, but even they wanted privacy safeguards to be institutionalised. The promise of holistic government, or the targeted provision of integrated services, was one in which most groups studied had little faith. When the lay public was studied, they themselves identified many of the risks listed above, and attached more emotion to them than they did to the benefits. Clearly, governments engaged in programmes to promote holistic working need to work hard to cultivate the support of citizens, and to reassure them about specific privacy issues. Often, of course, these privacy concerns are not specific to data sharing or initiatives in holistic governance, but are quite generic to the ways in which personal information is handled.

It is worth recalling that the protection afforded to privacy by firewalls around the functions by which government has been organised is not particularly impressive in its quality. For at the heart of data protection as a set of principles that have inspired legislation around the world is the concept of the purpose for which data are collected, stored and used. The firewall is supposed to be around that purpose, and can only be set aside for good reason – legitimate suspicion of involvement in crime, fraud, and so on. But the functionally defined purposes for data collection and use were always rather strained and occasionally quite bizarre when considered in the round as ways to define what people were to expect in exchange for their personal information. Firewalls in the way of information flow are essential to data protection, but it matters very much that they are in the right place. The holistic governance agenda is properly understood as suggesting better places to put them.

By the time the White Paper was published, one of us had already argued (6, 1998c) that the key question is not whether to permit data matching at all, but which data matching is acceptable, bearing in mind that keeping information within functional silos often did little for the *value* of privacy, and tended to become an exercise in following the letter of the law on those occasions where it suited officials to enforce it for other reasons, rather than its spirit. If it is possible to design guidance for single professions, single departments, single authorities on data protection, then it ought in principle to be possible, if a little more difficult, to design guidance to cover a wide variety of holistic initiatives. In 6 (1998c, chapter 18), some principles were set out that should cover data matching and mining and disclosures that should be embodied in a code of practice covering the whole of the public sector. These include the use of anonymous data wherever true identity is not necessary, rules against 'fishing expeditions' or unstructured blocking and pasting of data that might come in useful some day, clear grounds on which data matching is conducted, and greater clarity for the public about holistic and joined-up *purposes* for which data about individuals is collected, held and analysed, and, perhaps most important, constrained and defined rules of inference that govern how far matched and shared data can be used in making decisions about individual cases, proportionately to the intrusiveness and coerciveness of the powers to act that are in question in any decision.

Conclusion

In this chapter, we have shown that there are good reasons to think-that information and communications technologies can be used to support holistic working, but there is no independent factor called 'technology' that does this. Rather, to the extent that technologies are shaped, developed, commissioned, designed, used, misused, redesigned in use for this purpose, it is because there are social processes at work, which often take highly ritualised form, to support the kinds of political and policy judgment involved in holistic working.

The findings in this chapter support the larger argument of this book, that indeed holistic governance is demanding, but that there are at least some serious efforts being made to meet the challenge, especially at the level of electronic service provision. However, the development of electronic support remains weak for holistic policy-making. The theoretical argument of the chapter has suggested that the general fatalist case about the impacts of electronic government need not be accepted, although certainly there will always be cases of the sorts of futility to which fatalism points. Normatively, the holistic governance agenda raises ethical issues in connection with privacy that have so far only been addressed in a piecemeal manner. While it is wrong to conclude that privacy and holism cannot live together, working out ways in which they can be mutually supportive requires the development and institutionalisation of ethical practices, and to date, inadequate effort has been put into this.

Privacy represents the dimension of accountability for holistic governance of information to individuals, just as budgeting and special initiatives represent the dimension of accountability to the central institutions. In the next chapter, therefore, we consider in more detail the dilemmas of handling multiple accountabilities in holistic working, before considering afresh the issues of budget design.

8 Accountability

Holistic governance is above all else about accountability. The importance attached to the pursuit of outcomes, which distinguishes the holistic from the merely joined-up in public management, calls for a distinctive style and focus in accountability. The imperative to find workable settlements between the basic tropes about, and biases in, interorganisational rela-tionships (see Chapter 6) calls for a style of holding public officials to account that gives incentives to develop such settlements. The trust requirements, the distinctive skills involved and the range of risks in holistic public management also suggest that public officials need to be held to account for the degree to which they develop these kinds of relationships and skills, and to which they put in place measures to limit their exposure to these risks. We argue that this is an area for which we can identify the main conceptual outlines of what is required, but in which neither detailed development nor actual institutionalisation has yet been achieved.

The chapter begins with a short analysis of what is meant by accountability in general, which enables us to show clearly what difference holistic accountability is intended to make. Next we address the following three key clusters of questions about accountability that arise from the holistic governance agenda:

- Is the idea of accountability compatible with the aspiration for more holistic working in government?
- Do the existing forms of accountability represent insuperable obstacles to holistic working? And, if the answers to the these questions are 'yes' and 'no' respectively, then
- How can the inherited systems of accountability be reformed to support more holistic governance?

Finally, the chapter deals with two other more general challenges to holistic accountability. The first is that it leads to unacceptable paternalism, and the second that it leads to excessive centralism.

Understanding accountability

The attempt to hold others to account is at the heart of what it is to behave politically, and of what is a genuinely political institution. Indeed, the study of how rival projects for accountability interact is a better characterisation of what political science is and does than the conventional Weberian conception of politics as the science of behaviour and institutions that relate to the territorial state, for politics long preceded, has always outflanked and will long succeed the territorial state form (6, 1999a).

Accountability, in the governmental context, however, consists of several distinct activities. 4 activities of accountability

First, some *identifiable individuals or defined group must be held responsible* for a set of executive operations, and this responsibility should correspond to their actual span of control and capacity to act using those tools of governance that are vouchsafed them.

Second, it requires that executive public managers and officials be required to *maintain records* and then at appropriate or defined intervals to *present some summary account*, report or description of their use of their powers, resources and skills in execution of their mandate, with some explanation and justification of that use, and finally, to ensure the *availability of the records* as evidence for the summary account in case they are demanded (March and Olsen, 1995, chapter 5).

Third, accountability requires an institutionalised system of *appreciation, evaluation and appraisal*. Specifically, this involves someone or some group charged with receiving, considering the account and evidence, weighing performance and outcomes against appropriate and publicly deliberated upon standards and then coming to judgments of responsibility for performance and outcomes, and *publicly allocating praise and blame* accordingly.

Fourth and finally, accountability involves the possibility of the use of actual *sanctions and rewards* for behaviour in accordance with the judgments of praiseworthiness and blameworthiness (Hogwood *et al.*, 1998; Day and Klein, 1987).

Attempts to invoke accountability against public officials, managers and front line staff can be defeated at any of these four stages. It may be impossible for either theoretical or practical reasons to identify who is responsible, or those held formally responsible may be able to show that they did not have the requisite span of control and action to affect the performance or the outcome for the better. Second, it may sometimes be impossible for complete, accurate records to be kept, or for a process of verification to be undertaken that would check the summary account presented against evidence. Third, the competing priorities for that scarcest of all resources in government, attention to problems, may mean that the appreciation process is not undertaken, or undertaken only in the most cursory manner suggesting empty pretence rather than substantive consideration, for some or even many of the accounts presented from across the executive (Hogwood *et al.*, 1998). Even if appreciation is undertaken, there are many practical reasons why praise and blame may not in fact be capable of being awarded. Finally, it may prove practically unaffordable, too low a priority, politically too risky given the power of key stakeholders in the executive, or just technically too difficult to administer sanctions and rewards in the manner indicated by the appreciation process.

A helpful distinction (Day and Klein, 1987, p. 27) is conventionally made between accountability for

- *probity*, or regularity, which is principally concerned with propriety in the use of public monies;
- *efficiency* or 'value for money' in the narrower sense of the term, which is mainly about the relationship between outputs and inputs in the process of delivering public services or interventions; and
- *effectiveness* or *programme* accountability, which is centrally about holding the executive to account for the degree to which public interventions achieve their officially and publicly declared result or effect.

Effectiveness or programme accountability comprises two elements. The first is a negative element, in which the executive is held to account for the avoidance of specific failures and the successful management of key risks that programmes run; very often, it is in respect of specific failures ('policy fiascos') that effectiveness accountability is first invoked. The positive element is concerned with improved performance to attain greater impact and problem-solving above a basic threshold of minimally acceptable outcome.

Holistic accountability is centrally concerned with the elevation of effectiveness or programme accountability to the status of the highest priority, and with strategies both to make sure that probity and efficiency accountability do not conflict with this goal, and secondly, ideally to make them serve it by defining in outcome terms, *what* is to be done efficiently.

Finally, it is crucial to consider the organisational levels at which questions of accountability arise. For accountability is something which is sought

- at the *managerial* level through audit, expenditure control, budget planning, performance measurement and political scrutiny; at the political level through electoral accountability to voters;
- at the *legal* level, through the availability of administrative law oversight through judicial review and through civil law by way of actions for breach of statutory duty, and through alternative forms of legal dispute resolution such as the use of ombudspeople, special tribunals and quasi-judicial regulators; and

- at the *constitutional* level, through the definition of the accountability of elected public officials to the legislature, and through informally sanctioned constitutional norms such as expectations of when ministerial resignations are and are not required for particular kinds of disapproved outcomes.

The aspiration for more holistic governance raises numerous questions of how to design systems of programme or effectiveness accountability for each of the four activities of accountability identified above.

Figure 8.1 shows the structure of accountability issues. Ideally it ought to be possible to specify what activities are conducted in each cell to hold public officials to account, and what risks of defeat of accountability are run at each point. In practice, of course, the activities are so numerous that such a table could hardly be completed empirically save in outline form for any given field, except by the most exhaustive descriptive and evaluative research. However, the figure serves to exhibit the structure of the accountability problems that the holistic governance agenda must tackle.

Searching for accountability in holism

A reader examining Figure 8.1 might ask whether a programme for the development of holistic governance can be compatible with these requirements for accountability at all. In this section, we argue that it can.

The mix of accountability mechanisms in the UK was famously described as a 'cat's cradle' of confused and tangled lines of multiple accountability

Figure 8.1 *The structure of accountability*

Activities	*Nominating account givers: identifying responsibility*	*Making accounts: keeping records, presenting an account, verifying account against evidence*	*Appreciation of accounts: receiving considering, assessing responsibility for performance, praising and blaming*	*Granting sanctions and rewards: imposing penalties, rewards and incentives for performance responsibilities*

Levels
Managerial
Legal
Constitutional

(the comment was made by Lord Bancroft, the Head of the Home Civil Service who resigned during the Thatcher years, to describe the accountability arrangements for the then newly burgeoning agencies: Ferlie *et al.*, 1996, p. 119). This problem is magnified for those attempting to do anything that cuts across the functional lines of conventional public administration. Not only are there providers from different agencies and at different levels, with their own internal lines and cultures of accountability, but there may be no lines of accountability *between* contributors. It was this messiness in contexts where clear, bureaucratic, hierarchical lines of accountability have traditionally been revered that managers in our case studies found confusing and, more significant, frightening. In the cases of innovation in holistic working that we studied, it became clear that managers developed coping systems for the problems set for them by this tangled web.

How, our interviewees in our case studies asked, could they be held accountable for actions of others over which they had no control? How could they be expected to work across boundaries with others when those to whom they were accountable were still focused on maintaining clear lines of accountability for defined, core agency responsibilities? Who would be blamed if anything went wrong?

Some managers solved the problem by 'underground resistance' – taking chances and going to the brink of their mandates; some kept their heads down and just got on with their holistic working, sometimes constructing more or less convoluted justifications for their activities. For example, one manager said, '[Probation] is separate from the local authority and I report to the [Probation] Committee. I haven't formally reported the [difficult-to-explain event] to the committee because it doesn't impinge directly on the work of probation. It isn't "need to know" information.' This officer also acknowledged that 'if agencies aren't accountable in their own agency structure, it is just an add-on and dependent on people's time and particular interest'.

Others, not unreasonably, found the confusion and the risks too threatening and effectively opted out of integrated working on the grounds of legal and accountability requirements. If existing systems of accountability mean that implementation of holistic initiatives is dependent on the vagaries of individual manager's time, interest and bravery, then clearly there are limits to the innovation in holistic working that can be expected in such a system.

Perhaps the most immediate obstacle to the institutionalisation of holistic systems of accountability is the sheer institutional weight of the inheritance of functionally defined systems of accountability, which tend to privilege probity and functionally defined efficiency above effectiveness. Scrutiny committees in the legislature, ministerial and civil service accounting roles in the executive, even audit functions have all been defined for so long in functional terms that overcoming this inheritance is far from straightforward, although some promising efforts are being made (see below).

But even if this inheritance could be shed, the intrinsic challenge of designing holistic systems of accountability is not to be dismissed. In the first place, identifying responsibility for outcomes in wicked social problems is genuinely difficult. It is often impossible – even in theory, let alone with actually existing measurement systems – to identify what proportion of the variance in say, crime, poverty or low educational attainment, can be ascribed to which of the vast range of social forces acting to produce these miseries. Therefore, it is very difficult to determine, what responsibilities to allocate to each of the many public agencies with some leverage. Selecting the appropriate 'lead' agency is politically difficult. The best placed may not be the most holistically motivated; the agency with the most leverage may easily be the most functionally acculturated, and so on.

The collection of holistic measures of outcomes on wicked social problems presents significant difficulties (Smith, 1996). First of all, true outcome measures have to be defined. In some areas – personal social services, for example – this is inherently difficult. While scalar measures of outcome have been developed for some elderly care services, they are very expensive to collect and analyse, requiring skilled and expensive researchers rather than normal practitioner case recording techniques. Some outcome measures require expensive equipment to collect. For example, good indicators of environmental quality often require electronic sensors to be distributed around sensitive sites to relay information automatically either over cables or by satellite. Moreover, in some cases, their collection can be very intrusive upon the privacy of service users. In other areas, outcome measures are indeed available but they understate the true range of outcomes with which we are concerned. Secondary education is a good example: measurement of qualifications obtained is a very coarse measure indeed of all the things that citizens expect schools to achieve in the cultivation of young people. In some fields, the multi-dimensional character of outcomes makes for problems with the tractability of outcome data.

Relating outcome to input or even output data for public services is very difficult. Even where consistent time series data exist for both, regressions will not typically tell us much that forms a robust basis for decision-making about what impact the efforts of any given profession or service has upon an outcome, for it is very difficult to be confident that one has controlled for all the relevant factors and that models estimated are soundly based. Who can say with reasonable confidence that the relationships to be estimated between expenditure on probation officers, or the allocation of probation time in one way rather than another, with rates observed and convicted reoffending by any given sample of convicted persons, are indeed linear ones? And if so, why?

In such a setting, it is not surprising the managers become cynical. One of our interviewees in Southbrookborough, in a moment of both despair and splendidly mixed metaphor, described the focus on particular outcomes, given the uncertainties of measurement and of the impact of particular services, as a 'dead end fool's errand'.

Key problems in developing holistic appreciation systems for accountability include the conflict between political priorities such as manifesto commitments to services given in input or activity terms and more general commitments to joined-up and holistic working. The preference of elected politicians at the local – just as at the national level – for executive decision-making rather than scrutiny work is a problem, but one that reflects the career paths to high office for politicians. Being a select committee or scrutiny commission chair is a much less promising route to ministerial office or group leadership or party mayoral candidacy than chairing a spending committee or being a whip. However, party promotion systems are unlikely, at least in the short term, to be changed in response to the need to create more holistic systems of accountability at the policy level. Politics at this level is not driven principally by policy considerations and rationales. Here, as we would expect, is where we find the greatest signs of a trade-off, at least in the short term, between probity and efficiency accountability on the one hand, and holistic effectiveness accountability on the other. For in practice, its tends to be the same scrutiny bodies that are charged with oversight of all three measures on which public services and interventions are held to account, and this creates bottlenecks in access of accounts rendered to political scrutineers' attention. These bottlenecks can only be alleviated by more investment in oversight capacity, which requires public justification along the lines discussed above.

Appreciation also runs into other political barriers. There are conflicts between policy objectives that have so far only been made tolerable because the conflict is masked or fudged by the inadequacy of the accountability systems. Take the case of combating illicit drugs. Successful interception of shipments reduces supply and pushes up price. As supply falls and price rises, only the most sophisticated and hardest-to-catch-and-convict criminals remain in the business. Therefore, numbers of arrests fall. When numbers of arrests fall, even if they fall because actual crime has fallen (which in the case of the drugs trade in such circumstances, cannot be confidently asserted), popular feelings of safety do not rise, and in some cases may fall too. This can create a Catch-22 situation in which success-ful improvements in community safety can worsen public fears. This wreaks havoc with the attempt to allocate praise and blame holistically for community safety on drugs.

A key problem with appreciation in holistic accountability is the conflict between the perception of politicians that they need to be seen by the public and media to be allocating (rather than receiving) praise and blame in unequivocal ways, and the holistic imperative to recognise that often they need to hold people to account more for their efforts in joint working than for actual impacts on outcomes when a particular service can realisti-cally only beheld responsible for a very small part of the variance on the levels of, say, cancer, teenage pregnancy, car crime, or air pollution. To the extent that accountability systems are legitimate only because they are *unfair*, to the extent that they are publicly supported only because they make scapegoats of hapless public managers who then become highly risk averse, there are real roadblocks in the way of holistic working. We explore the larger significance of this issue below.

The difficulties found by the Treasury in conducting expenditure con-trol and legitimating rationing decisions on outcomes show the scale of the problems at the point of designing and operating reward and sanction systems for holistic accountability. Over many years, the Treasury has experimented with many systems of allocating funds to departments and exercising oversight over their spending. It has tried fixed formulae, indi-vidual negotiation, zero-based budgeting, incremental budgeting, both cash and resource accounting, centralising and devolving financial management responsibility. The design challenges are not necessarily easier in a context of holistic accountability. As we shall see in Chapter 9 on finance and budgeting, the relationship between outcome budgeting and line-item input expenditure planning, and the challenge of disciplining the latter to the requirements of the former, is neither more nor less complex than the current problems of budgetary control and subordinating expenditure to policy goals. Nevertheless, there are real design challenges to be faced.

Finally, the scale of the changes involved – and in particular, the quasi-constitutional changes – in an agenda for holistic accountability are proba-bly rather daunting to many politicians. While the principle of ministerial government need not conflict with holism, the relationship is uneasy. Reshaping the select committee system for the House of Commons along holistic lines involves major political upheaval that a government with an already huge constitutional change agenda has good reasons of political and policy management to want to delay. Similar arguments can be found replicated at local authority level for reshaping commission and committee systems that have only just gone through one major shake-up to meet the requirements of cabinet, mayoral or scrutiny models of local governance.

Design principles for holistic accountability

Accountability for what?

The central problem of holistic accountability can be simply stated: how to hold people to account for outcomes, conceived holistically, when no single minister or permanent secretary, no chief organisation, no single organisation, department, committee or agency can possibly have the span of control to influence outcomes alone?

In a way, this is only an exacerbation of the general problem of ascribing causal responsibility for anything. After all, few historical events can be put down entirely and solely to the leaders whose decisions are conventionally identified by secondary school history textbooks as making them responsible (March and Olsen, 1995, chapter 5). Yet this recognition of endless causal interdependence does not lead us to abandon the concept of responsibility, so necessary is it to the normative basis of social organisation, indeed to making sense of social and political behaviour at all. To ascribe responsibility to the sometimes vast, always ill-bounded and perhaps amorphous collectivities that have causal influence over outcomes, is, the reasonable suspicion readily has it, to attempt to disclaim one's own responsibility (Lucas, 1993, chapter 5).

What the challenge of holistic governance adds to this entirely general and eternal problem is a specific focus upon outcomes, defined as changes in moral priority dimensions of human being in territorially defined populations, and a restriction or boundary upon those who may be held jointly and severally liable, as contract lawyers say, to those within the public sector and its collaborators and contractors. As we shall see, this restriction does not entirely solve the problem of the unit to be held accountable, but it does at least provide a start.

The problem of design principles for holistic accountability is not conceptually insoluble. Indeed, the broad outlines of a reasonable strategy are clear enough; the problem is their implementation, development, fleshing out, and institutionalisation.

In general, if we cannot hold public managers in particular organisations responsible for outcomes, but outcomes are what we care about, then we can only hold them to account for the extent and quality of their efforts in the following activities. The following list of eight key programmes of holistic effort is constructed on an 'ideal narrative' basis from initial understanding through action to evaluation in order to secure a measure of completeness:

- their efforts made to *understand* their own existing and past causal contributions, and to develop appreciations (Vickers, 1995 [1963]) of their capabilities for influencing outcomes positively and negatively;
- their efforts to collect *intelligence and information* about outcomes, ideally quantitatively to measure trends in priority outcomes and to measure the impact that their actions, and their combined efforts with other agencies, are having upon those priority outcomes;
- their *setting* of *priorities,* within the sphere of discretion that will unavoidably be left by any overarching array of policies, between all of the dimensions of human well-being that they could seek to make efforts to influence;
- the *scale* of their efforts made to *influence* outcomes positively, insofar as their own span of control enables them to make such efforts, or lack of such efforts, or, in the worst cases, even for their positive acts that influence outcomes negatively;
- their attempts to *collaborate*, work with others, negotiate arrangements with others, that are so designed to enable more effective, and to overcome the particular obstacles they face to such collaboration (these, we would argue, are most helpfully measured using the tools set out in Chapters 2 and 6, and especially in Figures 2.5, 2.6, 6.1, 6.4 and 6.5);
- their particular *design choices* of interorganisational relationships upon which to negotiate with others, reflecting their understandings and their priorities, in order to influence the priority outcomes;
- their efforts to *institutionalise* within their organisations and their interorganisational arrangements, understandings, programmes of information and intelligence gathering priorities, efforts, commitments to collaborate, and so on;
- the quality of their periodic internal *appraisal and evaluation* of the appropriateness of their priorities between outcomes, and the efficacy of these arrangements in promoting those outcomes.

If this list is roughly complete, then it can be brought together with the four basic activities of accountability identified above and summarised in Figure 8.1, to provide a description of the specific challenge for holistic accountability. Figure 8.2 presents the resulting matrix. In a well-developed system of holistic accountability, it should be possible to make entries in every cell for any given organisation in the system of governance,

Figure 8.2   *The challenge for holistic accountability*

	Identifying responsible persons	*Making accounts*	*Appreciating accounts*	*Sanctions and rewards*
Understanding				
Intelligence				
Priorities				
Influencing				
Collaboration				
Interorganisational design				
Institutionalisation				
Appraisal				

describing its managerial, legal and constitutional accountability in relation to outcomes and holistic working.

Naturally, it is not possible to provide a completely general set of entries for the cells of Figure 8.2 of all organisations with a role in governance. Different people, for example, will be responsible for setting priorities and conducting appraisals in, for example, the Benefits Agency, from those who would be involved in these activities in, say, a local authority environmental health department. The account receivers (the third column) differ between tiers of governance, and the sanctions and rewards differ widely even within tiers of governance. However, we can say that the first stage in developing a holistic accountability system should be that it should be possible for someone to complete a matrix of this kind for any organisation within the system of governance.

This analysis of what is involved in holistic accountability also has the merit of making it clear, under what conditions the strategic decision described above, to impose holistic accountability over a functionally defined administrative structure, can be successful. For only if the account receivers, the appreciators of accounts rendered, are organised holistically, can they measure the quality of the programmes of holistic effort made by the functionally organised departments, agencies and authorities.

The consequence of this is that multiple accountabilities must be a normal reality for many organisations that have significant causal impacts upon several priority outcomes. This can be costly if different account receivers demand accounts in different forms, if their sanctions and rewards conflict with each other or at any rate with the overarching settlement of priorities between outcomes. Therefore, a central challenge is to ensure the holistic cohesion of holistic accountability, to prevent both conflicting accountabilities and to prevent the problems of excessive accountability that can lead to risk aversion and stifling innovation.

+ duplication.

Focus on the executive structure or on the legislature?

It is sometimes argued that holistic accountability is best achieved by reorganising the structure of departments and ministerial responsibilities. Many think-tanks frequently develop new blueprints for rearranging the furniture in the executive. However, the international experience suggests that this is typically not the most effective route.

Intellectually, a key weakness of this approach is that it misunderstands what holism is really about. Holism is not, as we have argued above, a Holy Grail of design in organisational structure. Rather, as we argued in Chapters 2 and 6, the key issues are about the relationships between the interventions made by different professions and departments, and the effects they have on the outcomes that citizens and politicians care most about. The point is not to overcome the division of labour. Holding professionals and organisations to account does not need to be done in ways that replicate the same division of labour; the problem with the reinvention programme was precisely that it assumed that it would, and this has been the source of fragmentation.

A comparison between the UK and New Zealand provides a case in point. At both the local and the national level, Britain, like New Zealand and most countries, has sought to pursue holism by trying to graft a variety of forms of accountability for impact upon holistically defined problems and goals, to a basically functionally organised executive structure. A strategic decision was taken, more or less explicitly, very early in the life of the New Labour government, and probably while still in opposition, not to pursue – at least in a first term – a major restructuring of the departments of the civil service and the agencies along holistic lines. Rather, the decision was taken to use holistic budgets, holistic target-setting, holistic spending assessments, holistic audit and encouragement for innovation in joint working as the principal tools for eliciting holistic working. The reorganisation at the beginning of the second term reflects many considerations and not only these of holism. In the same way, New Zealand has applied its overarching system of accountability for strategic goals over and above departmental structures. In some US states, comprehensive holistic budgeting, under the label of 'performance budgeting' has been a more far-reaching version of the same approach than has been applied in the UK (Osborne and Plastrik, 2000, pp. 43–56).

The reasons for this strategic decision are understandable. First, it can take huge amounts of time, ministerial attention and resources to undertake and implement a massive restructuring. To overlay holistic accountability systems upon functionally organised administration is certainly the cheaper and simpler option. Secondly, the history of structural reorganisation is not an encouraging one. It is easy to get bogged down very quickly in endless negotiations, and it is also very difficult to prevent such reorganisations from being captured by special interests. For it would involve breaking up powerful professions, and no government has attempted to take on all the professions at once. Third, the record of success in holistic restructuring is not impressive. There have been some experiments in applying holistic design principles to executive management structures, although not in British central government departments. For example, the London Borough of Hackney created a number of thematically defined roles for chief officers, and Honda experimented with thematic allocation of portfolios to the senior management. Neither of these cases was wholly encouraging, but it might be that there were special circumstances in each case that limited what was achieved or achievable. The experience of most reorganisations at the executive level in both public and private sectors is that they achieve little, are very costly to effect, distract vital managerial attention and energy from many more urgent problems, are readily captured by special interests and that even the symbolism proves shallow (Weiss, 1981; Brunsson and Olsen, 1993). If restructuring were to reduce the holistic government agenda, in the eyes of most people, to yet another management fad, then it would have failed and could damage the wider holistic governance agenda. Finally, it could have proven to be a major distraction by focusing all attention on rearranging the furniture at the centre, when the priority is often to achieve joined-up and holistic working at the points where citizens come to deal with public services.

In any democratic country, the legislature should not be permitted to evade its responsibility for creating a tier of account receivers organised around outcomes, and for putting in place some system of disciplining and controlling conflicts and excesses by those account receivers. In principle, there is no reason why a system of scrutiny or select committees could not and should not constitute the holistic account receivers, and a small number of cross-cutting and superior select or scrutiny committees could not provide that discipline for cohesion. However, the British House of Commons' system is still a very long way from this. Most committees are functionally defined and organised, and the cross-cutting committees such as Public Accounts, Public Administration and Liaison are not organised or equipped to fulfil the second overarching role. Unfortunately, the recent debates in the House about reform of the select committee system have not really addressed this challenge (Liaison Committee, 2000a,b; President of the Council and Leader of the House of Commons, 2000).

But even this is not enough. If, for example, the division of labour between the account receivers is one that separates work on health outcomes from that for public security, learning from prosperity, and so on, there is still some overarching system required that appraises the appropriate priorities between these outcomes both in general and for any given administrative organisation. Logically, this structure is most appropriately located at the centre of the executive in central government, but with quite specific oversight from an overarching agency of scrutiny within the legislature.

The centrality of this role in the executive does not, of course, imply administrative centralisation, or command-and-control methods of sanctions and rewards, for such systems are as limited and cumbersome in the context of holistic governance as they have been in any other setting. Rather, the role of that priority-setting structure is to develop overarching policies that reflect the trade-off(s) between outcomes that fit the priorities of the government of the day. It is a commonplace of politics that such trade-off(s) often cannot be stated publicly, because politicians are understandably reluctant to face the obloquy of a voting public that is unwilling to listen to the tragic truth that they cannot have all the good things together and that hard choices must be made. This is not the place to consider whether political life could be otherwise. However, even if the priorities and trade-off(s) are not stated publicly, it remains important that they should be made somewhere, for holistic governance depends crucially upon some degree of effort being made at least to mitigate the most egregious policy conflicts. That all conflicts cannot be eliminated, that once for all resolution cannot be hoped for, that the long term consequences of some trade-off(s) that seem worth making in the short term will be regrettable, may all readily be admitted. But this utopia of complete consistency and long term thinking is not what holistic governance calls for. All that is required is practical efforts to mitigate the worst conflicts.

The unit of accountability in holistic working

So far we have discussed holistic accountability for the single agency. However, a key question in all programmes of joint and holistic working is, what is the unit that should be held accountable for performance? The question has enormous importance, both practically and legally. For as holistic working becomes institutionalised, and as it moves towards the higher end of the spectrum set out in Figure 2.6 in Chapter 2, so the single agency becomes a less appropriate unit. Long-term partnerships can exhibit increasingly blurred boundaries of management and even financing. The practical issue for many contractors, scrutiny committees and auditors is then to determine with what or whom they should negotiate, what flows of resources they should measure, what activities they should gather information on. Legally, the question can assume great importance in the event that an aggrieved citizen, employee, contractor or company not awarded a contract wishes to challenge a decision; for them the issue becomes, against what or whom should, for example, judicial review proceedings be issued?

Satellite bodies, merged entities, formal partnership bodies are often created precisely in order to give explicit form to an arrangement in order to attract particular kinds of resources – political legitimacy, grant aid, contracts or other financial flows, legal capacity to enter into contracts in its own name and right, and so on. At this point, the only problem, for legal and constitutional accountability at least, is not a gap but the possibility of duplication: for example, a joint structure – such as some partnerships involved in some 'action zones' – created between a central and a local agency may be subject to inspection and audit through both the system of oversight of local government by the Audit Commission and quite separately by the National Audit Office. While duplication in scrutiny and oversight is irritating, wasteful and causes distraction of managerial effort and time for the body being audited, there are easier ways available of dealing with these problems than there are for problems of absence of accountability.

The real problem of lack of accountability tends to arise for arrangements that are much less formalised, where – at least as yet – no structure with a clear legal capacity has been created. Here the legal and constitutional accountability systems are a very coarse grid over actual activity. In the UK, for example, local authorities are held to account for their contribution to joined-up and holistic working to the extent that they are required to file with central government departments, a range – often a huge range – of plans for work on cross-cutting issues. But accountability for the preparation of a certain kind of document is a rather shallow scrutiny of the quality of what is actually done in the name of holism.

More serious at this level are the problems of managerial accountability. For arrangements that are relatively informal, whether deliberately and appropriately kept informal or else during the period of development into something more formal, the systems of managerial accountability are often either obstructive or else inadequate. Obstruction generally comes from the fact that organisations' or departments' accountability systems put pressure on key staff to be delivering traditionally defined services rather than developing joint initiatives, or else over-zealous pressure to move faster and further towards integration and pre-set outcomes that the fragile basis of trust in the relationships will not in fact bear, while inadequacy generally arises from the lack of oversight of what is done by way of negotiation, development and policy adjustment. Inadequacy can have very different effects upon different kinds of managers in different situations. Some of the braver, or those with more informal and quiet political backing, will find low or lax accountability exactly the environment they need in order to pursue holistic working in their own way. For these more entrepreneurial public managers, accountability arrangements are a nuisance, a brake, or at least a very blunt instrument for dealing with an extremely delicate task that requires the sensitivity of the individual risk-taking public manager. For the less courageous, or simply those whose own superiors show doubts about the priority for coordination and collaboration, the lack of accountability for such work gives clear signals that it would not be welcome and they should avoid putting more effort into it than is explicitly required to keep central government happy that something, however symbolic or modest in nature, is being done.

Individualisation of responsibility and sanctions for poor performance

Responsibility in public management has long been to some degree individualised. Individual ministers are, in the constitutional fiction, accountable to the legislature for everything that is attempted, achieved or neglected within the purview of their departments. Although ministerial resignations for mistakes made by departmental officials without the knowledge of the minister, where the minister's lack of knowledge could reasonably be excused, have become rare since the early 1980s, the constitutional fiction remains. Permanent secretaries are the accounting officers for their departments. In the British case, in actual political practice and effect, although access is not quite so restricted in theory, select committees that want to interview civil servants of any grade junior to the permanent secretary can only do so with both the permanent secretary's Consent and with the Consent of the less senior official from whom they want to hear. There are select committees that have struggled in vain for years to talk to anyone from a department except the permanent secretary. In the same way, the permanent secretary is the person responsible before the National Audit Office. In local government, individualisation is extended slightly in that all senior officers have fiscal responsibility in the event of malfeasance, but in many authorities, scrutiny committees who wish to, will have to work to establish their rights to call any officers to answer before them, who are much more junior than departmental deputy directors. The advent of elected mayors in London and other local authorities represents a further individualisation of responsibility.

What is the role of individual accountability in the context of holistic governance? When many agencies and departments have some, although limited, influence over an outcome, under what circumstances might a resignation reasonably be demanded? How might we want to change the constitutional situation?

Again, the question need not be hard to answer in principle, but operationalising and institutionalising those principles remains a demanding task, and one to which legislatures have yet to rise.

As a sanction that is more severe than many others in the standard ordering of sanctions – for example, reprimands, public shame, cuts in budget, mandatory modifications to a policy or the design of programme, reductions in span of control – presumably a requirement to resign is appropriate for a minister or any other senior public official in the executive, in the context of holistic accountability for effectiveness, whether elected or appointed, for a severe, egregious, foreseeable and preventable failure on any one of the eight programme areas of holistic effort, where the official could reasonably be held to be culpable.

It may reasonably be objected that no political system could ever be quite so straightforward, so utilitarian or so rational, and that political systems are viable only when they make some provision for scapegoating – in effect, that a measure of unfairness to senior public officials in the accountability system is the necessary condition of any viable system at all of political accountability to wider publics and the media. If this is right, then the challenge for accountability in holistic governance may be to design a new constitutional fiction in the candid recognition that it will be another fiction like the myth of ministerial responsibility that has prevailed hitherto. Indeed, this may well be true, and, consistent with our argument in Chapter 4, we have no wish to suggest that holism is a purely rational, utilitarian model of governance. That is a romantic view that we have set out throughout this book to undermine. Making settlements is a matter of raw politics, which sometimes just has to override considerations of rationality, reasonableness and fairness. No doubt particular settlements – made, for example, in different countries and at different times, or, indeed, in different cities for the accountability of their elected mayors – between the institutional styles identified in Chapter 4 will result in slightly different fictions about the scope of individual responsibility.

Recognising this, however, it is worth pointing out that there are some well-documented risks with fictions of accountability that are too stringent and that make it too easy to achieve the scapegoating of individuals for systemic failures over which their direct control can only be limited and partial. These are the ordinary risks of over-accountability. In order to avoid the sanctions they may too readily face in such settings, ministers and chief executives will tend to become risk averse, to limit innovation, to use high handed and authoritarian methods within the domain they do control directly, and to do everything they can to create institutions over which they have no control whatsoever in order to devolve blame for failures where they think it highly likely that they will occur, and in turn more junior staff will avoid telling such public officials the truth about what they are doing. Indeed, these are not new problems, nor are they in any way specific to the context of holistic governance. However, it is worth considering how far the risks of such problems, which are well known in contemporary functionally defined accountability systems, are an acceptable price to pay for being able to conduct a certain kind of politics in public.

Independent receivers of accounts in holistic accountability?

One interesting innovation in holistic accountability has been to shift the public responsibility for holding public managers to account away from legislature and indeed from politicians generally, towards independent agencies.

In some part, in the UK, the Audit Commission and the National Audit Office (NAO) represent a partial implementation of this strategy. However, because the NAO has to agree its reports with departments and agencies in all but the last resort, the measure of independence is more limited than it might be. In Australia the independent Industry Commission collects and publicises data on outputs and outcomes from the various states to provide management data for chief executives and to give the general public an idea how their state is doing on a mixed score card of measures. Considerable significance is attached to publication of data in an understandable form in the popular press, encouraging people to ask pertinent questions about the allocation of government resources, outputs and outcomes.

However, there are limits to this kind of strategy. Politicians have created so many independent agencies to make decisions that are credible precisely for being independent of politicians' control that voters may eventually begin to wonder for what politicians can be trusted to take responsibility. If it becomes clear that politicians are concerned principally to devolve blame to technocrats, voters may become suspicious that the aim of holistic government is not improved effectiveness and problem-solving but simply the management of public opinion.

Central–local relations: accountability, devolution, decentralisation and local governance

Next we consider the question of how far, in the context of holistic governance, local tiers of governance should be accountable to centre. If the centre is involved in setting priorities between outcomes and in producing policy frameworks that encourage innovation for the promotion of these outcomes, inevitably these policy frameworks will shape how local governments behave and, to some degree, limit their policy autonomy.

The locus of accountability is at the centre of the sometimes bitter argument conducted both by politicians and in academic circles about whether the holistic governance agenda is essentially and necessarily centralising or whether it can be and/or actually is in practice, capable of encouraging and supporting decentralisation, local pluralism and diversity.

Those who argue that it is inevitably centralising (Chandler, 2000; Rhodes, 2000) point to certain aspects of the accountability process as evidence for their claim. In the UK, the agenda has been driven forward from the Cabinet Office, which has expanded and at the same time greater proportions of its total staff report directly to the Prime Minister. Central government departments require plans for holistic working to be filed and approved from local authorities on a wide range of problems; many special budgets are created as tools by which the centre stimulates holistic working from local authorities and other agencies under appointed leadership working at local level with some measure of operational autonomy such as health authorities. In New Zealand, the centrally set strategic priority areas act as a discipline across all departments and public authorities, against which performance is assessed.

Indeed, there is evidence that at least some of the practice of holistic governance is centralising, at least to the extent that any agenda that uses sticks and carrots to reward some activity and sanction other behaviour must be partially disciplinary and in practice that discipline will be centrally set. Certainly some of the implementation problems that we have diagnosed in the early years of the British programme exhibit many of the symptoms of over-centralisation: initiativitis, excessive hoarding of learning at the centre, impatience, over-hasty setting in concrete of outcome measures for accountability that later prove to be inappropriate and become straitjackets, and so on (6 *et al.*, 1999). It may be that the activism of the centre in promoting this agenda, which gives the appearance of centralisation in policy, in fact reflects the relative weakness of that centre in its capability to direct, shape and influence the course of public management.

On the other hand, the use of the tools of government, and even of the stronger, more disciplinary tools, to attempt to promote a particular agenda is not the same thing as centralisation, and there are elements in the holistic governance agenda that point in a more decentralising direction. For example, although the centre often mandates some form of joint working, its choice of instruments allow considerable discretion to agency chiefs and local authorities about exactly which other bodies they work with, and over the particular determination and formulation of goals only the broad outlines of which are centrally specified. The British programme for local government service transformation called Best Value, which replaces compulsory competitive tendering of services with a more flexible regime under which authorities are under an obligation to assess the most effective way to parcel up services, combine them with those of other agencies and authorities, and to organise for their provision, allows local authorities at least some discretion in the selection of the goals, and more latitude in the selection of the particular ways in which they combine and cluster services.

The British constitutional reform programme of devolution to a parliament in Scotland and an assembly in Wales has certainly been decentralising for governance, despite the media attention that attempts to retain central political control within the governing party have obtained. If the critics of holism are correct, that it is indeed centralising, then we should expect devolution to run counter to, and perhaps even undermine, holism. Thus far, at any rate, there is little evidence that this is the case. While some integration around cross-border activities may in the long run be threatened, even in the border regions between southern Scotland and the northern English counties of Cumbria and Northumbria, at present coordination seems to continue at least to the degree that it did prior to the election of the devolved assemblies and the reconstitution of the executives in these nations. In fact, the Scottish executive in particular has been persuaded to see devolution as a major opportunity for more holistic working (McLeish, 1999; Leicester and Mackay, 1998).

Moreover, empirical evidence suggests there are good reasons to doubt that holism is necessarily centralising. In the United States, holistic governance has, under other rubrics, been the focus of attention during much of the 1990s, having returned to priority after the end of the Reagan period (Agranoff, 1991). The states, rather than federal agencies, have been the leaders and the innovators in joined-up and holistic working, and by and large, federal government has been the laggard. There is little evidence that when the second phase of Vice-President Al Gore's programme was designed to shift from what were by 1993 the well-tried methods of contracting out, purchaser–provider splits, performance efficiency audit, and so on, towards more integrated working, that the result was any reassertion of federal authority over the states. In general, and despite what the failed health care reforms of the first term might have meant had they come to fruition, policy has meant that federal agencies have been continuing to hand over power to the states during the Clinton years, as the well-known welfare reform legislation of 1996 showed very clearly.

Finally, on theoretical grounds, there are good reasons to believe that centralisation is a poor strategy with which to pursue holism, for reasons of all the well-known limitations of centralised decision-making. The centre cannot know enough about what the appropriate priorities are in different regions and localities, for different institutional settings, and so on, and when or how to respond to change. The motivation required of public managers to take risks cannot be stimulated and sustained under conditions of excessive central control.

But it does not follow that there is no role for the centre in domestic holistic governance, or that holism can be achieved without central encouragement, sanction and initiative. Indeed, the holistic governance agenda does require an activist central government with a clear policy direction, prepared to use the tools within its repertoire to stimulate innovation in coordination and integration, to put in place systems of holistic accountability, to underpin holistic working with support systems such as reform of public sector pay schemes to encourage people to develop careers across different professions, to develop financial incentives and to encourage research and development of outcome indicators of a kind that are tractable enough to be used in management accountability systems and routine data capture, and not only in expensive academic longitudinal research. A centre that works in these ways must move beyond 'enabling', in at least one of the common uses of that term, for it must attempt to institutionalise the positive answer to the question whether to pursue integration. On the other hand, a centre playing this activist role can certainly decentralise much of the decision-making about what, how and when to integrate.

Naturally, this does not represent a single 'correct solution' to the delicate problems of negotiating central–local relations. Nor would it be reasonable to expect the holistic governance agenda to deliver a single form of preferred interorganisational linkage between centre and locality. Where collaboration is appropriate, the whole spectrum in Figure 2.6 in Chapter 2 is available. Where conflict is appropriate, or at any rate cannot be avoided between centre and one or more local authorities, there is nothing so centralist in the holistic governance agenda as we have characterised it that would require locally elected authorities always and everywhere to submit to the supposedly superior wisdom of the centre. But nor is the activist centre given any such *a priori* authority with which to trump the locally mandated authority in every case. For constitutional accountability for probity remains important within fragmented and holistic governance alike.

Democracy and public accountability

Finally, we consider the question of whether there is any necessary conflict between holistic accountability systems and accountability of the whole system of governance to a public that also has preferences about inputs as well as outcomes.

One criticism that is sometimes made of the holistic government agenda is that it is undemocratic because it is paternalistic. The argument is that citizens have come to trust in the fragmented, silo-based government they have inherited, because particular professions have successful 'brands': it is, the critics argue, paternalistic to impose a structure upon government in the citizen's interest that they have not chosen. The critics' view is that the role of democratic government is to give citizens what they demand, irrespective of its effectiveness.

One argument that can be made in reply to this is that the general anti-paternalist stance makes almost any kind of governance impossible. Modern complex societies cannot be run either wholly on what majorities will support or by restricting the individual's encounter with the state to only that which he or she wishes. There are too many conflicting majorities to be assembled from the same body of public opinion for consistent policy-making, too many people content to delegate powers to politicians to find problems and solutions for simple passive response to majoritarianism to be viable, and too many areas where crime must be controlled and citizens' duties acknowledged to confine the relationship to what each citizen prefers.

A second, more promising, strategy is to accept that, indeed, governments may not legitimately do anything they deem to be in their citizens' best interests, but that there is a restricted and constrained space for acceptable paternalism. One of us has set out in detail an argument from first principles about exactly what the conditions are in which certain very limited kinds of paternalism are acceptable (6, 2000a). Very briefly, this argument is as follows.

Paternalism in general is defined (adapting from VanDeVeer, 1986) as:

> deliberate acts (or omissions) done by an agent – in the present case, a government agency – contrary either to the preferences or to the refusal of consent of an adult individual ('the subject'), and either coercing or heavily sanctioning their choices, or overriding their preferences or refusal of consent about services from or transactions with the agent, where normally that would not be morally acceptable but justified by the agent (or others) on the grounds that the action has the primary or sole aim of promoting what the agent sees as the subject's interests, good or benefit, or preventing what the agent sees as the subject's harm.

The general principle that is regarded by most political philosophers other than libertarians is the following, which I shall call the *extended consent principle* (adapted from VanDeVeer, 1986's 'principle of autonomy respecting paternalism'):

> An agent – in this case government – can be permitted to act in good faith for the best interests of a subject – in this case, a citizen or the citizenry – where specific explicit or tacit consent has not been given, *if those citizens would consent to the activity, if they were aware of all the relevant information and circumstances, given the particular preferences, values and commitments those actual subjects have, and provided the activity is the least invasive way to achieve the goal that would be consented to, and does no wrong to others.*

In order to get from this principle to a characterisation of the conditions of acceptable paternalism, we need to add at least the following principles of delegation and accountability:

> *Duty of enquiry*: Government is empowered and given a duty in the name of, and ultimately by, citizens, subject to specific limitations on its powers in constitutional and human rights law, to enquire into the circumstances, conditions, causes and possible solutions (prevention, palliation, cure, melioration) to the key problems (risks) that concern citizens.

Government must exercise that power with due diligence and in good faith to find out 'what works'.

Duty to tackle citizens priority risks: Government is further empowered and given a duty to propose, debate openly, consult upon, and, after due process, subject to limitations in constitutional and human rights law, to take specific legal powers to take such measures as it, acting in good faith, sees fit to tackle those priority problems (risks) in order to prevent the occurrence of avoidable and unacceptable harms, to reverse damage caused or to meliorate unacceptable effects.

Duty to inform citizens wherever possible and enable the exercise of public reason and to open up avenues of participation (derived from the extended consent principle): Government must make every effort to make the public aware of all the relevant information and all the relevant circumstances, and encourage free exercise of the rights of speech and deliberation on that information and its exercise of its duties. Therefore, the more government innovates in ways that might run counter to majority views or to individual preferences, the more it must be innovative in explaining and defending its case to the public and in giving the public ways to play a part in decision-making and in commenting on the quality of the results achieved.

Duty to be subject to lawful removal or sanction by citizens: For the exercise of their powers and the performance of duties they owe to the citizens collectively, elected officials of government shall be held periodically accountable, both in periodic free and fair elections, and continuously under rules of due process and ministerial accountability in the legislature, and may be required under those processes to yield power to others. In turn, appointed officials shall be held accountable to and through elected persons through specific mechanisms of reporting to, scrutiny and sanction by the elected legislature, including the elected opposition.

Reasoning together with these principles now in place, the extended consent principle yields the following *principle of emergency paternalism*:

Subject to constitutional and human rights law and under specific legal powers and subject to subsequent accountability, government is justified, having fulfilled its duty of enquiry, in not waiting to act upon the priority risks until the citizens have been given that information and given explicit consent which an 'actual' version of the extended consent principle would have required, if and only if the consequences of waiting that long would be unacceptably damaging to the interests of the citizens in securing that those priority problems (risks) are tackled effectively and in due time – for example, by causing such strain on the public purse or valued services that no reasonable citizenry would be willing to tolerate.

In addition, it would be reasonable to require that for holistic intervention to be justified as a case of acceptable paternalism, it should be just, not violate human rights, be constitutional and no more invasive than necessary, and should not create greater harms than those with which it is intended to deal.

Finally, it would be necessary to supplement these with an account of political trust, political obligation, the role of public reason in legitimacy and accountability, before one can claim to have buttressed the account against the libertarian critique or to have constructed a full, viable, coherent account of limited justified paternalism. However, this should suffice to characterise the principal conditions.

The principle of emergency paternalism defined here, subject to these constraints, does justify much of the holistic governance agenda. For the democratic legitimacy of holism rests on the claim that what citizens care most deeply and fundamentally about are outcomes, and that their preferences for inputs reflect either mistaken derived preferences, preferences that reflect professional capture, or else second best preferences that reflect mistrust. Clearly, without offering citizens additional bases and reasons for political trust, holistic governance would lack legitimacy. But effective conduct and implementation of holistic governance could be part of a credible claim to be trustworthy. However, an argument along these lines would justify holistic interventions even if citizens report when asked that they have preferences in input or throughput terms for scaling up fragmented services that would be less effective in achieving the goals they fundamentally care about, provided that certain other things are also being done by governments at national and local level. First, they must produce and disseminate widely the basis of evidence for its commitment to prevention and integration, monitor effectiveness and publish the results: specific charters, published league tables and comparisons between prevention and cure should be central to the information basis of government. Secondly, they must provide greater opportunities for local referenda and deliberative polling and other opportunities for participation in the decision-making about the appropriate local balance and deployment of resources.

Indeed, these are demanding conditions. It would be surprising for an argument that is grounded in liberal political philosophy if it were otherwise. It would not be too difficult to show that most governments pursuing the holistic governance agenda are failing to meet them all in full. The issue of invasiveness is one which is discussed in Chapter 7. However, if the argument is accepted, then it does show that there are conditions under which the holistic governance programme can be legitimate and democratically acceptable.

Conclusion

In this chapter we have considered accountability questions of three kinds – in which accountability represents in turn obstacles, strategies and normative requirements for holistic governance. Our conclusion is qualifiedly optimistic. It is indeed true that in many cases, present accountability systems are part of the problem, not part of the solution. On the one hand, reform is conceivable and could be designed, and the fatalists have not conclusively shown it to be infeasible. Nevertheless, the normative requirements of accountability – if we are to judge holistic governance by the standards of general liberal principles – are certainly high. On the other hand, they are no higher than are mandated on the same philosophical authority for other forms of reform of governance, or indeed for functionally organised governance. Accountability is an area of holistic governance in which we can say quite a lot about what needs to be done, but still rather little, at least on the basis of actual experience, about how to do it. In the next chapter we show that our understanding of intelligent budget design for holistic working is in much the same state – that is, we can specify some general principles, identify some risks, explore the lessons from some particular examples, but it would be premature to claim to have a fully developed body of experience.

9   Finance

It is often said that when money talks, it speaks with more authority than anything else. Therefore, many people would argue, bringing together budgets should be the high road to holism. This chapter analyses how far the evidence and the theory suggests that this claim is true. It begins with a discussion of the work that budgets do and why there has been so much attention paid to budget reform in government. This is followed by a review of some thirty years of effort in the reform of budgets in the hope of making finance into the key lever with which to influence coordination and integration. We then, present a classification of the main types of holistic budget instrument, before showing how different types of instrument were used and received by the public managers we interviewed in our local case studies. This leads us to conclude with an argument that the power of holistic budgeting is, in fact, easily overrated. Only when it is used in conjunction with other instruments can it be expected to be effective: on its own, a holistic budget is neither necessary nor sufficient for holism. This, we argue, is an important policy consideration because of the very great reliance placed upon holistic budgeting in many countries and states.

Budgeting serves several functions that are central to the conditions for effective coordination and integration. In particular, it provides a system of *accountability* of the executive to parliament and of the salaried executive to the political executive, and it sustains and underpins the system of short, medium and occasionally long term *planning*. Therefore, it should not be surprising to find that a debate about the role of budget design is one of the most important battlegrounds over government coordination today, just as it was in the 1970s.

In this chapter we are principally concerned with the expenditure side of budgeting and fiscal affairs, and we largely ignore the issue of taxation in its role as collecting resources to finance expenditure or in its role as a lever in macro-economic policy. However, there are of course many important uses of taxation – and in particular, for tax reliefs and tax expenditures (McDaniel, 1989) – which are of direct relevance to the organisation of expenditure and the integration of programmes, and we shall touch upon these. However, we are not concerned greatly in the present context with the means by which governments prevent levels of expenditure from rising

194

beyond acceptable levels, either absolutely or as a proportion of gross domestic product, or with the definitional problems of what counts as public expenditure (Corry, 1997).

In each generation of government reform, there has been a fresh focus on the reform of budgeting, the planning and oversight of expenditure planning on both the capital and revenue accounts. During the long decades of nineteenth-century reform of the civil service and the creation and reorganisation of local government, budget reform played a central role in underpinning the reform of administrative recruitment and structure. At that time, apart from the perennial challenge of controlling expenditure the growth, the key priorities were structuring budgets more transparently to enable greater ministerial and parliamentary scrutiny.

During the 1980s and 1990s in the 'reinvention' era, a quite different kind of budget reform moved centre stage. In the British financial management initiative of 1983, a new relationship was hammered out between the Treasury and the spending departments, to give greater Treasury control over defined objectives in return for some greater devolution to departments over micro-patterns of expenditure to meet those objectives, under more or less formal written agreements. This devolution of authorisation of routine expenditure and running costs was steadily extended, first, in the creation of the Next Steps agencies, and more recently under New Labour, in the establishment of the Public Service Agreements, to cover some flexibility in aspects of staff remuneration, notwithstanding the traditionally rigid and centrally negotiated civil service pay system. In New Zealand, the model was developed still further, with enforceable private law contracts between the centre and the departments.

However, the major change in the design of budget accountability from the reinvention era to the era of holistic governance has been in the terms in which budget objectives are framed. Aspirations have been raised from objectives set in terms of expenditures to be made in a defined period on certain services or staff to be put in placed (*inputs*), to programmes to be run (activities or *throughputs*), to specifying services to be delivered (*outputs*) and finally – at least in some countries and some fields – to real differences to be brought about in specific social problems, changes in the well-being of citizens and of the environment (*outcomes*).

Even as this shift has been made slowly, inconsistently, subject to great conflict and with real difficulty, there has been innovation at the input management end of the spectrum in budgeting. Many countries have moved from budgeting in the 1970s in real or inflation-adjusted terms (which proved itself to fuel inflationary expectations, not least among public sector employees and departmental chief), to cash terms in the 1980s, to resource-based or full accrual terms in the 1990s, in which both depreciation and the opportunity cost of capital – and the aspiration is eventually for all – resources measured by some summary monetary figure such as a capital charge, are both budgeted and accounted for (Pallot and Ball, 1997, p. 242). How far resource-based accounting serves the goals of coordination is open to debate, but at least in New Zealand and the UK, ministers have by and large believed the two are not at least in conflict. The principal benefits of resource-based accounting are in incentives for more efficient use of resources and especially of capital, in making flows of expenditure more transparent for ministers and select committee members. To make resource-based budgeting and accounting work for coordination, it is necessary to make sure that the specification of the ownership of assets and the units to which freedom to manage on inputs are devolved are designed in the most appropriate way. This shifts the focus of attention from the cost calculation basis for budgeting and accounting back to the organisational issues that are the main concern of this book.

In the next section we review the experience of the last thirty years in innovation in budgeting. This review shows that the predictions made by some commentators of outright failure for performance-based budgeting have not been borne out, but it also shows that budget reform is by no means a panacea, nor is it the easy and direct route to holism. This leads us to identify the range of options for budget reform to support coordination and integration. We present a case study of one of the most important early experiments in joint budget design and management in the UK, from which a number of lessons can be drawn. The chapter concludes with a review of the findings on the scope and limited uses of the tool of holistic budgeting.

A review of experience

There was a plethora of innovations in central budgeting in the 1960s under Johnson in the US, and in the 1970s in the UK, especially under the Heath administration. What is often today called performance budgeting has its roots long ago. In the US, the Hoover Commission in 1950 called for budgeting to move away from the classical line item structure that attached sums to particular inputs purchased, and to develop stronger connections with accounting for real performance. The 'Planning-Programming-Budgeting System' (PPBS) was a complex and comprehensive approach to output-based budgeting that was structured around cost-benefit comparisons, developed by McNamara and others at the RAND Corporation in the 1960s and was the subject of several reports to President Johnson who ordered its adoption (van Gunsteren, 1976). The Heath administration in the UK also attempted to make use of the technique.

The story of PPBS is, at least at first sight, a discouraging one for the hierarchical approach. It proved difficult to find and train enough expert budget analysts to make the system work. Political support for these programmes was erratic and commitment was not always developed across all the agencies that contributed to the budget process. Legislatures showed limited interest. Elected politicians knew how to play the politics of line item budgets and saw in these technocratic methods few opportunities for the kinds of populism at which they excel. Departmental chiefs, perhaps rightly, saw them as a threat to their turf and either resisted or quietly undermined them. Even in technocratic terms, the paperwork demanded by these systems in the 1970s, when computers lacked the capabilities that are taken for granted today, was awesome. Cut down versions of PPBS such as 'zero-based budgeting' championed by President Carter were experimented with, but suffered from the same problems of lack of consistent political support, subtle subversion by bureaucratic and legislator action, and sheer technical intractability. The UK Labour governments of Wilson and Callaghan in the second half of the 1970s experimented with budgeting in real, inflation-adjusted figures, but with inflation running at that time at unprecedented rates for the post-war period, the effect of this was to help to institutionalise expectations among departments, agencies and local authorities that budgets would be protected against inflation. This was widely recognised as contributing to inflationary pressures: the system was abandoned and, from the end of the 1970s, British governments budgeted in nominal figures. However, the use of inflation-adjusted figures was widely associated with the more ambitious forms of performance-based budget experiments and helped to discredit those programmes as well.

The experience of failed budget reform in the 1970s also left permanent scars upon the body of knowledge that constitutes political science. Commentators in the discipline quickly reached for fatalist explanations of these failures, and van Gunsteren's (1976) fatalist analysis became a classic of the discipline. It was natural to connect these failures with the politically increasingly important arguments against planning in general from Hayek (1944, 1960, 1978, 1973–1982), Popper (1949) and others (Challis *et al.*, 1988, chapter 1). It was argued, with all the authority that fatalism can muster, that what had in fact been tried only half-heartedly, proven too cumbersome too use, failed to secure political legitimacy from legislators and managers, *could only have* suffered this fate. The empirical premise of failure was supplemented with general theoretical accounts of the limits to rationality and cognition, of political short-termism leading to fragmentation, and of institutional gridlock, to yield the conclusion that failure in hierarchical holism and indeed any form of holism was guaranteed in advance.

But perhaps the fatalist explanation does not sweep all before it. That something did not succeed, for reasons that are, in retrospect, understandable, is not evidence that it could not have at least partly succeeded had circumstances been a little different. For example, recent experiments with comprehensive performance budgeting in Texas, Oregon and elsewhere have shown that the issues of tractability can be at least partly solved with the availability of cheap raw computing power and speed and better software, and that there are even ways in which the needs of politicians to find ways to exercise their role as populists can be fitted within the overall framework of holistic budgeting. There is no guarantee of the long term success of these experiments, and no doubt the academic fatalists will gloomily predict their failure sooner or later. But there is at least some reason to question whether the fatalist move from actual problems to the necessity of failure is a convincing and valid form of argument from premise to conclusion in the general case.

The 1970s were not the end of experiments in holistic budgeting planning, but in general the reforms of financial management in the 1980s were geared very differently. In the UK under the 1983 Financial Management Initiative (FMI), as in the USA under the series of Reagan reforms initiated by the Stockman régime, the aim was short-term expenditure control, the reassertion of Treasury control over departments, and a move away from long-range anticipatory planning. The bias of the 'reinvention' era reforms was towards the dedicated agency, accepting its fragmenting effects, and the bias in financial management was towards improved input-based budgeting and using performance measurement as a discipline that was essentially *external* to the content of agency or government-wide budgets, by contrast with the ambition of the 1970s that the two should be wholly integrated. There were, it is true, some very modest experiments in small discretionary joint budget exercises in the 1980s, but even these were essentially joined-up rather than holistic: that is to say, they were expressed in line item and input terms, not output, or, still less, outcome terms. For example, in the British case, the Department of Health was continuing to look for ways to overcome the problems that the institutionalised division between medical and social care inherited from the 1945 settlement created. One response, which was roughly contemporaneous with the FMI, was Joint Finance and Planning. Local health authorities and local authorities were required to create joint decision-making structures in order to access a capital and revenue budget that was earmarked for work that crossed the functional divisions. Again, most observers do not consider the Joint Finance programme a great success. However, it is at least not obvious that the by now familiar fatalist explanation for failure is the most compelling. In the case of Joint Finance, a disproportionately high number of projects were funded on limited duration revenue arrangements. This suggests that the initial expectation that Joint Finance could act as a pump-priming fund to stimulate the transfer and build up of resources was not always realistic in the very restrictive financial climate of the 1980s. Lack of response to the new extended financial arrangements after 1983 was probably due at least in part to the fact that commitments to ongoing revenue financing for projects funded in the early years was beginning to silt up the available funds, crowding out the resources for new projects.

During the early 1990s, in some local authorities and states in the USA, in Australia and a few years before that in New Zealand, there were major initiatives in all the countries that are moving towards holistic governance, to move towards some form of 'performance-based' or 'strategic' budgeting. This involves the allocation of monies not by 'line items' defined in terms of inputs or activities, but in terms of the quantities of outputs to be produced or the level of the outcomes to be achieved with the available resources at given prices (Osborne and Plastrik, 2000). The benefits are said to be greater clarity about the accountability of managers, greater focus on the things that really matter, more discipline upon politicians to make clear their priorities in rationing and to be honest about what they are prepared to afford with the appropriations of public money they are prepared to make, and more discipline to integrate all aspects of strategic planning with budget planning than are provided by input or 'line item' based budgeting systems.

A key decision in performance-based budgeting is whether to express budgets in outputs or outcomes. In the course of its major programme of government reform, New Zealand decided against trying to design budgets around outcomes, or to try to hold departmental and agency chief executives to account for outcomes, on the grounds that so many factors affect trends in community safety, environmental quality, health, prosperity or employability that are beyond the control of public officials, that it was thought this would be unfair (Pallot and Ball, 1997). No doubt there were other reasons too. It is genuinely and inherently difficult to specify with any rigour or accuracy the causal relationships between the activities of public services or regulatory agencies on the one hand, and some proportion of the variance in crime, unemployment, firm formation and bankruptcy rates, disease, pollution and degradation on the other, or to specify the periods of time over which such effects might be found (Smith, 1996), and to control for the 'deadweight' effects of those proportions of the problem that might have solved themselves without the intervention (for example, people on welfare to work programmes who would have got jobs in any case: OECD, 1991). To do this on a true resource accounting basis is even more difficult, for it involves specifying appropriate counterfactual situations in which the resources were put to alternative uses both on the same social problem and on others.

The problem can be made more manageable, if one is prepared to make big simplifying assumptions. For example, Osborne and Plastrik's (2000) discussion of performance budgeting in Texas suggests that the state is relying for performance-based budgeting in economic development on such indicators as the numbers of job opportunities announced and observed to be created in a given year by firms in receipt of subsidy, numbers of trainees graduating from programmes and so on. However, without controlling for jobs being created and destroyed elsewhere in the economy, deadweight effects in the trainee cohort, and without specifying the appropriate range of counterfactual scenarios for the numbers of job opportunities announced and created by the same and other firms in the absence of subsidy or with lower or higher levels of subsidy on the basis of some well-founded causal theory of the relationship between programme and economic activity, it is hard to know what to make of the budget and performance figures. Efforts are in fact made in Texas, Osborne and Plastrik report, to specify at least in outline what might be done with lower and higher levels of resource, and to do some kind of cost-benefit assessment of all programmes, but the assumptions about, for example, the shape of the expenditure–job yield curve that lie behind the claims of the possible effects of such change, in the example given, are of course open to challenge. Moreover, to conduct full and rigorous cost-benefit appraisals on the basis of specifying sufficient numbers of counterfactuals to estimate true opportunity costs, and to estimate expenditure–yield curves on the alternative assumptions of both linear and several non-linear relationships for every programme would be simply unaffordable for any government.

Another way to simplify and make tractable the process of handling outcomes, as recommended by Osborne and Plastrik (2000), is to look for outcomes that are closer to the level of programmes, rather than to look for outcomes in the true sense of the word, that have to be expressed in terms of valid and reliable scalar measures changes in human well-being or environmental quality.

Performance-based budgeting on the simplified basis typically conducted is in fact closer to output rather than outcome-based budgeting. This is not necessarily a criticism. Rather, it is a reasonable and practical solution. Indeed, there are good reasons for thinking that even this is an improvement over input-based line item budgeting. Indeed, it does enable politicians and managers to understand something about their performance. But it is important that politicians avoid both exaggerating its benefits, and that they are not misled by the relationships apparently observed, on a year on year basis, into believing that these are more robust descriptions of causal relationships between effort and outcomes than they really are. Very often, these relationships are 'tin openers for cans of worms', or prompts to ask other kinds of questions, rather than 'dials' that suggest a single action in reaction to a change (Carter *et al.*, 1993, p. 49). For example, decisions on what to cut and what to scale up should reflect not simply 'performance' as measured by a division of total turnover on an intervention by the number of the clientele observed to reach a certain level of outcome (duration without relapse into use of illicit drugs, duration without unemployment, and so on). Such decisions ought to reflect more careful thought about the range of available interventions, wider public feelings including the effects on fear of crime and fear of addiction as well as observed trends in actual crime or addiction. Analysis of the relationships between trends expenditure patterns and a particular selection of indicators chosen for a budget because of their tractability is not the same thing as a full cost-effectiveness evaluation, and should not be mistaken for the kind of research base required for holistic governance. But certainly, if the information is treated with due caution, performance-based budgeting of this kind represents an advance towards holistic governance.

Finally, it would be unsafe to ignore the effect of Goodhart's Law. Charles, now Lord, Goodhart is a Bank of England economist who observed the monetarist experiment at close quarters, when the Treasury and the Bank were attempting to target a particular level on one particular measure of the money supply, in the belief that this would show a robust and consistent relationship with inflation, lagged by two years at most. That assumption was found to be wrong, and worse still, the relationship between the particular measure of the money supply and lagged inflation seemed to grow less stable over the period it was being targeted (Jackson, 1992). Goodhart formulated, in all seriousness, a claim that might seem at first to be cynical or satirical one like Parkinson's Law, but is in fact well founded: *the effort of policy-makers to target an indicator in programmes will itself cause that measure over time to cease to be a good indicator of the underlying problem it was meant to capture.* The 'law' counsels not only against policy design targeting single indicators but also against interpreting performance on too narrow a set of indicators. The moral is as sound in measuring performance in personal social services or in vocational training as it is in monetary and macro-economic policy.

Unfortunately, it is not clear that politicians always or even typically do treat such information with this kind of caution. Osborne and Plastrik report that state legislators using performance-based budgets are often reluctant to accept recommendations from managers that the indicators should be changed, when they are found to have ceased to be appropriate. Moreover, they report, legislators also wanted fewer indicators, and were unwilling to be asked to consider more complex sets of indicators. This is not an uncommon story. The analysis by Hogwood *et al.* (1998) of efforts in accountability by British MPs in the 1992–7 Parliament suggests a similar and understandable reluctance to use more than a few simple indicators and some difficulty in appreciating the complexities of performance evaluation.

Sensible budgeting will always be built partly around some elements defined at the input level, and as a strategic tool should always be more strategic than a detailed management plan, therefore the outcome and output indicators will always appear in more summary form in a typical budget document. However, there are ways to provide politicians with more and more multidimensional information, using hypertext tools that they can use from their offices or even on screen during committee meetings. These tools enable information to be organised in such a way that budget setters and scrutineers can drill down to more detailed and complex information about relationships and trends, and see richer analyses of performance than the summary indicators presented at the top level. To date, most of the experimentation with hypertext budgeting is in the private sector, but the idea is far from new. Indeed, many French local authorities were using a tool that would support this as part of the 'SIAD Mairie' system as far back as the mid-1980s (Klein, Roux and Villedieu, 1991). Many software companies can now offer systems that will provide the facility for a 'dashboard' of basic indicators to be viewed on a top level screen, with a variety of options to drill down for more analyses and more detail without any requirement that the user be a sophisticated statistician or be capable of using an academic statistical data analysis package.

Performance-based budgeting has been attacked since the 1960s and 1970s as absurdly over-ambitious, as a quixotic or hubristic, but in any case doomed, attempt to produce synoptic rationality, as the last insanity of planning (van Gunsteren, 1976). Perhaps these were fair accusations to make against its advocates thirty and forty years ago: we cannot judge. Today, however, more modest claims are typically made for it – that it enhances, albeit incrementally, the capability of those holding the executive to account, that it reinforces the discipline of asking whether what is being done actually works, that it introduces a slightly more long-term element into a process that can be unnecessarily short-term. Few today would argue, as the critics of the 1970s suggested the advocates then did, that performance budgeting – still less performance budgeting alone – will optimise and rationalise policy.

Without doubt, however, outcome-based budgeting is information-intensive, research-intensive, time-consuming for managers and politicians. Traditional input-based 'line item' budgets take much less time to process, despite their limitations. The case that these resources should be found for this support for holistic working and that they represent value for money is made if the overall case for holistic governance is accepted.

Types of holistic budget strategy

So far, we have offered only a fairly gross taxonomy of styles of budgetary accountability. However, the place and limits of holistic budgeting become clearer when a more finely grained classification is considered, of the particular types of budget structure. Consider Figure 9.1: the rows represent spectra for which the extreme cases are provided, not binary alternative choices.

The 'funder' in Figure 9.1 may be central government, the centre of a single local authority, or a directorate general of the European Union. These differing measures of accountability distribute the burden of the

Figure 9.1 *Types of holistic budget by accountability*

	More budgetary accountability	Less budgetary accountability
1. *Source of specification*	Definition of outcomes, outputs activities or inputs to be combined is set by the funder	Definition of outcomes, outputs activities or inputs to be combined is set by the recipient, within broad parameters of programme
2. *Formula or competition*	Amount of funding and target recipients are set by formula	Target depends on decision of potential recipients to bid at all, and amount depends on quality of recipient's bid, in a competitive process
3. *Discretion*	Terms and conditions are set out in detail by funder, e.g. the budget is highly specific about activities to be undertaken	Recipients have extensive control over uses, e.g. the budget is specific about outcomes, leaving recipient discretion over selection of activities

transactions costs differently. Centralisation of specification shifts the programme design costs to the centre, but can increase the costs of compliance and reporting of the recipients at local level. Greater discretion can increase ownership and commitment to a programme of holistic working among recipients and may increase innovation, but performs less well in targeting and accountability.

Competitive bidding systems can, under certain circumstances, improve innovation and targeting of resources, but probably increase the total administrative costs relative to yield, because of the time cost of bid preparation, particularly for those potential recipients that are not successful.

In our programme of interviews for our own case studies, pooled budgets accessed by bidding were repeatedly described to us as 'a game'. Managers talked of the 'fantasy' and 'pretence' involved in budgeting and complience respectively.

Interviewees suggested that the skills required in playing the bidding game are very different from those involved in putting bid plans into action and making them work. But bidding timetables and the whole notion of being able to know what needs to be done and is feasible in advance mean that bidding remains a separate activity, and one which involves considerable creativity, wishful thinking, ambiguity, faith and fudge.

Budgets in the bidding game are also a matter of creativity and fudge. Budget timetables for matching funding are not synchronised and so, as one Midcaster manager out it, 'a lot of it is Emperor's clothes stuff. You have to say you're going to get this but you don't really know.'

One area of creativity in budget setting in the bidding game is to inflate the value of items provided in kind from partners who do not have either the resources or the commitment to contribute any 'hard' money. However, as one interviewee in hard-pressed Midcaster CCC involved in a number of bids pointed out: 'you have to be pretty shrewd to make sure that what they are so generously giving to the partnership is not something that you would have got as of right anyway – one of their core responsibilities.'

In some cases, participants in the bidding game will accept over-inflated contributions in kind if, for example, this is the only way to get a particular partner involved. As one interviewee in Southbrookborough pointed out, 'you have to realise that budget setting is a human and dynamic process. It's not just a mathematical calculation. It's about power and control.'

Combinations are possible between different rows in Figure 9.1, and this also brings specific trade-off(s). For example, low discretion combined with competitive bidding is quite commonly used, and this can run the risk of shallowness, because the specific functional organisations or departments form temporary alliances to bid for money, but when successful, simply funnel the additional resources down their existing separate structures rather than innovate in the development of any new holistic executive structures that might be more appropriate. In the British case, outcome specification by funders combined with extensive recipient discretion is rare. However, the New Zealand case allows for this in more instances. It can work well in good times, but when there are failures this combination is not politically very robust: the normal processes of politics tend to demand that such systems are revised to allow for more micro-management by central politicians.

Competitive bidding systems also tend to foster in the centre, practices and policy-making in a style that leads in localities to 'fragmented holism' and 'initiativitis', or the problems of trying to coordinate between large numbers of distinct programmes each intended to integrate different activities or around different outcomes but within the same geographical area or within the purview of a single recipient, all of which are competing for the attention and support of the ablest politicians and managers.

Our interviewees reported that in many cases, pooled budgets achieved through competitive bidding led to risks of holistic initiatives being seen as a special project which had nothing to do with the mainstream work of the organisation. In Southbrookborough one manager told us, 'if we became a complete separate entity, it would be easy [for the parent health and local authorities] to disown all the problems … we could have been scapegoated.' The partnership feared being 'out of sight, out of mind'. This was a particular danger if the pooled budget was seen as experimental or innovative, if it was time-limited, if it employed project workers and/or if it involved additional, separate funding. Joint work funded by contributions from existing departmental funds ran similar or different risks. Another way in which pooled budgets might 'drown' issues was by take-over. For example, it was suggested that the Single Regeneration Budget (SRB) is now seen as very much a programme defined and controlled by central government. Even though it was initially funded by contributions from other departments, the objectives of those departmental contributions, such as Regional Enterprise and Business Start-Up grants, have largely disappeared from SRB. But in other cases problems arose precisely because the contributing agencies would not let go of their stake in the joint venture. One interviewee in South-brookborough commented, 'we have a so-called pooled budget but each partner's contribution is ring-fenced and we have to account separately for each part and make sure that we contribute to each department's performance measures.' In these cases, separated budgets were pooled and then, in effect, re-separated to reproduce the old departmental silos.

Accountability pressures can push relationships over the peak of the curvilinearity problem. Accountability for pooled budgets was regarded by some respondents as, like bidding, something of a game. One respondent in Midcaster described accountability as a matter of 'feeding the beast with one set of stories while getting on with the real job of improving the quality of life of the people in this authority'. While some highlighted the dangers of multiple accountability which effectively reproduces the old departmental divisions leaving little more than pooled rhetoric. Others pointed to the risks of lack of real or effective accountability in some pooled budget structures, because of the difficulties of attributing responsibility for jointly generated outputs and outcomes, the dangers of double (or more) funding of the same or related activities, and the related dangers of 'double vision' in measuring outputs and outcomes.

Weak tools are needed to supplement, balance and give context to holistic budgets

The discussion above suggests that, while it can play a useful role in some settings, outcome-based budgeting – or even pooled budgeting defined by activities – is in itself not sufficient to ensure holistic governance and, specifically, that the well-known dangers of hubristic excessive rationalism and failure that attend all aspirations for synoptic planning could follow from any attempt to achieve holistic working relying principally on this tool. For budgetary planning and accountability are strong tools of governance, in the terms of the taxonomy set out in Figure 4.2, and indeed they belong to the hierarchical style as defined in Figure 4.1 in Chapter 4. The point is not that these strong tools have no place, but that styles of governance that rely exclusively upon them are brittle and liable to the peculiar failures that attend over-centralisation and hubristic rationalism.

From the individualist perspective, the feasibility (as opposed to the desirability) objection to reliance on the strong tools of governance is the classical objection that the agencies that wield those tools – which will inevitably, individualists argue, mean the state centre, whether holists like it or not – cannot possibly acquire sufficient information to know how it should deploy those strong tools: the argument can be traced back through the generally anti-state arguments of Hayek (1944, 1960, 1973, 1982) back to von Mises (1935, 1948). However, on this more moderate individualist view of intra-governance coordination, the deployment of the blunt strong tools merely crowds out and disempowers the capabilities of individual public managers from using their entrepreneurial ability to coordinate the fragmented resources of governance as best they might.

The communitarian case for the limits of holistic budgeting can be stated as follows, and we draw upon the evidence of our interviews with local practitioners for this. It is a variant of a 'weak constraint' argument that is in part shared with the individualist solidarity. The usefulness of holistic and pooled budgets is specific, limited and precise, and they should be seen as one component of the tool-kit: they are neither necessary nor sufficient in general for successful integration.

As one of our interviewees commented during our workshop, 'money can be an important condition or a trigger. But it's like a shotgun marriage. It will only work if you work at it together.' The greatest achievements of, for example, the British experiment with the Single Regeneration Budget (SRB), were to administer shocks and act as a trigger to bring together professions, organisations and agencies for the first time. The key SRB agencies dealt with physical infrastructure regeneration, transport, job training and community development. Where fresh initiatives were undertaken they were sustained not so much by the availability of the pooled budget, but because they created a common culture, goals, and, crucially, common bases of professional knowledge. In Midcaster, the role of pooled budgets was symbolic, rather than a budgetary discipline for joined-up working. Those who set up the programme had hoped to use the tool of European funding to demonstrate what the effects of new money would be, and to lever further funds from businesses, and the promise of new money was significant in gaining the city council's support. In the event the European funding bid failed, but by then the project had gained sufficient support to continue. Similarly, in Beltham an SRB bid was unsuccessful; but by the time the bad news came through, those working together had built up enough knowledge, trust and capabilities to guarantee the project's survival. However, the SRB in and of itself was not the driver of integration, but the occasion for it. It provided the arena on which integrators could work. In Midcaster, an officer remarked in the course of one of our interviews, 'Take SRB – the biggest and clearest example of holistic budgeting but it's less than 0.5% of our total budget. The main budget is the super tanker and SRB is just one little propeller.'

*A case study: financial tools for integration between
health and social care*

If the strong tools of holistic budgeting are the key ones, then we would expect the existing functionally organised budget structures to be the key barriers to holistic working. This is a proposition we can now test.

In fact, we argue, there are many cases of innovative and successful joint working between health and social services, despite the separation of budgets, that are based firmly on joint identity and knowledge. Where existing networks are weak and in need of reinforcement (in some cities sustainable urban development is an example), pooled budgets can have a one-off cementing effect. But it is the creation of common cultures, knowledge bases, identities and synergies in working patterns and roles that are the really powerful tools for sustaining – as opposed to initiating or disciplining priorities within – integration. If these are in place, the organisational process of accountability can sometimes get in the way of getting effective holistic working done.

This is a case with a longer history than most of initiatives to promote integration, including a longstanding Joint Finance scheme, which was linked to joint accountability through joint committees of local authorities and the National Health Service. Yet efforts to encourage joint planning and activity between health and social services in the 1980s were only a limited success. One District General Manager of a Health Authority analysed the achievements and the obstacles of joint planning machinery as follows: 'I do not rate the Joint Consultative Committee very highly and am doubtful if a single constructive idea has ever come out of it. It is the forum at which the local politicians have their say, robustly, and often with scant attention to fact or health and social need. This is where the political points are made, but the machinery exists and we have to use it' (Nichols, 1991, p. 2).

Joint planning showed no evidence of the comprehensive, joint client group strategies envisaged by the initial Circulars. There were, however, some successes in moving beyond the rhetoric of joint working. Four key factors were found to contribute to survival and success: 'clarity of purpose; commitment and shared ownership; robust and coherent management arrangements; and organisational learning' (Hardy *et al.*, 1993, p. 40). But jointly managed schemes remained fragile, vulnerable to organisational pressures that threatened their sustained development. They operated on the periphery of parent bodies and were viewed as either an administrative inconvenience or a threat to the professional or organisational status quo. They relied heavily on mutual trust and on the personal networks of their original champions' (Hardy *et al.*, 1993, p. 41).

There were several major barriers to interagency coordination. Organisational structures including interorganisational complexity and the fact that geographical boundaries do not coincide, were one set of obstacles. Procedural obstacles were also important, including differences in planning horizons and cycles and in budgetary cycles and procedures.

Differences in funding mechanisms and bases and in stocks and flows of financial resources were other barriers.

The experience of Joint Finance also illustrates the way in which wider and longer-term factors and considerations influence the effects of pooled budgets. Joint Finance was first envisaged as providing an appropriate balance between capital and revenue in order to contribute to both the transfer of resources to the community and a build-up of resources in the community. However, with increasing financial stringency imposed on local government budgets at the time many found it difficult to support the revenue consequences of capital projects. As a result the composition of joint finance programmes differed from initial expectations.

Projects fell into five main divisions related to their implications for future revenue commitments: capital projects with no revenue consequences; capital projects with associated revenue consequences of limited duration or requiring total commitment after a tapering process; revenue projects of limited duration lasting less than the standard seven year period; revenue projects with seven year periods during which the health authority contribution would be phased out; and projects up to a maximum of thirteen years (a new regulation introduced in 1983) in which sponsoring agencies could respond to the financial consequences of joint finance.

The disproportionately high number of projects funded on limited duration revenue arrangements suggested that the initial expectation that joint finance could act as a pump-priming fund to stimulate the transfer and build up of resources was not always realistic in the current financial climate. Lack of response to the new extended financial arrangements (after 1983) was probably due partly to implications for the remainder of the fixed joint finance programme, that is, funding over thirteen years would impede the rate of new projects in coming years.

But professional and political barriers were as important as structural, procedural and financial obstacles. Professional obstacles included differences in ideologies and values, professional self-interest and concern for threats to autonomy and domain, threats to job security, and conflicting views about clients' and consumers' interests and roles. Political barriers included issues to do with status and differences in legitimacy between elected and appointed agencies (Hardy *et al.*, 1993). Thus it appears that financial arrangements may be significant obstacles to interagency working, but they are not the only ones.

Nevertheless joint finance and planning was a limited success, although not in the terms originally envisaged (Webb, 1991). Its vision of comprehensiveness was probably unrealistic, not least because planning resources are scarce and need to be deployed selectively, and because joint planning itself needs to be sufficiently flexible to take account of changing local needs (Hardy *et al.*, 1993).

Although joint planning and finance failed to produce the tangible outputs envisaged, their value lay in the process initiated. What the process achieved was 'mutual organisational learning; a clarification of agency and professional differences; an upward spiral of trust; and growing consensus about aims, principles and priorities' (Hardy *et al.*, p. 40).

The case study shows that the key barriers were not in fact budgetary, and that better designed holistic budgets would not in and of themselves have created more incentives and conditions for holism. That is not to say that better designed financial structures would not have helped, but rather to point out that the strong tools alone would not have made the difference desired to the levels of coordination.

Conclusion: budgeting in its place

In this chapter we have shown that the principles of requisite variety and rough balance laid down in Chapter 4 are of central importance in budget policy. The response of the 'weak constraint' forms of organisation to the insistence on strong tools needs to be taken seriously. Holistic budgeting is neither necessary nor sufficient for bringing about holistic working. It would be wrong to conclude that it has no place: one cannot rely exclusively on weak tools any more than one can rely exclusively on strong ones. But used alone or in the wrong context, it can actually be counterproductive.

For politicians and public managers to put all their attention, faith, time and energy into designing and operating structures of budgetary accountability will not be enough, and actually be counterproductive for holism. The key challenge for implementation is the cultivation of shared culture, shared knowledge, shared experience between managers and professionals in different tiers and functions of governance. This is not achieved principally through systems of budgetary planning and accountability but through the weak tools of managing flows of information, using training, promotion and motivation systems to enable practitioners to develop these cultures and bodies of knowledge together.

The conditions under which budgetary accountability for holistic working is most likely to be counterproductive, and to redirect effort away from learning, towards creative accounting and redescription of existing initiatives and towards defensiveness, are when the culture of that accountability is one in which politicians are principally concerned to use budgetary accountability as a tool for the devolution of blame for the inevitable failures of any programme of public management onto salaried public managers and professionals, and when they are also concerned that innovations should be politically safe, and not run risks of failure. This has, unfortunately, been the political climate in which the holistic governance agenda has been pursued in Britain.

In this case, the polar opposite would not be New Zealand, but many of the states in the USA where holistic working, under various names, has been a high priority during the 1990s. While those cities and states where the blame culture of accountability remains dominant – New York City is an internationally known example – have made least progress, those cities and states – the city of Dallas, the states of Oregon, Vermont, Texas, for example – with political cultures sufficiently trusting of public servants to adopt the slogan of 'entrepreneurial government' (to which Osborne and Gaebler, 1992, attached great weight), with all its connotations of being willing to take risks, fail and then learn from those failures, have achieved more in integration.

In the medium term, it is the creation of this kind of risk culture in the wider democratic politics that is the key to enabling, motivating and supporting managers and professionals in creating joined-up culture and integrated knowledge. When performance or outcome-based budgeting is pursued without this, it can be positively unhelpful.

Having now explored many of the key specific dimensions of holistic working in government, we can bring the argument together in the next, and last, chapter to answer the question, how far can holistic governance be institutionalised?

10   The Prospects for Holistic Governance

In this final chapter, we argue that there is no reason to be as fatalistic as so much of political science and organisational sociology has been about the prospects for holistic governance. We show that it could be institutionalised as a paradigm in public management, just as other models have been in the past. The chapter begins by setting out the nature of the challenge to be met. We argue that the issue needs to be understood as one of institutionalisation. We therefore offer a fresh synthesis of the theory of institutionalisation, which enables us to identify the key factors for the institutionalisation of a paradigm in public management. This provides us with a way of analysing what has been achieved and what remains to be done, and how far it is feasible to imagine the challenge of institutionalising holism being met. We do not suggest that it has been met anywhere in full, but we conclude there is no reason in principle or in theory that prohibits it, and that there are encouraging signs. In short, there is an answer to the received fatalistic wisdom of so much of political science and public management debate.

The challenge

Holistic governance is a major commitment for the reform of policy-making, civil service and local government structures, budgets, work processes and professional networks, systems of staff development, management practices, information systems including the design and use of digital information technology, and for the accountability of public officials at every level. There have been several phases in the history of politics – principally those of twentieth-century centrist politics – and of public administration when this has been attempted, and there are lessons to be learned from the rise and fall of those initiatives. The current phase of the pursuit of holism has arisen largely in reaction to the perception of fragmentation in both policy and administration that flowed from the 'reinvention' or 'new public management' era, in which managerial focus was conceived as requiring dedicated, single-purpose agencies with objectives defined in activity or output terms only.

Nevertheless, we have acknowledged the fragility of holistic governance. To be sure, there are political pressures that lead politicians to introduce policies and commitments expressed in input and activity terms that conflict with the aspiration for holism. Motivating public managers to work across agency boundaries is difficult. The great functionally defined departments and professions have real institutional force and create incentives of status, career aspiration and expectation, and managerial turf the defence of the autonomy of which is worth something to many public managers and indeed to many politicians. Innovation in holistic systems of accountability has lagged behind innovation in holistic budget mechanisms. The ordinary coping mechanisms by which front line staff or street level bureaucrats manage their work pressures can sometimes cut against the grain of holistic working. It is all too easy for national politicians to focus on central structures, which they can affect directly and in relatively short periods of time. They are tempted to use the strong tools of governance, rather than local implementation networks over which they must deploy the weak tools over long period There are plenty of risks, problems of implementation, genuine difficulties in knowing how to proceed and areas of ignorance about 'what works'.

However, we have consistently argued in every chapter of this book, as we have examined each of these sources of fragility, that it does not follow that, in the face of these difficulties, the analyst of the trend should be fatalistic about its prospects. Indeed, there are no guarantees that the trend will be institutionalised, or that even if institutionalised in public management, it will deliver all the aspirations attached to it. But nor is it necessarily true that because something is fragile it must be doomed. We have offered a number of specific arguments against the fatalist case.

The first is historical. At the same point in the development of the 'reinvention' programme fatalist arguments had been made, yet that programme succeeded in institutionalising itself, even though in many ways it cut against the grain of the then inherited institutionalised styles of both governance and public management.

There is a theoretical underpinning to the historical argument against the fatalist. The fatalist point of view flows from a very particular kind of institutionalism. That is, first, it takes structure to be everything, agency little or nothing. Secondly, it takes institutions to be principally constraining and limiting, not productive or innovation-generating (Goodin, 1996, pp. 19–20) Third, it takes institutional explanation to lead to predictions of continuity (Zucker, 1977). Fourth, it takes institutions to be, in the general case, effective in securing the continuity or change to which they are committed (March and Olsen, 1989). Fifth, it takes institutions to produce homogeneity more often than diversity (DiMaggio and Powell, 1983). This, as Stinchcombe has recently (1997) argued, is a very recent view of institutions, and not one which the founders of institutional analysis in the social sciences – Durkheim, Weber, Commons, Veblen, Wigmore, the younger Selznick – would have recognized. This fatalistic view is deeply consonant with 'the new institutionalism', as formulated by such writings as Meyer and Rowan (1977), DiMaggio and Powell (1983), although some of these thinkers have modified their views since then (Powell, 1991).

The authors of the present volume, while differing in particular theoretical affiliations, share the view about the importance of institutional analysis, although we argue strongly that the fatalist view of institutions that emerges from some 'new' institutionalist writing is empirically and theoretically inferior to some of the older, subtler and more flexible institutional theories (6, 1999a; Stoker 2000; see also Peters, 1999). Institutions are productive as much as they are constraining; they are systems that open up possibilities as much as they close down. To argue that there is a dead weight of inherited institutional forces that would block an innovation is inadequate and a misreading of what institutional explanations are properly equipped to do.

A second argument is that there are now more powerful political, institutional and organisational commitments that make for holism than could have been observed, for example, during the 'national efficiency' aspirations of the centre ground in Edwardian times, or during the Carter and Heath governments in the US and the UK of the 1970s. Public expectations also seem to have risen, in respect of the problem-solving capabilities of governments, and this may explain in some part the roller coaster profile of the levels of public trust in government in recent decades. The political and organisational commitments can be observed in the new forms of budgeting, appraisal, training and performance measurement introduced to shape implementation, and in the new forms of policy coordination and meta-analysis based policy work being pressed from the centre in countries such as the UK and New Zealand. The effect of some of these organisational innovations is to create new learning networks. Together, these institutional forces are beginning to create new kinds of interests and preferences among public managers and at least some politicians.

A third consideration is technological. New information technologies have enabled the deployment of kinds of detectors required by holistic working, in ways that the lumbering information technologies of the 1970s could not. Also, new kinds of intellectual technologies are now available for those politicians and public managers willing to use them for holism, including new systems of outcome measurement, models of matrix management and of network steering (Kooiman, 1993; Kickert *et al.*, 1997) and the kinds of understandings of how to design a strategy for holistic working that we have outlined in this book and, more prescriptively, in our previous writings (6 *et al.*, 1999). Finally, the deepening commitment of governments to cross-national benchmarking and comparison in many fields of public policy is also beginning to build within government a set of evaluative practices that can support mutual learning for holism.

Taken together, these three general arguments against fatalism amount to a demonstration of the empirical possibility of change, some forces that make for willingness and some forces that make for ability to make changes in the direction of holistic governance. Taken together, they encompass all of the major categories of forces that political scientists consider to be important in understanding policy change – historical trajectories, institutions, organisational inheritance, networks, interests, ideas, technologies and tools (for instance, John, 1998; Rose and Davies, 1994; Hood, 1994; Rose, 1993).

But this is not the end of the argument against the fatalist. We still need to show that the fatalist claim that while holistic governance may indeed be tried quite seriously, it will not be institutionalised, for the forces of fragility will as steadily de-institutionalise it in both governance and in public management, and that as a result, fragmentation will return in other forms. The pendulum in the history of public management will swing back away from holism, leaving little behind that will substantially shape subsequent periods, just as previous waves of innovation in holism have left little that has not been overwhelmed by later forces for fragmentation.

In Chapter 4 we set out a general form argument to the effect that it is at least possible that the institutionalisation of holism could be achieved in ways that would leave behind something that could be robust against future cyclical forces for other styles of governance. In that chapter we argued that holistic governance can be conceived and could be practised in ways that meet the neo-Durkheimian test of viability – namely, that there can be within holism some reasonable, rough and ready, 'clumsy' balance between the four basic tropes, biases and institutional solidarities that govern styles of organisation. That is, the charge that holism is and must be merely a hierarchical style, or a single mechanical solidarity in Durkheim's terms, can be rejected.

We do not say – no one can say with any confidence – that holism will be institutionalised, that future contrary trends in governance will not in fact overwhelm its legacy, that the forces of fragility will not in practice prove too great to resist. What we do argue is that if holism does prove to have been a passing phase with limited lasting impact on governance, then there is and will have been no necessity about such an outcome, and that in explaining such a defeat, one should look to contingent, empirical failures of particular aspects of institutionalisation. To phrase a defence of possibility in such modest, even negative terms, might seem to provide the practitioner with only the coldest comfort, and might seem to offer the academic political scientist critic only a narrow concession. In our view, the significance of this argument, if it is accepted, is much larger. If the argument goes through, it should offer real encouragement to practitioners that there are things within their power to achieve, and to the academic critic, it offers a major challenge to the prevailing, indeed orthodox, view that management fads come and go and, in the words of Prospero in the *Tempest*:

> shall dissolve
> and, like this insubstantial pageant faded,
> leave not a wrack behind.
> (Act IV, Scene 1, lines 54–56)

Certainly, we would join with the fatalist and with many others in denying that the history of governance or of public management is a process of the cumulative development of knowledge, competence, efficacy, rationality, judgment, progress or 'modernisation' (Hood, 1998); this is far from the case. From that denial, however, it does not follow that phases succeed each other completely, or that rival forms wholly supplant one another and make their exits, leaving an empty stage on which the next act must start, as it were, from institutional scratch.

The bulk of this concluding chapter, then, is devoted to developing this argument about the nature and possibility of the institutionalisation of initiatives and paradigms in governance and public management, and of the holistic governance agenda in particular.

Institutionalisation and institutional change

In the limited space available here we can only present a schematic synthesis of accounts of institutionalisation. This draws on a variety of traditions of institutional analysis, but is guided by the Durkheimian principles of institutional analysis.

We can only identify from across the social sciences, factors that are at least jointly sufficient – and perhaps more than sufficient – for institutionalisation to occur, rather than a defined set of necessary factors. (Perhaps one might try arguing that if more than, say, one factor in each of the categories below is present, that would be just sufficient for institutionalisation, but this seems rather arbitrary.) However, for the purposes of the argument for the possibility of holism, only a set of factors that are jointly sufficient is required. Although political science knows many institutionalist theories, and studies many kinds of political institution, it is still true to say that the understanding of institutionalisation belongs much more to general sociology and to anthropological theory (Jepperson, 1991), than it does to political science. Therefore, we make no apology for borrowing – indeed, committing grand larceny – principally from these disciplines in order to present a minimal account of the sufficient conditions of institutionalisation.

For the present purpose, we shall say that something – either a particular initiative or a paradigm in governance and public management – has achieved *institutionalisation* when the following characteristics can be attributed to it:

- It has, in a given society, the status of established fact, something that must be dealt with by anyone operating in its particular field of endeavour, and which has at least a modest presumption of legitimacy.
- For many of those who work within particular formal organisations, roles or career paths, that are underpinned or organised in some way by the putative institution, the institution has the status of an accepted, legitimate and valid rule or norm, and not merely an arbitrarily adopted convention.
- It has some name or noun phrase in the language of the society in which it operates, by which it is generally known and recognized. Under that name the putative institution is taken to represent something with at least just enough internal consistency and coherence to be recognized in discussion.
- When faced with challenge to its establishment, legitimacy or persistence, the institution has been able to survive; that is, it has shown itself robust against rival institutions or projects for institutionalisation. This is the criterion of 'viability'.

These are demanding conditions, but it would not be too much to say that in many countries by the end of the 1980s or the early 1990s, the collection of commitments then collectively known as 'new public management' met this test. In the same way, by the end of the nineteenth century, the Northcote-Trevelyan model of a civil service or by the middle of the 1960s, the post-war model of the local welfare state, could both be said to have met these tests for institution-hood.

If something institutionalised is interesting, then it must also be distinct. This means that the noun phrase that describes it (the third characteristic above) must capture some distinctive characteristics of various kinds, which will be identified when we discuss the conditions for institutionalisation.

Institutionalisation of an initiative or a paradigm cannot be achieved instantly: typically, it takes at least a period of years, and in the case of the Northcote-Trevelyan model, it took many decades. While stage models may not very helpful, at the very least, there must be in the course of institutionalisation a stage of initiation, a stage of sustaining the institution, and there may eventually be a stage of de-institutionalisation.

The next section of this chapter consists of a list of what seem to be, based on the arguments of the principal texts on institutionalisation, at least sufficient conditions for it to occur. The account given draws on a wide range of traditions, including the classics. However, as will be expected from previous chapters of this book, the overall character of the account of institutionalisation is Durkheimian rather than Weberian: that is to say, the dynamics on which Weber focused are shown to be a special case of a larger process for which the work of Durkheim and of the tradition that has followed him, provide a better guide. The factors are organised into the following headings:

- socio-economic background;
- cognition or ideas;
- interests;
- organisation;
- emotional attachment; and
- practice.

This particular list should surprise no one. For these are the basic categories of factors used – albeit given different weight by rival theories – in political science in explaining policy change (e.g., John, 1998), in much of historical sociology in explaining macro-social change (e.g., Mann, 1986; Sztompka, 1993), in political sociology explaining the waxing, waning and the social and political impact of social movements (e.g., Johnston and Klandermans, 1995), and many other phenomena.

Under each element, we give examples from the major paradigms of governance and public management of recent decades from the Northcote-Trevelyan model of the civil service, through the New Liberal 'national efficiency' aspirations of Edwardian times to the post-war welfare state model and the reinvention era that is now ending. Having presented this account of what institutionalisation means for paradigms of governance and public management, we then use the analysis to consider the question of how far the holistic governance agenda can be said to be on the way towards institutionalisation.

Sufficient conditions for institutionalisation of paradigms of public management

We consider first the conditions for initiating institutionalisation. The first conditions concern the *socio-economic background.*

In order to be initiated and survive the 'liability of newness', a paradigm of governance and public management that is a credible candidate for institutionalisation must achieve a sufficient degree of 'fit', that is, be able to control, mask or manage dangerous inconsistencies with

1. other institutions, including macro-political institutions, for example, the constitution, and micro-political institutions such as style of state-craft, party organisation;
2. fiscal conditions of what is considered politically *affordable* by key opinion formers such as within broadcast and print media;
3. at least some prior self-recognized and vested *interests* of at least some actors, including leading politicians, parties, public sector professions, business sectors with a direct interest in providing consultancy or seek-ing service contracts with the public sector, and so forth; and with
4. prevailing conditions of *legitimacy*, such as key currents of public opin-ion, likely social movement activity, and so on.

Next are conditions for continuation of institutionalisation. To sustain itself long enough and with sufficient robustness to achieve the status of institu-tionalisation as defined in (1)–(4) above, a paradigm of public manage-ment must both to some degree fit within existing (the backward-looking element of institutionalisation) and also generate new (the forward-looking element that sustains both distinctiveness and institutionalisation) ideas, interests, styles of organisation, affect, and practice. Key to the sustaining of institutionalisation is the shaping *cognition* or *ideas*, that is to say, the construction of a 'tradition'.

A paradigm of public management must, like any institution (Durkheim, 1995 [1912]; Durkheim and Mauss, 1963 [1902–3]; Berger and Luckman, 1966; Bowker and Star, 1999), to some degree both work within *general cat-egories* in terms of which institutionally prescribed actions are appraised and at the same time adapt and innovate new general categories. In the 'reinven-tion' era, for example, 'the three Es' and the general categories of 'incentive' and 'performance' served this function, just as the idea of administration *sine ira et studio* and merit-based recruitment did for the Northcote-Trevelyan era in the UK and the Progressive era in the US.

An institution must provide more *particular narratives*, that is, it must offer an account of the nature of its world, or a 'cosmology' – what motivates human beings, what values are important, what kinds of things can be achieved – and also has to tell a range of particular stories. Indeed, for many writers one of the tests of whether something is institutionalised is whether, on being asked a question, the representatives or advocates of an institution typically answer with general claims about the nature of the world, human life and motivation, fundamental values and where history is expected to take us (Douglas, 1986, 1970; Durkheim, 1995 [1912]). For example, the myths of institutionalised altruistic human motivation re-told by Richard Titmuss in the 1960s and 1970s (e.g., 1971) played this role for the Beveridgean welfare state paradigm. Again the reinvention paradigm was grounded in an account of the motivation of both professionals and politicians as utility maximisers, of administrative history as a process of upheavals of rationalisation, of the fundamental ethical value of efficient service provision, or of the expansion of the role of proprietary firms in implementation. Stories are more particular. Some stories must be exemplars of the paradigm's categories (Douglas, 1993). For example, some of the case studies told by Barzelay with Armajani, 1992; or by Osborne and Gaebler, 1992, quickly gathered mythic status, and were re-told from a great many conference platforms. The New Zealand reform programme also acquired exemplar status for categories such as the move from status to contract and incentive.

In addition, an institution must develop a body of *formal teachable knowledge* in which people can become acculturated. In the post-war British welfare state, great efforts were made to codify the formal knowledge of the recently developed semi-professions such as land use planning and social work. By the end of the 1980s, and for the reinvention paradigm similar processes of codification – in which the creation of university accredited courses play a key role – went on for purchasing in the public sector.

The late Imre Lakatos argued (1970) that scientific research programmes – that is, internally consistent clusters of theories, experimental practices, bodies of people – are institutionalised when they are perceived, not only among their practitioners but more widely, as *progressive* rather than degenerating in the sense that they support a continuing stream of innovations and new capabilities. That is to say, an institution must generate its own *cognitive energy*. The same test is a powerful one when examining paradigms of governance. For example, the model of governance and public management that developed in the late eighteenth century in Prussia following the reforms of Frederick William produced not only innovations in centralisation, but as Hacking (1990) showed, a stream of innovations in statistics, and as Foucault (1991) argued, in the management of populations. Similarly, the post-war welfare state paradigm supported a stream of innovations well into the 1970s, in local governance and in the production of new professions of governance such as community work.

Institutions must not only produce new ideas; they must also *forget* old ones (Douglas, 1986; Halbwachs, 1992 [1941]). Some ideas are indeed deliberately challenged and rejected by institutions, and heroic victories declared. Other inconvenient ideas are simply quietly forgotten. For example, many commentators have suggested that the reinvention quietly forgot some aspects of the post-war welfare state paradigm's concepts of 'public service' as a category of basic motivation.

Institutions must, to sustain themselves, shape practices of *judgment* (Vickers, 1995 [1965]). One conception of judgment, for example, as a process of calculation that recurs every few decades from the aspirations of the eighteenth-century government statisticians through Bentham's felicific calculus to Herbert Simon's hopes for calculation-based artificial intelligence in policy-making in the 1950s to the e-governance movement of today (6, 2002 forthcoming). In general, this tends to speak from the institutionalised meta-paradigm of technocratic governance which has underpinned several of the succession of particular paradigms.

Institutions need to create soluble problems or manageable risks in order to sustain themselves. Selecting and highlighting the kinds of problems and risks that the institutionalised paradigm of governance is well equipped to solve – for example, budget management for the reinvention paradigm or risks of nepotism and corruption for Progressive era paradigms – is not sufficient. For the institution must also *specify what counts as relevant* to deciding what problems are worth worrying about, and what kinds of consideration are relevant to deciding how to solve them (Berger and Luckmann, 1966; Douglas, 1986). 'Garbage can' models in political science have sometimes been used to capture this aspect of institutionalisation (Cohen *et al.*, 1972). For example, the institutionalised criteria of the reinvention era specified that for most administrative problems, considerations of contract design, incentive structure, measurement and objective or target setting systems, were the key types of information to look for, and the key tests used to determine just how urgently in need of reform a field of public administration was.

Shaping cognition is not enough. Institutions cannot survive unless they can shape *interests*. The first stage in achieving this is that of creating *classifications of recognisable interests.* For interests do not spring fully formed in individual public managers or clients from forces entirely outside the systems of governance and public management. First, people can only have an interest in what is defined and recognized and available as the sort of thing that could be in someone's interest, and these systems of classifications are achieved through institutions. Institutionalised paradigms of governance and public management define, for example, the kinds of financial rewards that are thinkable for elected politicians, salaried public managers and private contractors; they define the kinds of valuable status that are recognized and available to be secured; they define what kinds of work count as 'interesting'. While individuals can sometimes defy some institutional classifications, typically they depend on rival institutions in order to offer themselves or others alternative goals. For example, the introduction of performance related pay during the reinvention era did not simply appeal to prior financial self-interest. Indeed, in many cases, it may not even have done that, for schemes were often subsequently withdrawn on the ground that they failed to motivate. But the purpose of the linkage was to redefine institutionally the range of available interests. Similarly, the high status attached to financial management responsibilities from the early 1980s during the first phase of 'reinvention' was achieved not principally by appealing to prior interests, but by reclassification of what counted as worth pursuing, what counted as control, what counted as influential, what counted as interesting work to secure.

Institutions sustain interests by specifying and attempting to enforce – without ever completely succeeding – sets of incentives and disincentives, *sanctions and rewards*, mandations, prohibitions and permissions. These may be very finely calibrated as in some of the more rococo reward and penalty schemes put in place through contracts for the private provision of blue collar services during the 1980s and 1990s, or they may be very coarse, as in the case of the British civil service grading structure prior to the mid-1980s. The function of such penalties and incentives is never simply, in a Pavlovian or Skinnerian manner, to stimulate and deter specific behaviours, but to institutionalise individuals and organisations into becoming governable through the kinds of tools and resources that the institutionalised paradigm of governance and public management is capable of deploying. The development of public sector audit is a good case in point, for the production of people and organisations capable of auditable performance is at least as important as the micro-manipulation of particular financial behaviours (Power, 1997).

Interests are shaped and institutions fixed by creating and organising particular *roles*, skills, capabilities, personnel development, career paths and professions. Commitment is produced to institutional goals and styles of organisation by defining roles, which in turn enable people to structure their career paths. In the nineteenth century, just as the Chadwickian conception of local government mobilised public and élite commitment through the development of such roles as the town clerk, the borough engineer and the sanitary inspector, so the Northcote-Trevelyan model of central government public management defined new key roles such as the accounting officer and the permanent secretary. In the twentieth century, the post-war welfare state paradigm created a plethora of new professions including those of planning and social work, and with the advent of human relations management disciplines in the 1950s quickly incorporated the new role of the personnel function. Similarly, the reinvention era gave new definition, prominence and career focus to such professional roles as financial management, audit, performance and project management. The career path definitions implicit in these professional roles were for the most part functionally defined, although a few very senior specialist professionals in local government, and a few senior economists in central government, could hope to move into general management. Implicit in such roles are very particular ways of linking together the skills of those occupying these roles, sequencing their different interventions, and ironing out inconsistencies and conflicts. These different functional models of governance have sometimes privileged the politician as the initiative-taker in development, as did the paradigm of city governance in the nineteenth century, or the professional town planner in the post-war welfare state, and thereafter defined the sequence of other professional interventions.

However, roles are not enough. It is also necessary for an institution to shape an *ethic* (Galaskiewicz, 1991). Institutions that appeal simply to crude conceptions of the self-interest of those whose energies they mobilise quickly run into problems of wider public legitimacy, as the Soviet Union found in its last two decades. Indeed, within the public sector, they also typically run into motivational problems among politicians and public officials, for the public sector can typically only raise the levels of revenue to afford the kinds of rewards that will motivate those interested principally in maximising their own income, when the private business sector is languishing to the point that it offers very little to the ablest and most ambitious. For a variety of reasons, therefore, the shaping of public ethics and of the ethics of politicians and public officials at every level is crucial to the process of institutionalisation. An ethic of economy (in Gladstone's famous phrase about the saving of candle ends) was combined in the late nineteenth century liberal model with an ethic of probity and propriety stressed in the Northcote-Trevelyan reforms to recruitment and promotion. The ethics of the Edwardian programmes that we disussed earlier are in fact helpfully read as motivated partly by an aspiration towards holistic governance. For at least some of the New Liberals' aspirations summed up in the phrase 'national efficiency' (a combination of liberal concerns with economy and the neo-mercantilist concerns with the duty of government to promote the interests of the nation) were widely shared from Joseph Chamberlain on the centre–right through to the Wells wing of Fabian thought on the centre–left, by way of Hobson and Hobhouse among the New Liberals. Distributive justice, grounded in the internalisation of altruism and compassion among the better off, came to be seen as the central ethic of the post-war welfare state, although the full ideological articulation of this had to wait until the work of Titmuss in the 1960s and early 1970s: in the internal context of public management, this was conceived as 'the public service ethic'. A second current of the ethic of that model, as articulated by Marshall (1992 [1950]), was one of citizenship, although this later proved vulnerable to the critiques of paternalism from both left and right (Deakin, 1994). As we have seen, the ethics of consumerism, economy, at least a rhetoric of choice, and a revived language of efficiency were combined with a strongly functional ethical conception of accountability in the reinvention era.

Institutions are patterns of social organisation. Therefore, to sustain themselves, they must create legible structures of *accountability*.

In the political context, this means first that institutions must define and secure acceptance for the *rules of decision-making* that reflect their basic commitments and style of organisation. March and Olsen (1989, p. 118ff) distinguish between aggregative and integrative decision rules as a basic way to classify types of institution. Aggregative institutions take the preferences of the represented group – voting or taxpaying citizens, clients of public services, professionals, party members – to be exogenously fixed and ordered, and look for ways to aggregate those preferences either through market institutions or through voting procedures, while integrative institutions attempt to shape those preferences through pedagogy, persuasion, apprenticeship, acculturation and so on, into a tradition. In practice, any viable institutionalised paradigm of governance must mix both types of decision rules, both in dealing with the wider tax-paying and voting public, and with actors within networks of governance, although they may give greater weight to one kind over another (March and Olsen, 1989, p. 140ff). While democratic aggregative institutions may prevail in formal relationships with voters, in practice, democratic governments must shape the preferences of citizens in a whole variety of ways (6, 1997b; Rose, 1999): the same holds true for relationships between the professionals, civil servants and party politicians that sustain institutionalised patterns of governance. Integrative institutions held a particular importance for the decision rules in the post-war welfare state, where styles of decision-making from local land use development to the use of public expenditure for redistributive purposes, were more or less openly justified on pedagogic and preference shaping grounds. In the reinvention era, particular stress was placed, at least in rhetoric, on aggregative institutions of choice and consumer accountability, although the practice was much more of choice for public managers engaged in purchasing services.

Holding individuals to account is at the heart of what institutions do (Douglas, 1986; March and Olsen, 1995, chapter 5), but they differ in the requirements against which individuals are held accountable and in the degree of accountability (key dimensions of which are captured in the distinction between the dimensions of constraint and bonds: Douglas, 1970, 1982, 1992). We can consider the case of the post-war welfare paradigm where public officials were principally held accountable to their peers in functionally defined professional structures, and more or less trusted to pursue overarching goals: micro-management by politicians or by the courts was not the normal style of governance in Britain from the 1950s to the late 1970s, although goals and resources were centrally fixed and activity held to account against those measures. The innovations that characterised the reinvention era have already been discussed, in measured performance accountability to a centre increasingly willing to engage in micro-management for accountability.

Institutionalised accountability requires a structure of powers that allocate decisions to particular agencies and actors: institutionalised paradigms of public management need not micro-manage, but they must at least implicitly allocate specific powers to groups, roles, professions, political structures. Sometimes, these powers may be explicit in written and published legislation or judicial decisions, but more often the important institutionally given powers are implicit until such time as they are challenged. Indeed, that implicit character may be the basis of the kind of ambiguity in which institutionalisation can sometimes only be achieved. This is of course, a generalisation to the institutional level of Machiavelli's argument about individual leaders; it has little to do with the larger 'dirty hands' problem about the need to use evil means to pursue morally warranted goals (Hampshire, 1978, Thompson, 1987; Buckler, 1993; Johnson, 1993) and much more to do with the political importance of exploiting uncertainty and ambiguity about the formal allocation of powers. The Northcote-Trevelyan paradigm of public management was very explicitly built around allowing specific powers to permanent secretaries as accounting officers, whereas the reinvention paradigm allocated powers more implicitly to auditors, financial managers.

Institutionalised paradigms of governance must offer a conception and a *style of leadership* that makes sense within their general commitments, which itself furthers the process of institutionalisation, preserves the distinctness of the institution and organises the social structure of the organisations within its sights, structures motivation as well as giving a public face to the systems of decision-making and authority embedded within that institution. Viable institutionalised paradigms must mix, balance and strike settlements between the pure forms or myths of leadership that each of the four solidarities identified in Chapter 4 produce. For example, Weber's (1968) model of charismatic leadership speaks to the processes by which egalitarian forms of organisation secrete fragile and distrusted forms hierarchy, which must be legitimate themselves within sectarian cultures of organisation by constantly mobilising the egalitarian affect of what Durkheim (1995 [1912], p. 218) called 'collective effervescence' (6, 2000e). Weber opposed that conception of leadership to the conception implicit in the ideal type of bureaucracy (Weber, 1958, p. 196ff) in which leadership is exercised through the hierarchical exercise of routinised information structures. One model of democratic governance imagines that the politics–administration split politicians can be institutionalised by allocating charisma to politicians and bureaucratic leadership to permanent secretaries. This quickly tends to produce instability and conflict or else processes of capture. But there is at least a third basic style of leadership, namely, the public entrepreneurial or individualist, which Weber did not emphasise, but which certainly the American reformers of the Progressive era did, and sought to contain by their project of the institutionalisation of precisely the bureaucratic principles of probity and propriety in leadership that Weber could diagnose from his German experience. The post-war welfare paradigm produced a particular settlement in leadership styles, in which *professional* leadership was highly prized in such fields as medicine, policing, town planning, municipal finance and, by extension, within the general civil service reconceived as a at least a semi-profession. The professional leader is expected to show the kind of mechanical solidarity (as the younger Durkheim (1984 [1893]) would have said) with junior colleagues that the charismatic leader must, by visibly coming from within the same community of practitioners and discipline, but must also exercise the skills of routinised bureaucratic communication necessary to the management of large organisations, as well as at least a modest degree of the policy entrepreneurship expected of the individualist leader. The reinvention era challenged the charismatic dimension of this professional model by arguing the impropriety of professional capture of management and policy. While the myth and rhetoric of the advocates of reinvention were firmly individualist and entrepreneurial (Osborne and Gaebler, 1992), the spiralling transaction costs of the organisation practice mean that leadership had to be increasingly bureaucratic in style in order to handle the operating demands of purchaser–provider splits, performance audit, and so on. This mismatch between the institutional myth and the practical weaknesses of the paradigm is exactly what the theory summarised in Chapter 4 would lead us to expect (see also Thompson, Ellis and Wildavsky, 1990; Hood, 1998).

Only when these things are in place does it become important for institutions to specify *styles of formal organisation and of interorganisational relations*. Many accounts of coordination and integration have rushed too quickly to this stage. However, at the heart of what an institution is as a set of rules for formal organisation, is an aspiration to achieve a certain style of organisation – hierarchical and regulated, individualist and governed by private deals, sectarian or controlled by a movement committed to shared values, or chance-driven and passive (Douglas, 1986; Thompson, Ellis and Wildavsky, 1990; Hood, 1998). It should need no further labouring here how the styles of organisation of successive paradigms of public management have sought to recast organisational and interorganisational relations.

All institutions, however much their myth and rhetoric reflect the situation of weak constraint, inevitably create *élites, centres and peripheries*, produce advantage and disadvantage, whether through regulation of authoritative roles, through the operation of arbitrage in the many political and administrative markets or through the secretion of charismatic leadership in more communitarian or sectarian structures. It is not too much to say that institutions may be classified by the form of embarrassment their defenders exhibit when it is pointed out what kinds of settlements they have had to make with rival institutional pressures in order to produce the particular patterns of centres and peripheries that have emerged. The vertically organised central national hierarchies of civil service departments created in the Northcote-Trevelyan era were constantly embarrassed by the emergence of multiple centres in local government and in the special agencies created by frustrated political entrepreneurs to bypass the regulatory reach of the centre, just as the professional élites of the post-war era were constantly embarrassed by the re-bureaucratisation of professional leaderships. In each institutional paradigm, then, centre–periphery conflicts emerge and are differently fought and contained (or not contained) according to the bias of the paradigm. The centre–periphery conflicts of the reinvention era in the UK were fought out over the terrain of what local government could and should be, what autonomy it could reasonably demand against pressures for performance accountability from the centre, whilst in the Reagan era of the first phase of reinvention in the US, the key conflict was between federal structures and the presidentially backed demands of the states.

Institutions need *enemies*, or rival forms that present threats, against which the putative institution can attempt to show itself robust: all institutions define themselves, mobilise support, create systems of classification, produce accounts of what motives and interests are available to people to take up, by opposing other institutions in the form of particular individuals who are held to represent them; blame, attributions of responsibility to others and the ousting of enemies are at the heart of any institution. Evans-Pritchard's famous move in anthropology in understanding the nature of the institution of witchcraft was to ask what role the accusation of witchcraft played in a society (Evans-Pritchard, 1937), and many analysts of institutions of every kind have since then come to understand all institutions through a generalised form of his approach, by exploring the risks that institutions induce fear about, and by exploring the role of fears in self-definition, mobilisation, classification and the production of interests (Douglas, 1986, 1992). This analysis is as true for settlements between the basic institutional biases or solidarities as it is for the particular solidarities themselves – that is, it applies to the organic as much as to the mechanical solidarities. (This is a version of the symmetry postulate advocated by many scholars in the field of science and technology studies, where the requirement is that sociological techniques for the understanding of the emergence of scientific categories should be applied to science accepted as true as much as to science rejected as false – see Bloor, 1991 [1976] – in the same way, the political science of institutions should explain the origins, development and waning of institutions to which the political scientists themselves cleave in the same way that they would explain the trajectories of those they may disdain. This methodological stricture centrally informs the approach of this book, and of the argument of this chapter in particular.)

Thus, the great era of Progressive era public management or of the Northcote-Trevelyan model in nineteenth-century Britain was the demon of nepotism and corruption, just as that of the Edwardian New Liberal centrist consensus was of the effete, inadequately modern, inadequately industrialised culture of the upper classes that made for inefficiency in governance and the degeneration of low aspiration that can set in at the height of power. The enemies of the post-war settlement were the individualistic forces that made for what was seen as the paternalism and patchiness of voluntary action, for unprofessional governance, for territorial inequity, and for inadequate coverage. For the reinvention era, the enemy so carefully produced was that of the self-serving professional, the unaccountable time-serving bureaucrat, the underachieving and complacent managerial cadre.

So far we have considered institutionalisation as a cognitive and organisational process. However, these aspects are underpinned and made possible by the way in which institutions shape *affect* or *emotion*. Contrary to the rather cerebral view of the 'new institutionalists', the 'old institutionalists' from Durkheim to Weber and Simmel to Veblen understood that institutions are intensely emotional things. Political science has in recent years rather neglected the study of the emotions that was so central to the field in, for example, the period when political sociologists such as Rokkan, Almond, Verba, Mills or, later, the second wave feminists, made so much impact on the discipline. In particular, the field of public management has conceived itself as the study of 'cool' organisations, institutions and relationships in which the understanding of affect is hardly necessary. Fears in organisational life have been sanitised as 'risk perception'; rage and frustration have been treated as mere epiphenomena of political and administrative 'projects' and manoeuvres; patterns of civic friendship and personal animosity, which Aristotle understood to be at the heart of all political organisation, have been dehydrated into 'network structures' (see especially the *Rhetoric*, Book 1381–2: Aristotle, 1991, p. 149ff); the *Nichomachean ethics*, Books VIII and IX: Aristotle, 1925, pp. 192–247; and the *Politics*, Book II, chapters 1–5 on the bonds of cohesion and Book II, chapter 13 on ostracism: Aristotle, 1962, pp. 55–68 and 129–35); while feminist political theory gives an important place to the study of guilt and indignation, it has come to be poor etiquette in much of the rest of political science to study the role of such emotions as envy, *Schadenfreude, amour-propre*, loyalty, resentment or shame (a recent honourable exception is Elster, 1999, but even this work stands at some distance from mainstream political science, although Elster, 1993 for some briefly sketched connections; loyalty, for example, is the least theorised element in Hirschman's 1970 classic study, and even subsequent accounts have hardly explored its affective dynamics). Even the recent work in political science on trust has treated this independently of the affect on which it is structured, by focusing either on calculative aspects (Bianco, 1994) or else only on the macro-political consequences or causes. It has been left to recent sociology and social psychology to explore the political significance of the emotions (see, for instance, Bendelow and Williams, 1998; Harré and Parrott, 1996; Joffe, 1999) Yet, as the old institutionalists understood very clearly, institutionalisation and the processes by which institutions sustain themselves are fundamentally processes by which a selection from the kinds of affect given above are produced and modulated, while others are disorganised (6, 2000e). For emotions are not primordial, pre-social, instinctual impulses that well up without social and political shaping and definition, nor are they without social and political consequence. Rather, they are a basic instrument by which forms of solidarity – markets, hierarchies, clans and sects, and the diffusion of isolates – are politically and socially sustained at the macro level, but also in the development of forms of organisation within and between governmental organisations.

Moreover, institutions shape experience. They determine what is available to perceived, what can be recognized, what kinds of things can be learned from experience. With the exception of the work of March and Olsen (1976, 1989), this dimension of institutional life has been rather downplayed by 'new' institutionalist theory which focuses principally on the structural aspects of institutional achievement, although older institutionalisms such as those of Durkheim, Collingwood and Oakeshott put this fact at the centre of their understanding of how institutions shape political life. In part, the shaping of experience is achieved, as we have seen above, through the production of systems of classification and the shaping of cognition and ideas, but it is also achieved crucially through the management, cultivation, channelling and mobilisation of emotions.

Each of the mechanical solidarities or basic biases produce their own typical syndromes of affect and the management of affect. Hierarchical institutions cultivate such positive emotions as *amour-propre*, respect, and negative emotions such as fear and anxiety in the face of challenge to, or violation of, compliance with rule, under the governance of self-control as the institutional style of emotional management. However, hierarchy sees an important role for fear of carefully graduated sanctions among subaltern groups as a motivator. More sectarian institutions cultivate effervescence, an exclusive but intense and fragile mutual loyalty, and disciplines of frequent emotional arousal to sustain commitment. Individualist institutions focus on the cultivation of positive affect such as hope and the less expressive norms of affect appropriate to acquaintanceship and weak tie networking. The affective bias of fatalist institutions is typically a more impassive and stoic management of emotions (on the distinction between expressive and impassive institutional styles of affect, see 6, 2000e).

Here we focus on just two general aspects of the dynamics of affect that are of particular importance to understanding the institutionalisation of paradigms of governance and public management.

Candidate institutions do not achieve institutionalisation only by securing fear of enemies. They must also secure positive commitment and *loyalty* of defenders, activists, people willing to operate according the constraints and motivations they call for within the style of social organisation to which they cleave. Commitment comprises a whole cluster – and indeed, a highly organised cluster – of emotional processes. Motivations must be produced, interests recognized and accepted; ambitions and aspirations must be created; ties of friendship and acquaintanceship and collegiality within and between formal organisations must be organised in ways that suit the organisational style of the institution; *anomie* must be dispelled or at least disorganised; a sense of affective membership in organisations that sustain the institution must be cultivated; in certain styles of institution, an effervescent, charismatic commitment must be cultivated among all members of a profession, an organisation or a particular group who must represent the organisation to the outside world. The means by which this is achieved are often themselves institutional: institutional classifications of available emotions are produced; norms are created that define what emotions are acceptable; sanctions are applied to those who cannot demonstrate the appropriate emotions, and so on. The post-war welfare settlement attached particular importance to the cultivation, in its egalitarian moment, of altruistic compassion and empathy, and among street level bureaucrats, to the emotions appropriate to collegial friendships within professional networks. Reinvention, in its individualist moment, certainly cultivated the high aspirations of hope, but in its more hierarchical dimension focused on what was seen as appropriate levels of fear of sanctions for failure.

Institutions must shape and manage people's *expectations* in two senses, namely their anticipations of the future, and the demands they believe it acceptable to make of others in the light of those anticipations. Hierarchical institutions such as those that dominated the nineteenth-century reforms of the central civil service in Britain put a premium on both securing the regularisation of expectations, and the institutionalisation of expectations of stability, the management of 'excessive' expectations (see Brittan, 1988 [1974]: compare Durkheim's formulation of *anomie* as the 'malady of the infinite', or expectations that are impossible to fulfil, which can be understood as the disappointment of the sectarian solidarity as people slip from it into isolate or fatalist biases: Durkheim, 1951 [1897] and 1961 [1925], especially chapters 3 and 4). Again, the millenarian expectations and high demands based on collective effort, of many sectarian movements and some communitarian forms of organisation can be contrasted with the more individualistic institutions that sustain high anticipations but low levels of positive demands of collectivity, but a great importance to the demand for negative freedom to be let alone, based upon personal self-confidence and self-efficacy.

Producing emotions and creating accountability is something that requires of institutions a way of creating appropriate *observable, bodily practices*, and this means *ritual*. Institutions can only be produced, reproduced and sustained in and through ritual, by which we understand the repeated, meaningful, bodily enactment before other people of images, metaphors and representations of social organisation (Durkheim, 1995 [1912]; Goffman, 1967, 1971; see also 6, 2000e). Ritual is not necessarily limited to public, formalised ceremonial (which latter is, unfortunately, the limited focus of most political science concerned with ritual such as Edelman, 1985 [1964]; Kertzer, 1988). Rather, as Goffman (1967, 1971) insisted, many quotidian, mundane behaviours should be understood as ritual. More important for our present purpose, as Durkheim (1995 [1912]) showed, institutionalisation cannot be achieved without some form of visible, tangible, bodily performance, which conveys the meanings and commitments of the institutions, both of those who are already in return committed to it, and to others more sceptical or hostile. The rituals of hierarchical institutions include such behaviours as making applications, meticulous circulation of information to all and only particular role-holders, the appropriate forms of deference of civil servants to elected ministers and of distant respect for elected opposition shadow ministers, highly formal memoranda and so on. By contrast, the rituals of individualist institutional forms include relentless formation and flexible abandonment of strategies, the production of business plans, the interaction rituals of self-conscious and deliberate 'networking' or the cultivation of weak ties (6, 1997c), and communication through brief, informal casual and telegraphic e-mail or simply verbally. More collegial ritual styles characterise the densely tied professional group, varying according to the degree of internal hierarchy (such as in medicine) or rough-and-ready equality (government statisticians, social workers, community development workers).

Finally, institutions need to cultivate a distinctive, preferred and admired style or *aesthetic* both of individual demeanour and of organisational design. Interestingly, the aesthetics of the one tend to reverse, perhaps even compensate for, those of the other. The rococo organisational design of hierarchical systems is matched by the sobriety of personal dress codes and the stiffness of deportment between professional and client, and between superior and subaltern. By contrast, the colourful variety and informality of the dress codes of individualist and egalitarian institutions and the only superficially 'informal' but actually florid, staccato verbal delivery of their conversation, contrasts with the utilitarian, even brutally simple organisational styles that are the organisational signatures of the weak constraint solidarities, which range from the opportunistically grown flat agency structure to the small egalitarian cell. As each of the principal paradigms of public management has represented some skewed or distorted settlement between these solidarities, we can expect the institutionalised styles to be mixed, perhaps differently among civil servants from between elected officials and officers, and so on. Typically, the post-war welfare paradigm promoted most collegial styles within the professional group and the most hierarchical between professionals and clients, whilst in the reinvention era, the aspiration and the myth was that some of the rolled-short-sleeve informality of the public entrepreneur would exhibit itself in behaviour towards service users, although the institutionalised reality of hierarchy here proved more resistant. As we have stressed, paradigms never replace each other and, as any institutionalist account would emphasise, the persistence of institutionalised aesthetics despite the aspirations of myths of subsequent periods and institutions, is exactly what we should expect.

This completes the set of elements that form, jointly, one set of sufficient conditions for institutionalisation of paradigms of governance and public management. The account shows that having once achieved institutionalisation, such paradigms are not replaced wholesale by subsequent waves of reform, but, as any institutionalist theory will recognize, shape the conditions under which subsequent reform can work.

How strong are the forces for the institutionalisation of holism?

We may now draw on our analysis of holistic governance to consider how far the agenda holistic governance is, at least as yet, from achieving institutionalisation on each of these measures. At this stage, we are concerned with institutionalisation of holism as a paradigm, and not with the institutionalisation of particular initiatives. Our assessment of the extent of institutionalisation for the UK is given in Figure 10.1. The situation may be more advanced in New Zealand and in some states of Australia and the US.

The assessment – broken down by the main categories of factors for institutionalisation – presented in Figure 10.1 suggests that, while institutionalisation is obviously incomplete, a significant and perhaps decisive challenge has been made in the UK to the institutionalisation of the reinvention paradigm. This is certainly the first step towards deinstitutionalisation of that model, although certainly not a sufficient condition.

Figure 10.1   *Signs of institutionalisation for holistic governance*

Categories of factors for institutionalisation	Early signs of factors for institutionalising holistic governance as a paradigm
A. Socio-economic background	
1. *Other institutions*	The formal accountability systems and central budget are not yet in place, but reforms are not ruled out. New Zealand's SRA and KRA structures or Oregon's outcome target system are probably more congenial than those of British budget and policy accountability.
2. *Affordability*	The debate about affordability has been thin. The focus on social exclusion rather than on poverty has been framed in ways that enable fine-grained targeting, which may make some potentially anti-poverty programmes more affordable.
3. *Interests*	Only a few politicians as yet see holism as in their personal interests; probably, however, more see it as a distraction than a threat.
4. *Legitimacy*	Public opinion priorities for government action suggest latent popularity for effective coordination. However, this can be overridden by popular support for particular stand-alone measures defined by e.g., increased expenditure or personnel input on particular services defined by activity.
B. Shaping cognition or ideas	
5. *General categories*	A body of general categories has been developed: coordination, integration, holism, 'joined-up', sectoral pragmatism, service pragmatism about 'what works', effectiveness as a key criterion, etc. At this level, there has been a decisive challenge to the institutionalisation of the reinvention agenda.
6. *Particular narratives*	A number of particular initiatives is beginning to attain iconic status, including 'success' stories from some zones, particularly innovative local authorities and central initiatives perceived as promising: e.g., action on rough sleepers.
7. *Body of formal knowledge*	Several bodies of codified managerial knowledge in coordination do exist, but knowledge about these is less well developed than in the USA.
8. *Cognitive energy*	Experience with urban regeneration, some networks of professionals working in zones, and in the social exclusion field suggests that there are signs of cognitive energy and fertility.

Figure 10.1 *continued*

Categories of factors for institutionalisation	Early signs of factors for institutionalising holistic governance as a paradigm
9. *Forgetting*	As yet, there are few signs of institutional forgetting of key categories of functional thinking.
10. *Judgment*	Specific judgment practices for holistic working are still under-developed. However, there are some promising early signs in the Comprehensive Spending Reviews, some zone-based policy-making processes.
11. *Criteria of relevance*	There are in a number of fields, such as community safety, young people at risk, public health and some aspects of social exclusion policy, now relatively well developed criteria for effectiveness assessment, for testing for the comprehensiveness of involvement of a range of agencies.

C. Shaping interests

12. *Classifications of recognisable interests*	A re-classification of who has an interest in holistic working is incomplete in the UK, and reinvention classifications probably remain dominant, especially among politicians. A few entrepreneurial, boundary spanning public managers are beginning to see a career interest in holistic working, but many conventional professionals do not, at least as yet. However, the aspiration at local level that local authorities should move to a role of 'community governance' may be creating interest in certain kinds of holistic networking and policy formulation.
13. *Sanctions and rewards*	This is one of the better developed aspects of the UK experiment. A range of discretionary budget incentives has been introduced, and there are some steps being taken towards at least soft sanctions around promotion for senior civil servants and local government chief and senior officers to encourage holistic working. However, most incentives bite on organisations rather than individuals; individual level sanctions and rewards tend to be principally functionally defined.
14. *Roles*	Boundary spanning roles are beginning to emerge at local level in fields such as community safety, young people at risk, social exclusion and some clientele based programmes,

Figure 10.1 *continued*

Categories of factors for institutionalisation	Early signs of factors for institutionalising holistic governance as a paradigm
	and through zones. At the political level, most committee chair and ministerial roles remain functionally defined, although there are some promising experiments in some local governments.
15. *Ethic*	A professional and managerial ethic of holistic working as a personal and organisational responsibility, and an ethic of comprehensiveness and effectiveness in service design is not yet fully developed. There are senior civil servants and local government officers who have internalised this to some degree, but this has probably yet to motivate a majority of street-level bureaucrats.

D. Shaping organisation

16. *Decision rules*	Decision rules for holistic governance are beginning to emerge. For example, comprehensive budgeting procedures represent one kind of decision rule in budget setting; consensus-based decision rules are beginning to emerge in some zones and partnerships.
17. *Accountability*	Holistic political accountability remains poorly developed, particularly in the House of Commons, where the remit of most select committees is still defined, at least in their implicit curricula, in functional terms.
18. *Powers*	The creation of specific powers for the development, cultivation and evaluation of holistic initiatives is at an early stage in the UK. Most job descriptions and most professional responsibilities have some joint working clause, but typically in a position that indicates a low priority.
19. *Leadership*	Holistic working still has a leadership deficit. Although the Prime Minister has repeatedly called for joined-up government, and Chancellor (Finance Minister) Brown has given political weight to the holistic elements of the Comprehensive Spending Review, even for these senior figures in the government, holistic working often takes second place to functionally defined efforts. More political

Figure 10.1 *continued*

Categories of factors for institutionalisation	Early signs of factors for institutionalising holistic governance as a paradigm
	leadership can be identified at local government level, among more innovative authorities.
20. *Styles of organisational structure and inter-organisational relations*	The holistic governance agenda has been developed sufficiently in the UK for most practitioners to have a reasonably clear idea of what kinds of relationships and organisational styles would be required. Many professional media – newsletters, web sites, training courses, etc. – are available to promulgate understanding of the holist style.
21. *Élites*	To date, there are still few signs of élites and putative centres organising around holistic working.
22. *Enemies*	The holistic working agenda in the UK has very clearly identified its enemies, in the form of certain professions, certain political defenders of the functional principle of government, and, more generally, the reinvention programme's commitment to the 'dedicated agency' model.

E. Shaping affect or emotion

23. *Loyalty*	The primary loyalties of public officials probably remain defined in functional terms, but there are some emerging networks associated with the zones and the social inclusion agenda where new networks, ties and alliances are beginning to be forged.
24. *Expectations*	Expectations about the institutionalisation of holistic working among many practitioners are still fragile. Many seem to fear that it will be overwhelmed by other pressures. However, as one moves up the seniority scales both centrally and locally, practitioners speak of higher expectations for institutionalisation in respect of evaluation, sanction and reward and eventually political accountability for holistic governance.

F. Observable, bodily practice

25. *Ritual*	Most of the rituals of public governance probably sustain functional paradigms of governance. However, some of the rituals associated with agency consultation and involvement, with certain kinds of political rhetoric, with

Figure 10.1   *continued*

Categories of factors for institutionalisation	Early signs of factors for institutionalising holistic governance as a paradigm
	applying for certain kinds of high-profile grants or status, do suggest that the ritual dimension of holistic governance could be developed.
26. *Aesthetic*	While the literature on partnership arrangements suggests that a certain rather rococo style in organisational design is emerging, it is not clear that a personal aesthetic associated with holistic work is yet emerging.

In sum, Figure 10.1 shows that, in our assessment of the British case:

- (A) Many of the socio-economic conditions are in place for holistic working;
- (B) The intellectual case has been made for holism, and concepts of coordination and integration and 'partnership' have been developed;
- (C) There is in principle no reason why interests cannot be shaped, but the New Labour administration has had less success in this respect, for many of the reasons identified in Chapter 5, but also because it has focused insufficiently on roles and ethics;
- (D) There remain significant gaps in the holistic accountability structure, except in respect of interorganisational relations, which reflect the traditional approach to integration;
- (E) and (F) Far too little thought has been given to the affective and ritual issues, and this represents a source of serious weakness in the motivational basis of institutionalisation of holistic governance in the UK.

However, the key question to ask at this stage is, what is the relevant comparison? Surely to compare the state of institutionalisation in the UK of the holistic governance agenda in 2000 with the institutionalisation of the reinvention agenda is quite inappropriate, since one can date the reinvention agenda from at least 1980, when compulsory competitive tendering was introduced for local government, or at least 1983 when the Financial Management Initiative was brought forward in central government. If holism and reinvention are to be compared, then a more useful point of comparison would be with the degree to which the reinvention model in the UK was institutionalised in, say, 1982 in local government or 1985 in central government. At that stage, in fact, one might argue that many of the categories, particular narratives, interests and decision rules that came to characterise the mature reinvention agenda of, say, 1991 or 1992, were not only not yet in place, but were less clear than are the categories, narratives, interests and decision rules of holism in 2000. Moreover, the degree to which the institutionalisation of the post-war local or central welfare state was under direct challenge, rather than merely rhetorical criticism, was far from clear in the early 1980s.

In one key respect, however, the assessment summarised in Figure 10.1 probably understates the power of the forces for institutionalisation of holistic governance. For it shows only the balance of forces domestically. As we have seen, however, an exit from the reinvention paradigm and a shift in varying ways and degrees towards holistic governance is being made in many countries. This creates opportunities for voluntarily initiated learning from other countries, benchmarking and the sharing of information, experience, lessons and the making of comparisons that may support the development of 'best practice'. In addition, one impetus for policy change that is not very powerful but nonetheless has some motivational force is the desire among political élites to achieve an international reputation for innovation and a leading role in reform. Over the last few decades as the borrowing of policy ideas has itself come to be, at least to some degree, an institutionalised practice in governance (Rose, 1993; Dolowitz *et al.*, 1999), political élites have felt under scrutiny from other governments. In addition, the growth of international management consultancy companies with public sector divisions offering advice, comparison and information has facilitated the passage of comparison and borrowing. The growth in the numbers of intergovernmental organisations and in inter-parliamentary linkages in recent decades is also a force for policy transfer and reputation effects. Finally (and we do not exaggerate the importance of this factor by comparison with more direct inter-government forces for policy transfer), think-tanks may have played some role in the making of comparisons and the movement of ideas between governments and political parties internationally (Denham and Garnett, 1998; Stone, 1996).

Holistic governance is, then, not fully institutionalised in Britain. Concerning some of the conditions of institutionalisation identified in this chapter, it may be more so, and in others, less so than in other countries. There remain significant barriers to be surmounted before it could be said that holism has achieved the degree and depth of institutionalisation that the Northcote-Trevelyan, the post-war welfare and the reinvention paradigms achieved. Previous initiatives in holistic governance have achieved some degree of institutionalisation, but neither the New Liberal 'national efficiency' programme nor the Heathite coordination drive and reform of the policy process achieved the full and near-hegemonic institutionalisation that the 'big three' paradigms in governance and public management did. Nevertheless, these previous initiatives in holism did leave their mark on governance and public management. The Haldane Committee of 1918 did not bury the New Liberal agenda, but reached a settlement between its aspirations and the already institutionalised pressures for functional organisation. Similarly, the reinvention programmes of the Thatcher governments did not wholly oust the legacy of the Heathite aspirations for coordination, and by the Major administration, the Conservatives felt forced to move towards coordination themselves in such programmes as the Urban Development initiative, the late electronic government initiative and in some areas of social policy such as community safety. The imperative for coordination and integration wells up cyclically, but powerfully and regularly in governance, not only in the UK but in almost any complex and ramified governmental system subject to democratic scrutiny.

Therefore, it is not fatalistic to note that previous waves of holism have not achieved near-hegemonic institutionalisation. If the argument of this chapter is accepted, then it is at least possible that holistic governance could become institutionalised in the UK and elsewhere. For there is a measure of political will and greater understanding than has existed previously of the organisational requirements of holism, as well as technological capabilities that were not available to previous generations for processing information necessary for analysing expenditures by outcome and by estimated opportunity cost and practical experience. This represents more than just 'a start'.

However, it will remain crucial to ask, as we have argued in Chapters 2 and 4, exactly what kind of holism is institutionalised. In Figures 2.2 and 2.3 in Chapter 2 we showed how the holistic ('by exactly what set of relationships can this outcome be promoted or, ideally, secured?') is distinguished from the merely joined-up ('what can we do together?'). Institutionalisation of joined-up governance is much easier to achieve, but, if the basic argument for holistic governance is accepted, of much less value.

Suppose, at least for the sake of argument, that a very full form of holistic governance were to be institutionalised. Would that represent the last work in the reform of government, the public management equivalent of Fukuyama's (1992) claim about the 'end of history'? Clearly not. But that which is not fully institutionalised may nevertheless be sufficiently institutionalised to leave a lasting mark on subsequent patterns of governance. No doubt there will at some future time be a cyclical swing back in interest towards some model of governance and public management which, at least implicitly, undermines coordination and integration in favour of some other value. That may not be productive efficiency and targeting as was the case in the reinvention era, or redistribution as was the case in the post-war welfare model. But the possibility cannot be ruled out.

Do such cycles in the waxing and waning of holistic governance over the history of public management reflect the fact that politicians and public managers implicitly switch to and from coordination and integration at roughly the point where the balance of gain and loss on each of the main trade-off(s) discussed in Chapter 3 tips towards or away from the worthwhileness of holism or other kinds of focus? Transaction cost models of political action (North, 1990) would suggest that this could be the case. But the various constructivist models (Thompson, Ellis and Wildavsky, 1990; Wynne, 1989; Latour 1996; Yanow, 1996; Hood, 1998) would suggest that the ways in which people recognize costs and benefits reflect their situation, their prior commitments to certain kinds of social organisation, the point in the organisational trajectory at which they make their judgment, the consequences of prior institutional legacies, the pressure of the networks in which they work, the effect of prevailing symbols and ideas, and so forth, rather than any implicitly accurate sensing of objective costs and benefits. The 'efficient history' hypothesis of paradigm change, whether grounded in transaction costs arguments or otherwise, is essentially another form of fatalism. It provides a pre-written script for change in, for example, public management, but utterly fails to acknowledge the fact of contingency.

Conclusion

Will the present wave of effort towards holistic governance wane, as have so many before it, or will it, by contrast, be institutionalised for a sustained period of time, as have been the functional model and the reinvention model? We have argued here that at least it could be institutionalised, even if it has not yet been. That will depend on the continuation of favourable political conditions that make centrism possible, as well as upon achieving a more sophisticated and pluralistic approach to public management that recognizes the role for weak as well as strong tools. It will require commitment to use the stream of shocks and untoward events as opportunities, just as we found the most astute public managers able to do at local level. No doubt, to those of a radical sensibility, centrist politics, better balanced public management, more astute political policy and managerial judgment seem tame. However, there is a good case to be made, as we showed in Chapter 3, that integration and coordination respond better than function-ally fragmented systems to the concerns of the public. It remains a central challenge for politicians and public managers now to sustain their com-mitment and to build institutions without giving way again to fatalism.

References

Adams, J. (1995) *Risk* (London: UCL Press).

Agranoff, R. A. (1991) 'Human services integration: past and present challenges to public administration', *Public Administration Review*, 51, 6, 533–42.

Agranoff, R. A. and Pattakos, A.N. (1979) *Dimensions of service integration: service delivery, programme linkages, policy management, organisational structure, human services* (Washington DC: Monograph), Series 13, Project SHARE and US Department of Health, Education and Welfare.

Alexander, A. with Orr, K. (1995) *Managing the fragmented authority* (Luton: Local Government Management Board).

Alexander, E. R. (1995) *How organisations act together: interorganisational coordination in theory and practice* (Amsterdam: Gordon and Breach).

Alter, C. and Hage, J. (1993) *Organisations working together*, Sage Library of Social Research 191 (California: Sage Publications).

Altman, D. (1991) 'The challenges of services integration for children and families', in Schorr, L. B., Both, D. and Copple, C. (eds) (1991) *Effective services for young children: report of a workshop* (Washington DC: National Academy Press).

Amin, K. and Oppenheim, C. (1992) *Poverty in black and white*, (London: Child Poverty Action Group).

Anheier, H. K. (ed.) (1999) *When things go wrong: organisational failures and breakdowns* (London: Sage).

Annie E. Casey Foundation (1995) *The path of most resistance: lessons learned from New Futures* (Baltimore, Maryland: Annie E. Casey Foundation).

Appadurai, A. (1996) *Modernity at large: cultural dimensions of globalisation* (Minneapolis, Minnesota: University of Minnesota press).

Aristotle (1925) *The Nichomachean ethics*, tr. Ross, D. (Oxford: Oxford University Press).

Aristotle (1962) *The politics*, tr. Sinclair, T. A. (Harmondsworth: Penguin).

Aristotle (1991) *The art of rhetoric*, tr. Lawson-Tancred, H. (Harmondsworth: Penguin).

Audit Commission (1994) *Seen but not heard: co-ordinating child health and social services for children in need* (London: HMSO).

Audit Commission (1996) *Misspent youth: young people and crime* (London: Audit Commission).

Audit Commission (1999) *Safety in numbers: promoting community safety* (London: Audit Commission).

Ballantine, J. A. and Cunningham, N. (1999) 'Strategic information systems planning: applying private sector frameworks in UK public healthcare', in Heeks, R. (ed.) (1999) *Reinventing government in the information age: international practice in IT-enabled public sector reform* (London: Routledge) pp. 293–311.

Barber, B. (1983) *The logic and limits of trust* (New Jersey: Rutgers University Press).

Bardach, E. (1996) 'Turf barriers to interagency collaboration', in Kettl, D. F. and Milward, H. B. (eds) (1996) *The state of public management* (Baltimore: Johns Hopkins University Press) pp. 168–92.

Bardach, E. (1998) *Getting agencies to work together: the theory and practice of managerial craftsmanship* (Washington DC: Brookings Institution).

Barry, A., Osborne, T. and Rose, N. (eds) (1996) *Foucault and political reason: liberalism, neo-liberalism and rationalities of government* (London: UCL Press).

Bartlett, C. and Ghoshal, S. (1989) *Managing across borders: the transnational solution* (Boston: Harvard Business School Press).

Barzelay, M. with Armajani, B. J. (1992) *Breaking through bureaucracy: a new vision for managing in government* (Berkeley: University of California Press).

Baum, J. A. C. and Singh, J. V. (eds) (1993) *Evolutionary dynamics of organisations* (New York: Oxford University Press).

Bellamy, C. and Taylor, J. A. (1998) *Governing in the information age* (Buckingham: Open University Press).

Bemelmans-Videc, M.-L., Rist, R. C. and Vedung, E. (eds) (1998) *Carrots, sticks and sermons: policy instruments and their evaluation* (New Brunswick: Transaction Books).

Bendelow, G. and Williams, S. J. (eds) (1998) *Emotions in social life: critical themes and contemporary issues* (London: Routledge).

Berger, P. L. and Luckmann, T. (1966) *The social construction of reality: a treatise in the sociology of knowledge* (Harmondsworth: Penguin).

Bergeson, T., Kelly, T., Riggers, M. and McElro, C. (1999) *Washington State readiness to learn: school linked models for integrated family services, evaluation report 1997–98* (Seattle, Washington State: Olympia Washington State Superintendent of Public Instruction).

Berlin, I. (1990) *The crooked timber of humanity: chapters in the history of ideas* (London: Fontana).

Berry, F. S., Berry, J. D., Foster, S. K. (1998) 'The determinants of success in implementing an expert system in state government', *Public Administration Review*, 58, 4, pp. 293–305.

Bianco, W. T. (1994) *Trust: representatives and constituents* (Ann Arbor: University of Michigan Press).

Bijker, W. E. (1997) *Of bicycles, bakelites and bulbs: toward a theory of sociotechnical change (inside technology)* (Cambridge, Massachusetts: Massachusetts Institute of Technology Press).

Bijker, W. E. and Law, J. (eds) (1992) *Shaping technology / building society: studies in sociotechnical change* (Cambridge, Massachusetts: Massachusetts Institute of Technology Press).

Bilton, K. and Jones, A. (1994) *The future shape of children's services* (London: National Children's Bureau).

Blank, M. and Hoffman, A. (1994) *Services integration in the United States: an emerging agenda,* (Washington DC: Institute for Educational Leadership).

Bloor, D. (1991 [1976]) *Knowledge and social imagery*, second edition (Chicago: University of Chicago Press).

Blunden, M. and Dando, M. (eds) (1994) *Rethinking public policy-making: questioning assumptions, challenging beliefs – essays in honour of Sir Geoffrey Vickers on his centenary* (London: Sage).

Borins, S. (1998) *Innovating with integrity: how local heroes are transforming American government* (Washington DC: Georgetown University Press).

Boston, J., Martin, J., Pallot, J. and Walsh, P. (1996) *Public management: the New Zealand experience* (Auckland: Oxford University Press).

Both, D. and Copple, C. (eds) (1991) *Effective services for young children: report of a workshop* (Washington, DC: National Academy Press).

Bovens, M., T'Hart, P., Dekker, S. and Verheuvel, G. (1999) 'The politics of blame avoidance: defensive tactics in a Dutch crime-fighting fiasco', in Anheier, H.K. (ed.) (1999) *When things go wrong: organisational failures and breakdowns* (London: Sage) pp. 123–47.

Bowker, G. C. and Star, S. L. (1999) *Sorting things out: classification and its consequences* (Cambridge, Massachusetts: Massachusetts Institute of Technology Press).

Bradshaw, J. (1990) *Child poverty and deprivation in the UK* (London: National Children's Bureau).

Bright, J. (1997) *Turning the tide: crime, community and prevention* (London: Demos).

Brittan, S. (1988 [1974]) 'The politics of excessive expectations', in Brittan, S. (1988) *The economic consequences of democracy*, second edition (Aldershot: Wildwood House) pp. 247–78.

Brown, J. S. and Duguid, P. (1994) 'Organisational learning and communities-of-practice: toward a unified theory of working, learning and innovation', in Tsoukas, H. (ed.) (1994) *New thinking in organisational behaviour: from social engineering to reflective action* (London: Butterworth Heinemann) pp. 165–87.

Brunsson, N. and Olsen, J.-P. (1993) *The reforming organisation* (London: Routledge).

Buckler, S. (1993) *Dirty hands: the problem of political morality* (Aldershot: Avebury).

Bugler, D. T. and Bretschneider, S. I. (1993) 'Technology push or program pull? Interest in new technologies within public organisations', in Bozeman, B. (ed.) (1993) *Public management: the state of the art* (San Francisco: Jossey-Bass) pp. 275–93.

Bunker, J. P., Frazier, H. S. and Mosteller, F. (1994) 'Improving health: measuring the effects of medical care', *Milbank Quarterly*, 72, pp. 225–58.

Burchardt, T., Le Grand, J. and Piachaud, D. (1998) 'Social exclusion in Britain today', paper presented at an ESRC conference, 3rd December 1998.

Burchell, G., Gordon, C. and Miller, P. (eds) (1991) *The Foucault effect: studies in governmentality* (Hemel Hempstead: Harvester Wheatsheaf).

Burns, D., Hambleton, R. and Hoggett, P. (eds) (1994) *The politics of decentralisation: revitalising local democracy* (Basingstoke: Macmillan – now Palgrave).

Burt, R. S. (1992) *Structural holes: the social structure of competition* (Cambridge, Massachusetts: Harvard University Press).

Bynner, J. (1998) 'What are the causes of social exclusion affecting young children?', paper presented at the cross-departmental review of provision for young children (London: London Ministerial Seminar, Joseph Rowntree Foundation).

Cabinet Office (1998) *The people's panel* (London: Cabinet Office).

California State Department of Education, Healthy Start and After School Partnerships Office (1999) *Healthy Start works: a state profile of Healthy Start sites*, California State Department of Education.

Caprara, G. V. and Rutter, M. (1995) 'Individual development and social change', in Rutter, M. and Smith, D. J. (eds) *Psychosocial disorders in young people: time trends and their causes* (Chichester: John Wiley and Sons) pp. 35–66.

Carter, N., Klein, R. and Day, P. (1993) *How organisations measure success: the use of performance indicators in government* (London: Routledge).

Challis, L. (1990) *Organising public social services* (Harlow: Longman).

Challis, L., Fuller, S., Henwood, M., Klein, R., Plowden, W., Webb, A., Whittingham, P. and Wistow, G. (1988) *Joint approaches to social policy: rationality and practice* (Cambridge: University Press, Cambridge).

Chancellor of the Duchy of Lancaster (1996) *Government.direct: a prospectus for the electronic delivery of government services*, Cm (3438) (London: The Stationery Office).

Chandler, J. A. (2000) 'Joined-up government: "I wouldn't start here if I were you" ', paper given at the annual conference of the Political Studies Association, 10–13.4.00 (London: London School of Economics).

Chartered Institute of Housing (1998) *Rehousing sex offenders: a summary of the legal and operational issues* (Coventry: Chartered Institute of Housing).

Checkland, P. B. (1989) 'Soft systems methodology', in Rosenhead, J. (ed.) (1989) *Rational analysis for a problematic world: problem structuring methods for complexity, uncertainty and conflict* (Chichester: John Wiley and Son) pp. 71–100.

Checkland, P. B. (1994) 'Systems theory and management thinking', in Blunden, M. and Dando, M. (eds) (1994) *Rethinking public policy-making: questioning assumptions, challenging beliefs – essays in honour of Sir Geoffrey Vickers on his centenary* (London: Sage) pp. 75–91.

Checkland, P. B. and Scholes, J. (1990) *Soft systems methodology in action* (Chichester: John Wiley and Sons).

Chisholm, D. (1989) *Coordination without hierarchy: informal structures in multi-organisational systems* (Berkeley: University of California Press).

Clark, T. N. (ed.) (1994) *Urban innovation: creative strategies for turbulent times* (London: Sage).

Clarke, M. and Stewart, J. (1997) *Handling the wicked issues*, INLOGOV Discussion Paper, Institute for Local Government Studies, University of Birmingham.

Cockburn, C. (1977) *The local state: management of cities and people* (London: Pluto Press).

Cohen, M. D., March, J. G. and Olsen, J.-P. (1972) 'A garbage can model of organisational choice', *Administrative science quarterly*, 17, 1, reprinted in March, J.G. (1988) *Decisions and organisations* (Oxford: Blackwell), pp. 294–334.

Comptroller and Auditor General, (1999) *Government on the web*, HC 87 (London: Stationery Office).

Corry, D. (ed.) (1997) *Public expenditure: effective management and control* (London: Dryden Press and Harcourt Brace Jovanich).

Coulson, A. (ed.) (1998) *Trust and contracts: relationships in local government, health and public services* (Bristol: Policy Press).

Coyle, D. J. (1993) 'The theory that would be king', in Coyle, D. J. and Ellis, R. J. (eds) (1993) *Politics, policy and culture*, (Boulder: Westview Press), pp. 219–39.

Coyle, D. J. and Ellis, R. J. (eds) (1993) *Politics, policy and culture* (Boulder: Westview Press).

Crane, J. (ed.) (1998) *Social programs that work* (New York: Russell Sage Foundation).

Cupitt, R., Whitlock, R. and Williams Whitlock, L. (1997 [1996]) 'The [im]mortality of international governmental organisations', *International organisations*, 21, 4, reprinted in Diehl, P. F. (ed.) (1997) *The politics of global governance: international organisations in an interdependent world* (Boulder: Lynne Rienner Publishers), pp. 7–23.

Daines, R., Lyon, K. and Parsloe, P. (1990) *Aiming for partnership* (Illford, Essex: Barnardo's).

Day, P. and Klein, R. E. (1987) *Accountabilities: five public services* (London: Tavistock Publications).

Deakin, N. (1994) *The politics of welfare: continuities and change* (Hemel Hempstead: Harvester Wheatsheaf).

Dean, M. (1999) *Governmentality: power and rule in modern society* (London: Sage).

Denham, A. and Garnett, M. (1998) *British think tanks and the climate of opinion* (London: UCL Press).

Dennehy, A., Smith, L. and Harker, P. (1997) *Not to be ignored: young people, poverty and health* (London: Child Poverty Action Group).

Department for the Environment, Transport and the Regions (1998) *Building partnerships for prosperity: sustainable growth, competitiveness and employment in the regions* (London: DETR).

Department of the Environment, Transport and the Regions (1999) *Cross-cutting Issues affecting local government* (London: DETR), available at http://www.local-regions.dtlr.gov.uk/cross/indx.htm

Department of Health (1998) *Working together to safeguard children: new government proposals for inter-agency working* (London: Department of Health).

Devons, E. (1950) *Planning in practice* (Cambridge: Cambridge University Press).

DiMaggio, P. J. and Powell, W. W. (1983) 'The iron cage revisited: institutional isomorphism and collective rationality in organisational fields', *American Sociological Review*, 48, pp. 147–60.

Dolowitz, D. P., Hulme, R., Nellis, N. and O'Neal, F. (1999) *Policy transfer and British social policy: learning from the USA* (Buckingham: Open University Press).

Douglas, M. (1966) *Purity and danger: a study of the concepts of pollution and taboo* (London: Routledge).

Douglas, M. (1970) *Natural symbols: explorations in cosmology* (London: Routledge).

Douglas, M. (1972) 'Self-evidence', reproduced in Douglas, M. (1999 [1975]) *Implicit meanings: selected essays in anthropology*, second edition (London: Routledge), pp. 2252–83.

Douglas, M. (ed.) (1982) *Essays in the sociology of perception* (London: Routledge and Kegan Paul).

Douglas, M. (1986) *How institutions think* (London: Routledge and Kegan Paul).

Douglas, M. (1992) *Risk and blame: essays in cultural theory* (London: Routledge).

Douglas, M. (1993) 'Rightness of categories', in Douglas, M. and Hull, D. (eds) *How classification works: Nelson Goodman among the social sciences* (Edinburgh University Press) pp. 239–71.

Douglas, M. (1994), 'Institutions are the product', paper presented at the conference of the Society for the Advancement of Socio-Economics, Paris, Hautes Études Commerciales July 15–17.

Douglas, M. (1996a) *Thought styles* (London: Sage).

Douglas, M. (1996b) 'Istituzioni: problemi teorici', *Enciclopedia delle scienze sociali* (Rome: Fondata da Giovanni Trecanni), pp. 126–134.

Douglas, M. and Ney, S. (1998) *Missing persons: a critique of personhood in the social sciences* (New York: University of California Press, Berkeley, with Russell Sage Foundation).

Dowding, K. M. (1991) *Rational choice and political power* (Aldershot: Edward Elgar).

Drèze, J. and Sen, A. (1989) *Hunger and public action* (Oxford: Oxford University Press)

Dunleavy, P. (1991) *Democracy, bureaucracy and public choice* (Hemel Hempstead: Harvester Wheatsheaf).

Dunleavy, P. (1999) comments made orally at LSE seminar, 19.2.99.

Durkheim, É. (1951 [1897]) *Suicide: a study in sociology*, tr. Spaulding, J. A. and Simpson, G. (London: Routledge).

Durkheim, É. (1961 [1925]) *Moral education: a study in the theory and application of the sociology of education* (New York: Free Press).

Durkheim, É. (1983 [lectures 1913–14]) *Pragmatism and sociology*, tr. Whitehouse, J. C. (Cambridge University Press) selections, reprinted in Wolff, K. H. (ed.) (1960) *Essays on sociology and philosophy by Émile Durkheim et al. with appraisals of his life and thought* (New York: Harper Torch, Harper and Row) pp. 386–436.

Durkheim, É. (1984 [1893]) *The division of labour in society*, tr. Halls, W. D (Basingstoke: Macmillan – now Palgrave).

Durkheim, É. (1995 [1912]) *Elementary forms of the religious life*, translated by Fields, K. E. (New York: Free Press).

Durkheim, É. and Mauss, M. (1963 [1902]) *Primitive classification* edited by Needham, R. (University of Chicago Press).

Eccles, R. G. and Nohria, N. (1992) *Beyond the hype: rediscovering the essence of good management* (Boston: Harvard Business School Press).

Edelman, M. (1985 [1964]) *The symbolic uses of politics*, second edition (Urban: University of Illinois Press).

Edelman, M. (1988) *Constructing the political spectacle* (Chicago: University of Chicago Press).

Edelman, P. and Radin, B. (1991) 'Effective services for children and families: lessons from the past and strategies for the future', in Schorr, L. B., Both, D. and Copple, C. (eds) (1991) *Effective services for young children: report of a workshop* (Washington DC: National Academy Press).

Eisenstadt, S. N. and Roninger, L. (1984) *Patrons, clients and friends: interpersonal relations and the structure of trust in society* (Cambridge: Cambridge University Press).

Ellis, R. J. and Thompson, M. (eds) (1997) *Culture matters: essays in honour of Aaron Wildavsky* (Boulder: Westview Press).

Elster, J. (1989) *The cement of society: a study of the social order* (Cambridge: Cambridge University Press).

Elster, J. (1993) *Political psychology* (Cambridge: Cambridge University Press).

Elster, J. (1999) *Alchemies of the mind: rationality and the emotions* (Cambridge: Cambridge University press).

Emerson, R. M. (1962) 'Power-dependence relations', *American sociological review*, 27, pp.31–40.

Evans-Pritchard, E. E. (1937) *Witchcraft, oracles and magic among the Azande* (Oxford: Clarendon Press).

Fairtlough, G. (1994) *Creative compartments: a design for future organisation* (London: Adamantine).

Fardon, R. (1999) *Mary Douglas: an intellectual biography* (London: Routledge).

Ferlie, E., Ashburner, L., Fitzgerald, L. and Pettigrew, A. (1996) *The new public management in action* (Oxford: Oxford University Press).

Forester, J. (1993) 'Learning from practice stories: the priority of practical judgment', in Fischer, F. and Forester, J. (eds) *The argumentative turn in policy analysis and planning* (London: UCL Press) pp. 186–209.

Foucault, M. (1991) 'Governmentality', in Burchell, G., Gordon, C. and Miller, P. (eds) *The Foucault effect: studies in governmentality* (Hemel Hemstead: Harvester Wheatsheaf), pp. 87–104.

Fox, A. (1976) *Beyond contract: work, power and trust relations* (London: Faber and Faber).

Fox, N. and Roberts, C. (1999) 'GPs in cyberspace: the sociology of a "virtual community"' *Sociological review*, 4, pp. 643–71.

Fukuyama, F. (1992) *The end of history and the last man* (New York: Free Press).

Fukuyama, F. (1995) *Trust: the social virtues and the creation of prosperity* (Harmondsworth: Penguin).

Galaskiewicz, J. (1991) 'Making corporate actors accountable: institution-building in Minneapolis-St.Paul's', in Powell, W. W. and DiMaggio, P. J. (eds) *The new institutionalism* in *organizational analysis* (Chicago: University of Chicago Press).

Gambetta, D. (ed) (1988) *Trust: making and breaking co-operative relations* (Cambridge: Cambridge University Press).

Garrity, A. and Moore, S. (1999) 'University of Kentucky Winburn Community Academy: a three year analysis', *Universities and Community Schools*, 16 pp. 1–2.

Geddes, M. (1999) *Partnership against poverty and exclusion? Local regeneration strategies and excluded communities in the UK* (Bristol: Policy Press).

Goffman, E. (1967) *Interaction ritual: essays on face-to-face behaviour* (New York: Doubleday/Anchor Books).

Goffman, E. (1971) *Relations in public: micro-studies of the public order* (New York: Basic Books).

Golden, O. (1991) 'Collaboration as a means, not an end: serving disadvantaged families and children', in Schorr, L. B., Both, D. and Copple, C. (eds) *Effective services for young children: report of a workshop* (Washington DC: National Academy Press).

Goldman, H. H., Morrissey, J. P. and Ridgely, M. S. (1994) 'Evaluating the Robert Wood Johnson program on chronic mental illness', *Milbank Quarterly*, 72, pp. 37–48.

Goodin, R. E. (1986) 'Laundering preferences', in Elster, J. and Hylland, A. (eds) *Foundations of social choice theory* (Cambridge: Cambridge University Press) pp. 75–102.

Goodin, R. E. (1996) 'Institutions and their design', in Goodin, R. E. (ed.) *The theory of institutional design* (Cambridge: Cambridge University Press).

Gosling, P. (1997) *Government in the digital age* (London: Bowerdean).

Govier, T. (1998) *Dilemmas of trust* (Montreal: McGill-Queen's University Press).

Graham, J. D. and Wiener, J. B. (eds) (1996) *Risk vs risk: trade-offs in protecting health and the environment* (Cambridge: Harvard University Press).

Granovetter, M. S. (1973) 'The strength of weak ties', *American Journal of Sociology*, 78, May, pp. 1360–80.

Greene, R., Boyd, D. J. and Davis, E. I. (1998) *Reforming the delivery of children's services: a study of the implementation and effects of the New York State Coordinated Children's Services Initiative* (New York: Nelson A. Rockefeller Institute, Albany).

Grønbjerg, K. A. (1993) *Understanding nonprofit funding: managing revenues in social services and community development organisations* (San Francisco: Jossey-Bass).

Grønhaug, K. and Kaufmann, G. (eds) (1988) *Innovation: a cross-disciplinary perspective* (Oslo: Norwegian University Press).

Gross, J. L. and Rayner, S. (1985) *Measuring culture: a paradigm for the analysis of social organisation* (New York: Columbia University Press).

Hacking, I. (1990) *The taming of chance* (Cambridge: Cambridge University Press).

Hagen, M. and Kubicek, H. (2000) (eds) *One-stop-government in Europe: results from 11 national surveys* (Bremen: University of Bremen Press).

Hager, M., Galaskiewicz, J., Bielefeld, W. and Pins, J. (1999) ' "Tales from the grave": organisations' accounts of their own demise', in Anheier, H. K. (ed.) *When things go wrong: organisational failures and breakdowns* (London: Sage), pp. 51–70.

Halbwachs, M. (1992 [1941]) *On collective memory*, tr. and ed. Coser, L. (Chicago: University of Chicago Press).

Ham, C. and Hill, M. (1993 [1984]) *The policy process in the modern capitalist state*, second edition (Hemel Hempstead: Harvester Wheatsheaf).

Hammer, M. and Champy, J. (1995) *Re-engineering the corporation: a manifesto for business revolution* (London: Nicholas Brearley).

Hampshire, S. (1978) *Public and private morality* (Cambridge: Cambridge University Press).

Hanf, K. and Scharpf, F. W. (eds) (1978) *Interorganisational policy making: limits to coordination and central control* (London: Sage Publications).

Hannan, M.T. and Freeman, J. (1989) *Organisational ecology* (Cambridge, Massachusetts: Harvard University Press).

Hardin, R. (1993) 'The street-level epistemology of trust', *Politics and Society*, 21, 4, pp. 505–29.

Hardy, B., Turrell, A. and Webb, A. (1993) 'Collaboration and cost effectiveness', in Robbins, D. (ed.), *Community care: findings from Department of Health funded research, 1988–1992* (London: HMSO), pp. 39–43.

Harré, R. and Parrott, W. G. (eds) (1996) *The emotions: social, cultural and biological dimensions* (London: Sage).

Harries, J., Gordon, P., Plamping, D. and Fischer, M. (1998) *Projectitis: a whole systems view* (London: Kings Fund).

Hasan, H. and Hasan, S. (1997) 'Computer-based performance information for executives in local government', *Australian Journal of Public Administration*, 56, 3, pp. 24–9.

Hayek, F. A. von (1944) *The road to serfdom* (London: Routledge and Kegan Paul).

Hayek, F. A. von (1960) *The constitution of liberty* (London: Routledge).

Hayek, F. A. von (1973–1982) *Law, legislation and liberty: a new statement of the liberal principles of justice and political economy*, vols I–III (London: Routledge and Kegan Paul).

Hayek, F. A. von (1978) *New studies in philosophy, politics, economics and the history of ideas* (London: Routledge).

Hayes, N. and Walsham, G. (2000) 'Competing interpretations of computer-supported cooperative work in organizational contexts, *Organisation*, 7, 1, pp. 49–67.

Heeks, R. (ed.) (1999) *Reinventing government in the information age: international practice in IT–enabled public sector reform* (London: Routledge).

Heinrich, C. (1999) 'Do government bureaucrats make effective use of performance management information?', *Journal of Public Administration Research and Theory*, 9, 3, pp. 363–94.

Hirschman, A. O. (1970) *Exit, voice and loyalty: responses to decline in firms, organisations and states* (Cambridge, Massachusetts: Harvard University Press)

Hirschman, A. O. (1991) *The rhetoric of reaction: perversity, futility, jeopardy*, Belknap Press of the (Cambridge, Massachusetts: Harvard University Press).

HM Chief Inspector of Prisons for England and Wales, (1997) *Young prisoners: a thematic review* (London: HM Stationery Office).

HM Treasury (1998) *Modern public services for Britain: investing in reform – comprehensive spending review: new public spending plans 1999–2002* (London: HM Treasury).

HM Treasury (2000) *Spending review 2000*, available http://www.treasury.gov.uk/sr2000/

Hodgkin, R. and Newell, P. (1996) *Effective government structures for children: report of a Gulbenkian Foundation enquiry* (London: Gulbenkian Foundation).

Hogwood, B. W. and Gunn, L. (1984) *Policy analysis for the real world* (Oxford: Oxford University Press).

Hogwood, B. W., Judge, D. and McVicar, M. (1998) 'Agencies and accountability', paper given at the Whitehall Programme conference, University of Birmingham, December 1998.

Hollis, M. (1998) *Trust within reason* (Cambridge: Cambridge University Press).

Holman, K. (1999) *New connections: joined-up access to public services* (London: Community Development Foundation).

Home Office, Department of Health and Welsh Office, (1995) *National standards for the supervision of offenders in the community* (London: Home Office Probation Service Division).

Hood, C. C. (1983) *The tools of government* (Basingstoke: Macmillan – now Palgrave).

Hood, C. C. (1994) *Explaining economic policy reversals* (Buckingham: Open University Press)

Hood, C. C. (1998) *The art of the state: culture, rhetoric and public management* (Oxford: Oxford University Press).

Hood, C. C. and Jackson, M.W. (1991) *Administrative argument* (Aldershot: Dartmouth Publishing).

Hood, C. C. and Jones, D. K. C. (eds) (1996) *Accident and design: contemporary debates in risk management* (London: University College London Press).

Hornbeck, D. W. (1991) 'Outcome measurement as a tool to provoke systems change', in Schorr, L. B., Both, D. and Copple, C. (eds) (1991) *Effective services for young children: report of a workshop* (Washington DC: National Academy Press).

Jackson, P. M. (1992) 'Economic policy', in Marsh, D. and Rhodes, R. A. W. (eds) *Implementing Thatcherite policies: audit of an era* (Buckingham: Open University Press) pp. 11–31.

Jackson, T. (1996) *Material concerns: pollution, profit and the quality of life* (London: Routledge).

Jenkins, D. (1998) *Partnerships and power: leadership and accountability in urban governance*, Working Paper no 4 in the series, *The richness of cities: urban policy in a new landscape* (London: Comedia in association with Demos).

Jennings, E. T. Jr and Ewalt, J. A. G. (1998) 'Interorganisational coordination, administrative consolidation and policy performance', *Public Administration Review*, September–October 58, 5, pp. 417–28.

Jepperson, R. L. (1991) 'Institutions, institutional effects and institutionalism', in Powell, W. W. and DiMaggio, P. J. (eds) *The new institutionalism in organisational analysis* (Chicago: University of Chicago Press), pp. 143–63.

Joffe, H. (1999) *Risk and 'the other'* (Cambridge: Cambridge University Press).

John, P. (ed.) (1998) *Analysing public policy* (London: Pinter).

Johnson, P. (1993) *Frames of deceit: a study of the loss and recovery of public and private trust* (Cambridge: Cambridge University Press).

Johnston, H. and Klandermans, B. (eds) (1995) *Social movements and culture* (London: UCL Press).

Jordan, G. (1994) *The British administrative system: principles versus practice* (London: Routledge).

Joseph Rowntree Foundation (1998) *The role of social services in maintaining children in school* (York: Joseph Rowntree Foundation).

Jupp, B. (2000) *Working together: creating a better environment for cross-sector partnerships* (London: Demos).

Kable (1995) *Wired Whitehall* (London: Kable).

Kable (1996) *Tomorrow's town hall* (London: Kable).

Kable (1997) *Citizen direct* (London: Kable).

Kagan, S. L., Goffin, S. G., Golub, S. A. and Pritchard, E. (1995) *Toward systemic reform: services integration for young people and their families*, (Falls Church, Virginia: National Center for Service Integration).

Kagan, S. L. and Neville, P. (1993) *Integrating services for children and families: understanding the past to shape the future* (New Haven: Yale University Press).

Kalafat, J., Illback, R. and Sander, D. (undated) *Evaluation of Kentucky's School-based Family Resource and Youth Service Centers, Part I and Part II* (Louisville, Kentucky: REACH).

Kant, I. (1983, [1795]) 'To perpetual peace: a philosophical sketch', in Kant, I. (1983) *Perpetual peace and other essays on politics, history and morals*, tr. Humphrey, T. (Indianapolis: Hackett Publishing Co.) pp. 107–144.

Kertzer, D. I. (1988) *Ritual, politics and power* (New Haven: Yale University Press).

Kickert, W. J. M., Klijn, E.-H. and Koppenjan, J. F. M. (eds) (1997) *Managing complex networks: strategies for the public sector* (London: Sage).

Kingdon, J. W. (1995 [1984]) *Agendas, alternatives and public policies*, second edition (London: HarperCollins).

Klein, M., Roux, D. and Villedieu, T. (1991) 'Decision support for municipality financial planning in France: recent progress with "SIAD Mairie", a knowledge based DSS', in Traunmüller, R. (ed.) *Governmental and municipal information systems II*, proceedings of the second IFIP TC8/WG8.5 Working conference on governmental and municipal information systems, Balatonfüred Hungary (Amsterdam: North-Holland), pp. 117–30.

Klein, R. (1995) *The politics of the National Health Service*, third edition (Harlow: Longman).

Knoke, D. (1990) *Political networks: the structural perspective* (Cambridge: Cambridge University Press).

Koebel, C. T., Steinberg, R. and Dyck, R. (1992) 'Public–private partnerships for affordable housing: definitions and applications in an international perspective', paper prepared for the Federal Mortgage Corporation (Virginia: Virginia Polytechnic Institute and State University, and Indiana: Indiana University, Purdue University at Indianapolis).

Kooiman, J. (ed.) (1993) *Modern governance: new government–society interactions* (London: Sage).

Kraemer, K. L. and Dedrick, J. (1997) 'Computing and public organisations', *Journal of Public Administration Research and Theory*, 7, 1, pp. 89–112.

Kramer, R. M. and Tyler, T. R. (eds) (1996) *Trust in organisations: frontiers of theory and research* (London: Sage).

Lakatos, I. (1970) 'Falsification and the methodology of scientific research programmes', in Lakatos, I. and Musgrave, A. (eds) *Criticism and the growth of knowledge*, proceedings of the International Colloquium in the Philosophy of Science, London, (1965) vol. 4, pp. 91–196.

Landbergen, D., Coursey, D. H. Loveless, S. and Shangraw, R. F. Jr, (1997) 'Decision quality, confidence and commitment with expert systems: an experimental study', *Journal of Public Administration Research and Theory*, 7, 1, pp. 131–57.

Lane, C. and Bachman, R. (eds) (1998) *Trust within and between organisations: conceptual issues and empirical applications*, (Oxford: Oxford University Press).

Latour, B. (1996) *Aramis, or the love of technology* (Cambridge, Massachusetts: Massachusetts Institute of Technology Press).

Lawrence, P. R. and Lorsch, J. W. (1967) *Organisation and management: managing differentiation and integration*, Graduate School of Business Administration Press (Cambridge: Harvard University Press).

Lawson, G. (1998) *Netstate: creating electronic government* (London: Demos).

Leadbeater, C. (1999) *Living on thin air: the new economy* (London: Viking).

Leadbeater, C. and Goss, S. (1998) *Civic entrepreneurship* (London: Demos and Public Management Foundation).

Leat, D. and 6, P. (1997) *Holding back the years: how Britain can grow old better in the twenty-first century* (London: Demos).

Le Grand, J. (1989) 'Markets, welfare and equality', in Le Grand, J. and Estrin, S. (eds) *Market socialism* (Oxford: Oxford University Press).

Lee, A. S. (1994) 'Electronic mail as a medium for rich communication: an empirical investigation using hermeneutic interpretation', *Management Information Systems Quarterly*, 18, 2, pp. 143–58.

Leeuw, F. L., Rist, R. C. and Sonnichsen, R. C. (eds) (2000) *Can governments learn? Comparative perspectives on evaluation and organisational learning* (New Brunswick, New Jersey: Transaction Books).

Le Grand, J. (1989) 'Markets, welfare and equality', in Le Grand, J. and Estrin, S. (eds) *Market socialism* (Oxford: Oxford University Press).

Lehman, A. F., Postrado, L. T., Roth, D., McNary, S. W. and Goldman, H. H. (1994) 'Continuity of care and client outcomes in the Robert Wood Johnson program on chronic mental illness', *Milbank Quarterly*, 72, pp. 105–22.

Leicester, G. and Mackay, P. (1998) *Holistic government: options for a devolved Scotland* (Edinburgh: Scottish Council Foundation).

Liaison Committee (2000a) *Shifting the balance: select committees and the executive*, First Report, Session 1999–2000, Report and Proceedings of the Committee, 2 March 2000 (London: House of Commons).

Liaison Committee (2000b) *Independence or control? The government's reply to the Committee's First report of Session 1999–2000* 'Shifting the balance: select committees and the executive', Second Report, Session 1999–2000, Report together with the Proceedings of the Committee and Minutes of Evidence, 20 July 2000 (London: House of Commons).

Lindblom, C. E. (1955) 'Bargaining: the hidden hand in government', in Lindblom, C.E. (1988) *Democracy and market system* (Oslo: Norwegian University Press), pp. 139–70.

Lindblom, C. E. (1959) 'The science of "muddling through"', *Public administration review*, 19, 2, pp. 78–88, reprinted in Lindblom, C.E. (1988) *Democracy and market system* (Oslo: Norwegian University Press), pp. 171–90.

Lindblom, C. E. (1979) 'Still muddling, not yet through', *Public Administration Review*, 39, Nov–Dec, 517–26, represented in Lindblom, C. E. (1988) *Democracy and market system* (Oslo: Norwegian University Press), pp. 237–59.

Lindblom, C. E. (1990) *Inquiry and change: the troubled attempt to understand and change society* (New Haven: Yale University Press).

Lipsey, R. G. and Lancaster, K. J. (1956) 'The general theory of the second best', *Review of Economic Studies*, 64, pp. 11–32.

Lipsky, M. (1980) *Street level bureaucracy: dilemmas of the individual in public service* (New York: Russell Sage Foundation).

London Housing Unit, (1998) *Housing benefit: making the links* (London: London Housing Unit).

Luban, D. (1996) 'The publicity principle', in Goodin, R. E. (ed.) *The theory of institutional design*, (Cambridge: Cambridge University Press), pp. 154–98.

Lucas, J. R. (1993) *Responsibility* (Oxford: Oxford University Press).

Mackenzie, D. and Wacjman, J. (eds) (1985) *The social shaping technology: how the refrigerator got its hum* (Buckingham: Open University Press).

Mann, M. (1986) *The sources of social power, volume 1: a history of power from the beginning to A.D. 1760* (Cambridge: Cambridge University Press).

Mannheim, K. (1936) *Ideology and utopia: an introduction to the sociology of knowledge* (San Diego: Harcourt and Brace).

March, J. G. (1988) *Decisions and organisations* (Oxford: Blackwell).

March, J. G. and Olsen, J.-P. (1975) 'The uncertainty of the past: organisational learning under ambiguity', *European Journal of Political Research*, 3, pp. 147–71, reprinted in March, J. G. (1988) *Decisions and organisations* (Oxford: Blackwell), pp. 335–58.

March, J. G. and Olsen, J.-P. (1976) *Ambiguity and choice in organisations* (Bergen: Universitetsforlaget).

March, J. G. and Olsen, J.-P. (1989) *Rediscovering institutions: the organisational basis of politics* (New York: Free Press).

March, J. G. and Olsen, J.-P. (1995) *Democratic governance* (New York: Free Press).

Margetts, H. and Dunleavy, P. (1995) 'Public services on the world markets', in *Missionary government, Demos collection* (London: Demos) 7, pp. 30–2.

Mars, G. (1982) *Cheats at work: an anthropology of workplace crime* (London: Allen and Unwin).

Marsh, D. (ed.) (1998) *Comparing policy networks* (Buckingham: Open University Press).

Marsh, D. and Rhodes, R. A. W. (eds) (1992) *Policy networks in British government* (Oxford: Oxford University Press).

Marshall, T. H. (1992 [1950]) *Citizenship and social class* (London: Pluto Press).

Martin, J. (1992) *Cultures in organisations: three perspectives* (New York: Oxford University Press).

Matheson, A. (1998) 'Governing strategically: the New Zealand experience', in *Public Administration and Development*, 18, pp. 349–63.

McDaniel, P. R. (1989) 'Tax expenditures as tools of government action', in Salamon, L. M. with Lund, M. S. (eds) *Beyond privatisation: the tools of government action* (Washington DC: Urban Institute), pp. 167–96.

McGuire, J. (ed.) (1995) *What works: reducing re-offending: guidelines from research and practice* (London: Wiley).

McLeish, H. (Minister for Home Affairs, Devolution and Local Government, The Scottish Office) (1999) Keynote address the Scottish Council Foundation conference, *The Interactive Scot: Public Services in the Information Age*, Thursday 18 March, Edinburgh, available at www.scottishpolicynet.org.uk.

Meštrović, S. G. (1993 [1988]) *Émile Durkheim and the reformation of sociology* (Lanham, Maryland: Rowman and Littlefield).

Meyer, J. W. and Rowan, B. (1977) 'Institutionalised organisations: formal structure as myth and ceremony', *American Journal of Sociology*, 83, pp. 340–63.

Miller, G. J. (1992) *Managerial dilemmas: the political economy of hierarchy* (Cambridge: Cambridge University Press).

Mintzberg, H. and Waters, J. A. (1994) 'Of strategies, deliberate and emergent', in Tsoukas, H. (ed.) *New thinking in organisational behaviour* (London: Butterworth Heinemann), pp. 188–208.

Mises, L. von, (1935) 'Economic calculation in the socialist commonwealth', in Hayek, F. A. von, *Collectivist economic planning: critical studies in the possibilities of socialism* (London: G. Routledge), pp. 87–130.

Mises, L. von, (1948) *Human action: a treatise on economics* (London: Henry Regnery).

Misztal, B. A. (1996) *Trust in modern societies: the search for the bases of social order* (Cambridge: Polity Press).

Moore, M. H. (1995) *Creating public value: strategic management in government* (Cambridge: Harvard University Press).

Moore, N. (1998) *Better information age government: the big picture* (London: Kable).

Morgan, K., Rees, G. and Garmise, S. (1999) 'Networking for local economic development', in Stoker, G. (ed.) *The new management of British local governance* (Basingstoke: Macmillan – now Palgrave), pp. 181–96.

Morgan, T. (1993) 'Phased decision conferencing: how a sequence of decision workshops helped a local authority to evaluate budget options', *OR Insight*, 6, 4, October–December, pp. 3–12.

Morrissey, J. P., Calloway, M., Bartko, W. T., Ridgley, M. S., Goldman, H. H. and Paulson, R. I. (1994) 'Local mental health authorities and service system change: evidence from the Robert Wood Johnson program on chronic mental illness', *Milbank Quarterly*, 72, pp. 49–8.

Mountfield, R. (2000) 'Civil service change in Britain', paper given at the Political Studies Association Conference (London: London School of Economics), pp. 10–13.4.00.

Mulford, C. L. (1984) *Interorganisational relations: implications for community development* (New York: Human Sciences Press).

Murray, R. (1998) *Reinventing waste: towards a London waste strategy* (London: Ecologika).

Murray, R. (1999) *Creating wealth from waste* (London: Demos).

Naidoo, J. and Wills, J. (1998) *Practising health promotion: dilemmas and challenges* (New York: Balliere Tindall).

Nedovic-Budic, Z. and Godschalk, D. R. (1996) 'Human factors in the adoption of geographic information systems: a local government case study', *Public Administration Review*, 56, 6, pp. 554–67.

Nichols, G. (1991) 'Collaboration or conflict in community care planning: a health service perspective', in Allen, I. (ed.), *Health and social services: the new relationship* (London: Policy Studies Institute), pp. 1–6.

Nicol, C. (1998) 'Collaboration and co-ordination in local government: lessons from practice in housing and planning departments', *Local Government Studies*, 24, 3, pp. 51–66.

Nidumolu, S. R., Goodman, S. E., Vogel, D. R., Dankowitz, A. K. (1996) 'Information technology for local administration support: the Governorates Project in Egypt', *Management Information Systems*, June, 20, 2, pp. 197–225.

Niskanen, W. (1971) *Bureaucracy and representative government* (Chicago: Aldine-Atherton).

Nohria, N. and Eccles, R. G. (eds) (1992) *Networks and organisations: structure, form and action* (Boston: Harvard Business School Press).

North, D. (1990) *Institutions, institutional chance and economic performance* (Cambridge: Cambridge University Press).

Nozick, R. (1974) *Anarchy, state and utopia* (Oxford: Blackwell).

Oakeshott, M. (1947) 'Rationalism in politics', in Oakeshott, M. (1953) *Rationalism in politics and other essays* (London: Routledge).

Organisation for Economic Cooperation and Development (OECD) (1991) *Evaluating labour market and social programmes* (Paris: OECD).

Organisation for Economic Cooperation and Development (OECD) (1996) *Building policy coherence: tools and tensions* (Paris: OECD).

Osborne, D. and Gaebler, T. (1992) *Reinventing government: how the entrepreneurial spirit is transforming the public sector* (New York: Plume [Penguin]).

Osborne, D. and Plastrik, P. (2000) *The reinventor's fieldbook: tools for transforming your government – practical guidelines, lessons and resources for revitalising schools, public services and government agencies at all levels* (San Francisco: Jossey Bass).

Overman, E. S. and Loraine, D. T. (1994) 'Information for control: another management proverb?', *Public Administration Review*, pp. 193–6.

Pallot, J. and Ball, I. (1997) 'What difference does resource accounting make? The case of New Zealand', in Corry, D. (ed.) *Public expenditure: effective management and control* (London: Dryden Press and Orlando, Florida: Harcourt Brace Jovanic), pp. 237–52.

Parston, G. and Timmins, N. (1998) *Joined up management* (London: Local Government Management Board).

Performance and Innovation Unit (2000) *E-gov: electronic government services for the twenty first century*, Performance and Innovation Unit (London: Cabinet Office).

Performance and Innovation Unit (2001) 'Better policy delivery and design: a discussion paper', Performance and Innovation Unit, Cabinet Office, London, available at http://www.cabinet-office.gov.uk/innovation/whatsnew/betterpolicy.shtml.

Peters, B. G. (1998) 'Managing horizontal government: the politics of coordination', *Public Administration*, 76, summer, pp. 295–311.

Peters, B. G. (1999) *Institutional theory in political science: the 'new institutionalism'* (London: Pinter).

Pfeffer, J. and Salancik, G. (1978) *The external control of organisations: a resource dependence perspective* (New York: Harper and Row).

Philliber Research Associates (1999) *Progress in caring communities; preliminary findings from the 1998 evaluation* (Accord, New York: Philliber Research Associates).

Phillips, L. D. (1990) 'Decision analysis for group decision support', in Eden, C. and Radford, J. (eds) *Tackling strategic problems: the role of group decision support* (Newbury Park: Sage), pp. 142–50.

Polanyi, K. (1944) *The great transformation: the economic and political origins of our time* (Boston: Beacon Press).

Popper, K. (1949) *The poverty of historicism* (London: Routledge and Kegan Paul).

Porter, D. (1999) *Health, civilisation and the state: a history of public health from ancient to modern times* (London: Routledge).

Porter, D. O. and Hjern, B. (1981) 'Implementation structures: a new unit of analysis', *Organisation Studies*, 2, pp. 211–27, reprinted in abridged form in Hill, M. (ed.) (1993) *The policy process: a reader* (Hemel Hempstead: Harvester Wheatsheaf), pp. 248–65.

Powell, W. W. (1991) 'Expanding the scope of institutional analysis', in Powell, W. W. and DiMaggio, P. J. (eds) *The new institutionalism in organisational analysis* (Chicago: University of Chicago Press), pp. 183–203.

Power, M. (1997) *The audit society: rituals of verification* (Oxford: Oxford University Press).

Pratchett, L. (1999) 'New technologies and the modernisation of local government', *Public Administration*, 77, 4, pp. 731–50.

President of the Council and Leader of the House of Commons (2000) *The Government's response to the First Report of the Liaison Committee on 'Shifting the balance: select committees and the executive'*, Session 1999–2000, Cm 4737, (May 2000, President of Council and Leader of the House of Commons London).

Pressman, J. L. and Wildavsky, A. (1973 [1968]) *Implementation, or how great expectations in Washington are dashed in Oakland; or why it's amazing that federal programs work at all, this being the saga of the Economic Development Administration as told by two sympathetic observers who seek to build morals on a foundation of ruined hopes*, second edition (Berkeley: University of California Press).

Prime Minister and Minister for the Cabinet Office (1999) *Modernising government*, Cm 4310 (London: Stationery Office).

Prinz, W. and Syri, A. (1997) 'Two complementary tools for the co-operation in a ministerial environment', *Journal of Universal Computer Science*, 3, 8, pp. 843–64.

Provan, K. G. and Milward, H. B. (1995) 'A preliminary theory of interorganisational network effectiveness: a comparative study of four community mental health systems', *Administrative Science Quarterly*, 40, (March) pp. 1–33.

Pugh, G. and McQuail, S. (1995) *Effective organisation of early childhood services* (London: National Children's Bureau).

Raab, C. (1997) 'Privacy, information and democracy', in Loader, B. D. (ed.) *The governance of cyberspace: politics, technology and global restructuring* (London: Routledge), pp. 155–74.

Ralls, J. and Thomson, C. (1999) *The Scotland index: visionary governance for a small nation* (Edinburgh: Scottish Council Foundation).

Rawls, J. (1993) *Political liberalism* (New York: Columbia University Press).

Rayner, S. (1992) 'Cultural theory and risk analysis', in Krimsky, S. and Golding, D. (eds) *Social theories of risk*, (Connecticut: Praeger, Westport), pp. 83–116.

Reinicke, W. H. (1998) *Global public policy: governing without government?* (Washington DC: Brookings Institution).

Reschenthaler, G. B. and Thompson, F. (1996) 'The information revolution and the new public management', *Journal of Public Administration Research and Theory*, 6, 1, pp. 125–43.

Reynolds, R. (1997) *The trust effect: creating the high trust, high performance organisation* (London: Nicholas Brearley Publishing).

Rhodes, R. A. W. (1997) *Understanding governance: policy networks, governance, reflexivity and accountability* (Buckingham: Open University Press).

Rhodes, R. A. W. (2000) 'Governance and public administration', in Pierre, J. (ed.) *Debating governance: authority, steering and democracy* (Oxford: Oxford University Press), pp. 54–90.

Romm (Livermore), C. T. (1999) *Virtual politicking: playing politics in electronically linked organisations* (Cresskill New Jersey: Hampton Press).

Rose, N. (1999) *Powers of freedom: reframing political thought* (Cambridge: Cambridge University Press).

Rose, R. (1993) *Lesson drawing in public policy: a guide to learning across time and space*, Chatham House, Chatham, New Jersey.

Rose, R. and Davies, P. L. (1994) *Inheritance in public policy: change without choice in Britain* (New Haven: Yale University Press).

Sabatier, P. A. (1986) 'Top down and bottom up approaches to implementation research: a critical analysis and suggested synthesis', *Journal of Public Policy*, 6, pp. 21–48, reprinted in slightly abridged form in Hill, M. (ed.) (1993) *The policy process: a reader* (Harvester Wheatsheaf, Hemel Hempstead) pp. 266–93.

Sabatier, P. A. (ed.) (1999) *Theories of the policy process* (Boulder: Westview Press).

Sabatier, P. A. and Jenkins-Smith, H. C. (eds) (1993) *Policy change and learning: an advocacy coalition approach* (Boulder: Westview Press).

Sako, M. (1992) *Prices, quality and trust: inter-firm relations in Britain and Japan* (Cambridge: Cambridge University Press).

Salamon, L. M. (ed.) (1989) *Beyond privatisation: the tools of government action* (Washington DC: Urban Institute Press).

Scharf, T. and Wenger, G. C. (eds) (1995) *International perspectives on community care for older people* (Aldershot: Avebury).

Schutz, A. (1967) *The phenomenology of the social world* (Evanston: North Western University Press).

Schwarz, M. and Thompson, M. (1990) *Divided we stand: redefining politics, technology and social choice* (Philadelphia: University of Pennsylvania Press).

Scott, W. R. (1992) *Organisations: rational, natural and open systems*, third edition (Englewood Cliffs: Prentice Hall).

Scott, W. R. and Christensen, S. (eds) (1995) *The institutional construction of organisations: international and longitudinal studies* (London: Sage).

Scott, W. R. and Meyer, J. W. (eds) (1994) *Institutional environments and organisations: structural complexity and individualism* (London: Sage).

Seligman, A. B. (1997) *The problem of trust* (Princeton: Princeton University Press).

Senge, P. M. (1990) *The fifth discipline: the art and practice of the learning organisation* (London: Century Business (Random House)).

Shapiro, D., Hughes, J., Harper, R., Ackroyd, S. and Soothill, K. (1991) 'Policing information systems: the social context of success and failure in introducing information systems in the police service', in Traunmüller, R. (ed.) *Governmental and municipal information systems II*, proceedings of the second IFIP TC8/WG8.5 Working conference on governmental and municipal information systems, Balatonfüred, Hungary, North-Holland, Amsterdam, pp. 183–97.

Silberman, B. S. (1993) *Cages of reason: the rise of the rational state in France, Japan, the United States and Great Britain* (Chicago: University of Chicago Press).

Smith, M. J., Marsh, D. and Richards, D. (2000) 'Departmentalism, the core executive and joined-up government', paper given at the annual conference of the Political Studies Association, pp. 10–13.4.00 (London: London School of Economics).

Smith, P. (1996) *Measuring outcomes in the public sector* (London: Taylor and Francis).

Snellen, I.Th.M. (1998) 'Street level bureaucracy in an information age', in Snellen IThM and van de Donk, W. B. H. J. (eds) *Public administration in an information age: a handbook* (Amsterdam: IOS Press), pp. 497–508.

Social Exclusion Unit (1998) *Bringing Britain together* (London: Social Exclusion Unit).

Stinchcombe, A. (1997) 'On the virtues of the old institutionalism', *American Review of Sociology*, 21, pp. 1–18.

Stoker, G. (ed.) (1999) *The new management of British local governance* Basingstoke: Macmillan – now Palgrave.

Stoker, G. (2000) 'Urban political science and the challenge of urban governance', in Pierre, J. (ed.) *Debating governance: authority, steering and democracy* (Oxford: Oxford University Press), pp. 91–109.

Stone, D. (1996) *Capturing the political imagination: think tanks and the policy process* (London: Frank Cass).

Sztompka, P. (1993) *The sociology of social change* (Oxford: Blackwell).

Sztompka, P. (1999) *Trust: a sociological theory* (Cambridge: Cambridge University Press).

Tapscott, D. (1997) 'The digital media and the reinvention of government', *Canadian Public Administration*, 40, pp. 328–45.

Tarlov, A. R. (1996) 'Social determinants of health: the sociobiological transition', in Blane, D., Brunner, E. and Wilkinson, R. (eds) *Health and social organisation: towards a health policy for the twenty-first century* (London: Routledge), pp. 71–93.

Thomas, T. (1995) *Privacy and social services* (Aldershot: Arena).

Thompson, D. (1987) *Political ethics and public office* (Cambridge: Harvard University Press).

Thompson, J. D. (1967) *Organisations in action* (New York: McGraw-Hill).

Thompson, M. (1982) 'The problem of the centre', in Douglas, M. (ed.) *Essays in the sociology of perception* (London: Routledge and Kegan Paul).

Thompson, M. (1997a) 'Rewriting the precepts of policy analysis', in Ellis, R. J. and Thompson, M. (eds) *Culture matters: essays in honour of Aaron Wildavsky* (Boulder: Westview Press), pp. 20–216.

Thompson, M. (1997b) 'Cultural theory and technology assessment', in Fischer, F. and Hajer, M. (eds) *Living with nature: environmental discourse as cultural politics* (Oxford: Oxford University Press).

Thompson, M. (1997c) 'Cultural theory and integrated assessment', *Environmental Modelling and Assessment*, 2, pp. 139–50.

Thompson, M. Ellis, R. J. and Wildavsky, A. (1990) *Cultural theory* (Boulder: Westview Press).

Thompson, M. and Tayler, P. (forthcoming) 'Old question, new answer', unpublished manuscript, Department of Comparative Politics (Bergen: University of Bergen).

Titmuss, R. M. (1971) *The gift relationship* (London: Allen and Unwin).

Tocqueville, A. De (1988 [1856]) *The ancien regime*, tr. Bonner, J. (London: JM Dent & Sons).

US Department of Justice, (1997) 'Keeping young people in school: community programs that work', *OJJDP Juvenile Justice Bulletin*, June.

United States General Accounting Office (1992) *Integrating human services: linking at-risk families with services for more successful systemic reform efforts* (Washington DC: US General Accounting Office).

Utting, D. (ed.) (1998) *Children's services now and in the future*, London: National Children's Bureau and York: Joseph Rowntree Foundation.

van de Donk, W.B.H.J. (1998) 'Beyond incrementalism? Redistributive policy making, information systems and the revival of synopticism', in Snellen, IThM. and van de Donk, W. B. H. J. (eds) *Public administration in an information age: a handbook* (Amsterdam: IOS Press), pp. 381–404.

van Gunsteren, H. R. (1976) *The quest for control: a critique of the rational–central rule approach in public affairs* (London: Wiley).

VanDeVeer, D. (1986) *Paternalistic intervention: the moral bounds of benevolence* (Princeton: Princeton University Press).

Veale, J. and Morely, R. (1999) *SBYSP school based youth services program* (Iowa: Iowa Department of Education).

Vickers, Sir G. (1973) *Making institutions work* (London: Associated Business Programmes).

Vickers, Sir G. (1995 [1965]) *The art of judgment: a study in policy making*, centenary edition (London: Sage).

Walsh, J. (undated) *The eye of the storm: ten years on the front lines of New Futures*, Baltimore, Maryland: The Annie E. Casey Foundation.

Webb, A. (1991) 'Coordination: a problem in public sector management', *Policy and Politics*, 19, 4, pp. 229–41.

Weber, M. (1947) *Theory of social and economic organisation*, translated by Parsons, T. Basingstoke: Macmillan – now Palgrave.

Weber, M. (1958) 'Bureaucracy', from *Economy and society*, in Gerth, H. H. and Mills, C. W. (eds) (1958 [1946]) *From Max Weber: essays in sociology* (New York: Galaxy / Oxford University Press), pp. 196–245.

Weber, M. [Eisenstadt, S.N. ed], (1968) *Max Weber on charisma and institution building: selected papers* (Chicago: University of Chicago Press).

Weber, M. (1976) *The Protestant ethic and the spirit of capitalism*, tr. Parsons, T. (London: Allen and Unwin).

Weinberg, A. M. (1997 [1972]) 'Can technology replace social engineering?', *University of Chicago Magazine*, LIX, October 6–10, reprinted in slightly abridged form in Teich, A. H. (ed.) (1997 [1972]) *Technology and the future*, seventh edition (New York: St. Martin's Press), pp. 55–64.

Weiss, J. A. (1981) 'Substance and symbol in administrative reform: the case of human services co-ordination', *Policy Analysis*, 7, 1, pp. 21–46.

Weissberg, R. P., Gullotta, T. P., Hampton, R. L., Ryan, B. A. and Adams, G. R. (eds) (1997) *Establishing preventive services* (London: Sage).

Wenger, G.C. (1998) 'Nurturing networks', in *Demos collection 12, The wealth and poverty of networks: tackling social exclusion* (London: Demos).

White, T. (1999) *Agencies together* (Essex: Barnardo's).

Whitney, J. O. (1996) *The economics of trust: liberating profits and restoring corporate vitality* (New York: McGraw Hill).

Wiener, J. (1999) *Globalisation and the harmonisation of law* (London: Pinter).

Wiener, N. (1948) *Cybernetics: the emerging science at the edge of order and chaos* (New York: Simon and Schuster).

Wildavsky, A. (1988) *Searching for safety* (New Brunswick, New Jersey: Transaction Books).

Wilkinson, D. and Applebee, E. (1999) *Implementing holistic government* (Bristol Policy Press: and London: Demos).

Wilkinson, R. (1996) 'How can secular improvements in life expectancy be explained?', in Blane, D., Brunner, E. and Wilkinson, R. (eds) *Health and social organisation: towards a health policy for the twenty first century* (London: Routledge), pp. 109–22.

Williams, J. and Williams, P. (date unknown) *Pass me a boundary spanner* (Liverpool: Society of Local Government Chief Executives (SOLACE)).

Wilson, D., Hickson, D. J. and Miller, S. J. (1999) 'Decision overreach as a reason for failure: how organisations can overbalance', in Anheier, H.K. (ed) *When things go wrong: organisational failures and breakdowns* (London: Sage).

Wilson, F. (1999) 'Cultural control within the virtual organisation', *The Sociological Review*, 4, pp. 672–94.

Wilson, J. Q. (1989) *Bureaucracy: what government agencies do and why they do it* (New York: Basic Books).

Wood, C. (1989) *Pollution: prevention or cure?* (New York: Heinemann Newnes).

Wood, M., Pervan, G. and Schmidenberg, O. (1998) 'The impact of computer modelling on the development of commitment to action in the application of decision conferencing to strategic issues: preliminary results from a field study', paper given at the Australiasian Conference on Information Systems, 1998 conference.

Wynne, B. (1989) 'Frameworks of rationality in risk management: toward the testing of naïve sociology', in Brown, J. (ed.) *Environmental threats: perception, analysis and management* (London: Belhaven Press), pp. 33–47.

Yanow, D. (1996) *How does a policy mean? Interpreting policy and organisational actions* (Washington DC: Georgetown University Press).

Ytterstad, P. and Watson, R. T. (1996) 'Teledemocracy: using information technology to enhance political work', *Management Information Systems Quarterly*, September 20, 3, 347, full details at <http://misq.org/discovery.home.html>.

Zigurs, I. and Kozar, K. A. (1994) 'An exploratory study of roles in computer supported groups', *Management Information Systems Quarterly*, 18, 3, pp. 277–98.

Zucker, L. G. (1977) 'The role of institutionalisation in cultural persistence', *American Sociological Review*, 42, 5, pp. 726–43, reprinted in Powell, W. W. and DiMaggio, P. J. (eds) (1991) *The new institutionalism in organisational analysis* (Chicago: University of Chicago Press), pp. 83–107.

Zucker, L. G. (1986) 'Production of trust: institutional sources of economic structure, 1840–1920', in Bacharach, S. (eds) *Research in organisational behaviour* (Connecticut: JAI Press, Greenwich), 8, pp. 53–111.

Zuurmond, A. (1998) 'From bureaucracy to infocracy: are democratic institutions lagging behind?', in Snellen, IThM. and van de Donk, W.B.H.J. (eds) *Public administration in an information age: a handbook* (Amsterdam: IOS Press), pp. 259–72.

6 P. (1997a) *Holistic government* (London: Demos).

6 P. (1997b) 'Governing by cultures', in Mulgan, G. J. (ed.) *Life after politics: new thinking for the twenty-first century* (London: HarperCollins), pp. 260–85.

6 P. (1997c) *Escaping poverty: from safety nets to networks of opportunity* (London: Demos).

6 P. (1998a) 'Ownership and the new politics of the public interest services', *Political Quarterly*, 69, 4, October–December pp. 404–14.

6 P. (1998b) 'Problem-solving government' in Hargreaves, I. and Christie, I. (eds) *Tomorrow's politics: the third way and beyond* (London: Demos).

6 P. (1998c) *The future of privacy, vol I: private lives and public policy* (London: Demos).

6 P. (1998d) 'Housing policy in the risk archipelago: toward anticipatory and holistic government', *Housing Studies*, 13, 3, pp. 347–75.

6 P. (1999a) 'Neo-Durkheimian institutional theory', paper for the conference *Institutional theory in political science*, at Ross Priory, Loch Lomond, 17–18 October, University of Strathclyde.

6 P. (1999b) 'Suppose you wanted more independent local government... how would you go about it?', paper given at the Local Government Association

Policy Seminar, *The Local Challenge*, at the *New Statesman* annual conference, 8–9.9.99 (London: London School of Economics).

6 P. (2000a) 'The morality of managing risk: paternalism, prevention, precaution and the limits of proceduralism', *Journal of Risk Research*, 3, 2, pp. 135–65.

6 P. (2000b) *London_Mayor@your_service: how the directly elected Mayor of London can use new technologies to communicate with Londoners* (London: A New Voice for London).

6 P. (2000c) 'E-governance: Weber's revenge?', in Dowding, K., Hughes, J. and Margetts, H. (eds) forthcoming, *Political Studies Association Yearbook 2000: the challenges to democracy* (Basingstoke: Macmillan – now Palgrave), pp. 220–36.

6 P. (2000d) 'The governance of affect: the ritual organisation of emotion and the limits of emotional emancipation', paper given at the final University of East London seminar in the series *Affect, ethics and citizenship* (London: Birkbeck College), 1.6.00.

6 P. (2001) 'E-governance: do digital aids make a difference in policy making?', in Prins, J.E.J., (ed.) (2001) *Designing e-government: on the crossroads of technological innovation and institutional change* (The Hague: Kluwer Law).

6 P. (2002 forthcoming) *E-governance: styles of political judgment in the information age polity* (London: Institute for Public Policy Research).

6 P. and Randon, A. (1995) *Liberty, charity and politics: non-profit law and freedom of speech* (Aldershot: Dartmouth Publishing).

6 P., Leat, D., Seltzer, K. and Stoker, G. (1999) *Governing in the round: strategies for holistic government* (London: Demos).

6 P., Stoddart, P., Penston N., Shire, C. and Laird, A. (2000) *If you are serious about modernising government...* (Cambridge: Smart Card Club).

Index